RED GUIDES

BUYING A P
Florida 2005

THE ULTIMATE GUIDE TO BUYING, SELLING AND LETTING IN FLORIDA

Merricks Media Ltd

THE UK'S NO.1 PUBLISHER FOR BUYING PROPERTY ABROAD

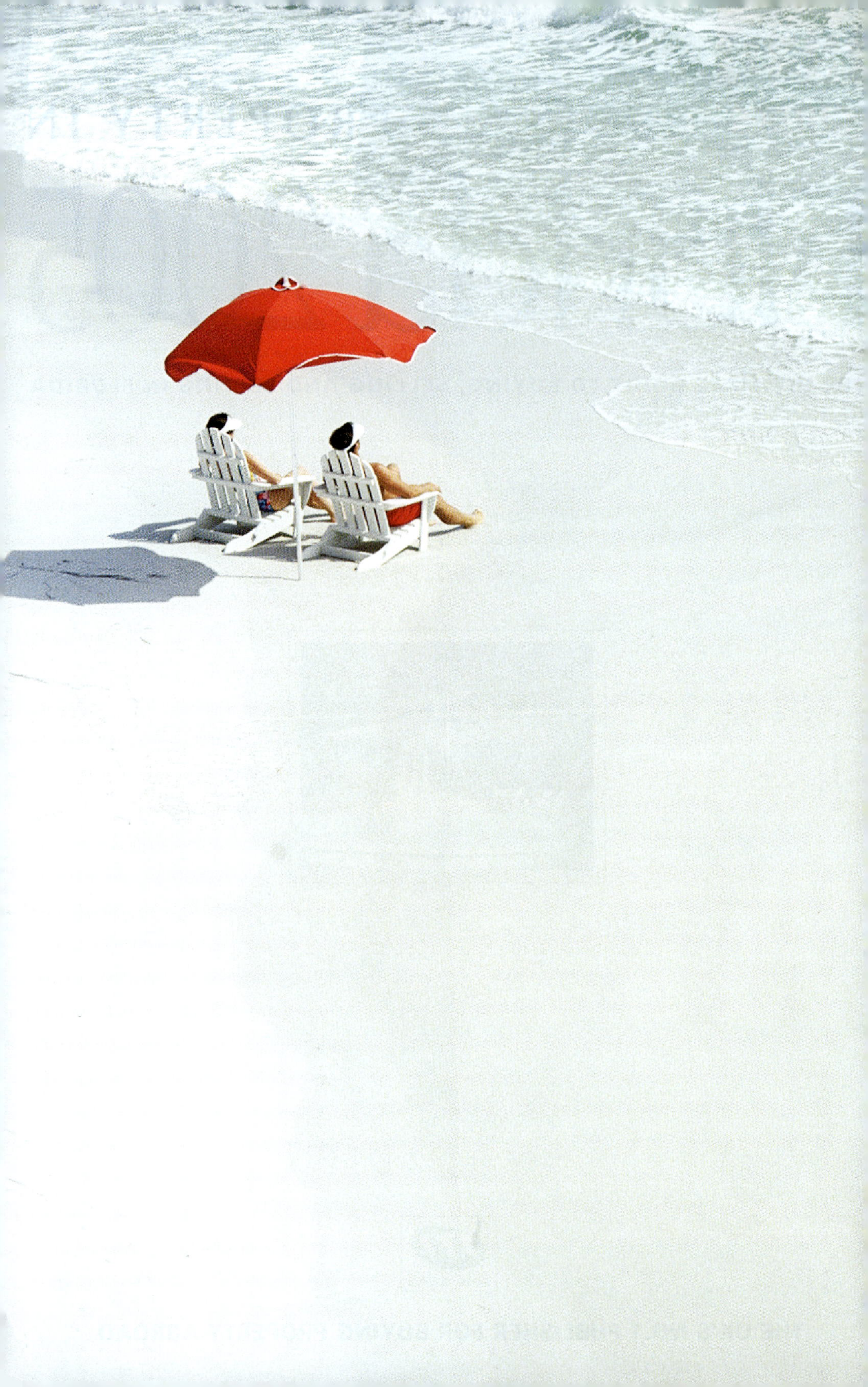

RED GUIDES

BUYING A PROPERTY IN
Florida 2005

THE ULTIMATE GUIDE TO BUYING, SELLING AND LETTING IN FLORIDA

EDITOR
Sarah Woods

Merricks Media Ltd

THE UK'S NO.1 PUBLISHER FOR BUYING PROPERTY ABROAD

FLORIDA CHOICE
ORLANDO & NAPLES
BUY TO LET HOLIDAY/INVESTMENT HOMES

Florida Choice
PROPERTY SALES, MANAGEMENT AND RENTALS

4/5 DAY INSPECTION TRIPS FROM £199-£399 PER PERSON

- Condos, townhouses & pool homes from £125,000
- Locations just minutes to Disney
- In-house management & rental services
- Rentals backed by B.A. & Thomas Cook

Property roadshows held throughout the U.K.
For more details of your nearest show or for your FREE colour brochure, visit our website at:

www.choice-properties.net
FREEPHONE Choice Properties 0800 897 479

ACKNOWLEDGEMENTS

A big thanks to all the Florida financial and property experts who contributed to this guide

Kevin M. Burke	Bennetts Solicitors and Attorneys	01934 862404
Andrew Bartlett	Realtor	0871 2221745
Kevin Fleury	Conti Financial Services	01273 772811
Garrett Kenny	Coldwell Banker Team Realty	+1 866 668 8326
Z. Joe Kulenovic	Enterprise Florida	+1 407 316 4690
Nick Thake	Florida Choice Realty	01702 529600
Janette Thorne	Homes of America Ltd	01244 579076
Lee Weaver	Mid-Atlantic Group	+1 407 396 9914
Liz Zitzow	British American Tax	020 8989 0088
Richard Robinson	Robinson O'Connell	020 7834 4162
Patrick Burgess	World of Florida	+1 863 207 3360
Barbara Lilley	Southdale Properties Inc	+1 561 644 1041
Dave Huband	Villages of Citrus Hills	+1 352 465 0380
Dave & Pauline Ford	Sunset International Management	+1 941 755 4489
Lesley Hare	Travel Masters International	+1 941 497 0709
Trevor Bright	TJS Realty Inc	+1 941 262 3000
Margaret Barnes	American Caribbean Real Estate	+1 305 664 4960
Margaret Barnes	Marr Properties	+1 305 451 4078
Graham Pyle	Florida Countryside	08456 444747

BUYING A PROPERTY IN
Florida 2005

THE ULTIMATE GUIDE TO BUYING, SELLING AND LETTING IN FLORIDA

Compiled, edited and designed by **Merricks Media Ltd**, Cambridge House South, Henry Street, Bath BA1 1JT. Tel: 01225 786800
redguides@merricksmedia.co.uk   www.redguides.co.uk

Managing Director Lisa Doerr
Production Manager Graham Prichard
Group Sales Manager Julie Stagg
Group Editor Ali Stewart
Sales Executive Barney Pearson
Consultant Editor Rebecca Spry
Managing Editor Daphne Razazan
Editor Sarah Woods
Senior Researcher Leaonne Hall
Researcher Helen Hill
Sub Editor Steve Bradley
Art Director Jon Billington
Art Editor Nigel Morrison
Design Louise Hillier, Hayley Liddle
Advertisement Design Becky Hamblin

All rights reserved. No part of this work may be reproduced or used in any form or by any means, electronic or mechanical, including photocopying, recording or any information storage and retrieval system, without the prior written permission of the publishers.

We cannot accept responsibility for any mistakes or misprints. While every care has been exercised in the compilation of this guide, neither the authors, editors nor publishers accept any liability for any factual inaccuracies or for any financial or other loss incurred by reliance placed on the information contained in **Buying a Property in Florida 2005**.

Dollar prices quoted are subject to fluctuations, and were correct at time of going to press. Current exchange rates should always be sought. The exchange rate used for this publication was 0.55 dollars to the pound, and has been rounded to the nearest pound.

RED GUIDES is a trademark of **Merricks Media Ltd**

Cover image © **PhotoDisc** Regional maps by Jamie Symmonds © **Merricks Media Ltd** Full Florida Map © **HarperColllins**

Illustrations by Felix Packer © Copyright 2004 **Merricks Media Ltd**. All rights reserved.

Printed and bound in Croatia by Zrinski's

Copyright © 2004 **Merricks Media Ltd**
ISBN 0-9543523-5-1 British Library Cataloguing in Publication Data.
A catalogue record for this book is available from the British Library.

The No.1 publisher in the travel and property sector

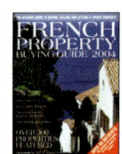

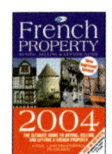

Merricks Media is the UK's number one publisher in the travel and property sector, publishing five dedicated magazine titles and a wide range of property-buying guides. We are the experts in helping you find and buy your dream home, worldwide. Tel: 01225 786800; **www.merricksmedia.co.uk**

EDITOR'S INTRODUCTION

Welcome

Sarah Woods

FOR ME, FLORIDA IS AMERICA'S LEISURE AND PLEASURE CAPITAL WHERE carefree relaxation and lazy, hazy days reign supreme. Few destinations can lay claim to 360 days of glorious sunshine per year, yet Florida manages this with ease. Sun-soaked days drift effortlessly into balmy nights with year-round temperatures that rarely drop below an average of 73 degrees. Everything from white sand beaches and wetlands to the most famous theme-park on the planet comes sun-drenched, earning America's south-easterly strip the nickname 'Sunshine State' with good reason. Yet Florida isn't just a suntrap – far from it. You can swim with dolphins, hit the fairways on 1,400 golf courses, enjoy some of the finest seafood in America and experience unforgettable sunsets. Florida also boasts some of the most magnificent wildlife on earth in a landscape of lagoons, marshlands, palm forests and ochre creeks – and if all this gets too much, you're never more than 60 miles from a beach.

More Britons visit Florida than any other foreign nationality and many love it so much they snap up a place of their own. Looking for a home with 'wow factor?' Then take a peak at the poolside architecture, which blends Southern-style design with Caribbean-cum-European touches. Keen to find Old South charm? Look no further than a country ranch nestled amidst citrus trees and stud farms, complete with rocking chair and porch. Hankering after a Hemingway-esque hideaway? Then follow in the footsteps of generations of novelists to the quirky Conch homes of the Florida Keys. From beachfront condo, lakeside villa and rural hacienda to island getaway and houseboat – Florida has it all.

> **Sun-soaked days drift into warm, balmy nights, with year- round temperatures rarely dropping below an average of 73 degrees**

Thanks to TV property shows, purchasing a pad in the Sunshine State has become the aspiration of many. Buyers are blessed with a tried and tested market, free of the burden that a foreign language brings. What's more, Florida's 'here to help' service makes the process simple.

However, a dream Florida purchase can become a financial nightmare, and like any overseas investment it requires consideration and planning. I have spoken to hundreds of Britons in Florida; those who familiarised themselves with the market properly have seen a return on their investment, while those who jumped straight in were not only owners of properties that failed to live up to lifestyle expectations, they also gained little financially. So, ensure you do plenty of homework, take expert advice, and benefit from the experiences of other British buyers.

You'll find all this and more in the first ever *Red Guide* to Florida. It's full of practical advice on how to find the perfect home and packed with a wealth of sun-drenched properties.

Sarah Woods Sarah Woods, Editor

EDITOR'S BIOGRAPHY British travel and property writer, Sarah Woods, has lived and worked in Florida and writes for 20 magazines. She is author of *Florida Homes* and a judge in Florida for the Homes Overseas Awards. Her best piece of advice for potential buyers is, "take time to pinpoint your location – remember Florida is the size of a small European country."

Contents

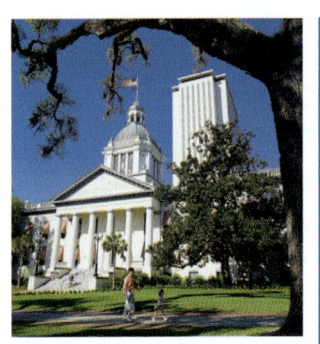

Although not as well known as Miami, Tallahassee has been the state capital of Florida since 1824

Walt Disney World Resort, SeaWorld and Universal Studios attract millions of visitors all year round

Florida is home to hundreds of miles of fantastic, white sandy beaches – regarded as the best in the United States

■ MARKET OVERVIEW

Editor's welcome	9
Map of Florida	12
Touring map and Florida facts	14

■ BUYING GUIDE AND CASE STUDIES

Buyer's guide introduction	18
Property market 2005	20
Florida's economy	22
Buying and selling	24
Letting property	26
Choosing a home	28
Florida's transport network	30
Steps to buying in Florida	33
We did it... Buying in Florida	52
We did it... Buying to let	54
Living and working in Florida	56
We did it... Relocation	72
We did it... A few years on	74

■ REGIONAL PROFILES AND PRICE GUIDES

Property guide introduction	76
The Panhandle	81
The North East	93
The Gulf Coast	107
Central Florida	125
The South East	143

CONTENTS

The Everglades	**159**
Miami	**171**
Florida Keys	**189**

■ FACTS, FIGURES AND CONTACT DETAILS

Buyer's reference guide	**206**
House sale prices	**208**
Apartment prices	**210**
Letting prices	**212**
Glossary	**214**
Useful contacts directory	**218**
Real estate agent index	**232**
General index	**236**
Meet the panel of experts	**240**
Advertisers index	**242**

There are around 1,200 restored buildings from the 1930s in Miami Beach's Art Deco Historic District

REGIONAL MAP

ALABAMA • GEORGIA

Pensacola • 98 • Fort Walton Beach • Destin • Panama City Beach • Panama City • Tallahassee • 10 • 98 • Keaton Beach • St George Island • Dog Island • Gainesville • 75 • Cedar Key • 98

Apalachicola • Suwannee • Withlacoochee • 19

GULF OF MEXICO

Tampa • Clearwater • St Petersburg • 75 • Bradenton • Sarasota • Venice • Englewood • Boca Grande • Cape Co...

KEY
- Hotspots
- Major towns/cities
- 66 Road numbers

12

REGIONAL MAP

The Regions

1. THE PANHANDLE
- Fort Walton Beach • Pensacola • Destin
- Panama City Beach

2. THE NORTH EAST
- Daytona Beach • New Smyrna Beach
- St Augustine • Ormond Beach
- Ponte Vedra Beach

3. THE GULF COAST
- Clearwater • St Petersburg • Sarasota
- Englewood • Venice • Naples • Fort Myers
- Bradenton • Punta Gorda • Cape Coral

4. CENTRAL FLORIDA
- Orlando • Kissimmee • Davenport

5. THE SOUTH EAST
- West Palm Beach • Fort Lauderdale • Port St Lucie
- Hollywood • Boca Raton

6. THE EVERGLADES
- Everglade City • Plantation Island
- Chokoloskee Island

7. MIAMI
- South Beach • North Miami Beach • Biscayne Bay
- Aventura • Bal Harbour • Surfside

8. THE FLORIDA KEYS
- Islamorada • Key West • Key Largo • Tavernier
- Layton • Marathon

13

TOURING MAP AND FACTS

Facts and figures

POPULATION

- Florida is the fourth most populous state in America with 16 million residents
- There has been a 26 per cent increase in the population since 1990
- Florida's population is concentrated around the coast
- Only 49,200 of Florida's population are native Americans, 0.3 per cent of the state's entire population
- The most populous metropolitan area is around Miami–Fort Lauderdale with a population of 3,192,582
- Florida has a healthy multicultural society, notably the strong Afro-Caribbean and Cuban presence in Miami

GEOGRAPHY

- Florida covers 58,560 square miles and it is the 22nd largest state in the country
- The coastline stretches for 1,197 miles, with 1,100 miles of beaches
- Of Florida's 67 counties, Palm Beach county is the largest at 2,578 square miles
- The state capital is Tallahassee
- Offers every possible geographical climate, but generally speaking very flat, with the highest peak being 350 feet above sea level
- Flanked by the Atlantic on the east coast and the Gulf of Mexico in the north west, Florida is 792 miles from the Panhandle to Key West
- Florida has two Intracoastal Waterways; the Atlantic Intracoastal Waterway runs along the east coast, while the Gulf Intracoastal Waterway along the west coast
- The freshwater marshlands of the Everglades dominate the south of Florida

CLIMATE

- Florida is the third wettest state in the United States
- Between December and May temperatures average 15°C to 24°C, with rainfall averaging a mere 51.05mm
- Florida's summer months are extremely hot and humid; June is the wettest month with an average rainfall 237mm

ECONOMY

- Florida is the fourth largest economy in the US, with tourism being the state's largest industry, generating $48 billion a year
- The median income per household is $37,998
- Florida is also the country's leading market gardener, agriculture being the second largest industry
- International trade accounts for 16 per cent of Florida's gross state product
- Florida's unemployment figures in 2004 were 5.3 per cent, lower than the national average of 5.6 per cent

BUYER'S GUIDE

How to use the property book

Inside you'll find a wealth of expert advice, covering every aspect of finding, buying and letting a home in Florida, whatever your budget

Part One: Buyer's Guide
This section offers the latest facts and information about the financial and legal process of buying a property in Florida. It includes a number of articles written by our panel of experts (see page 7) and a comprehensive Steps to Buying chapter, which takes you through every stage of the Florida conveyancing system, from appointing a lawyer to closing a sale. A section on Living and Working provides detailed advice on visas and taxes, as well as information about healthcare, education and renovating a property.

Part Two: Property Guide
Divided into eight regional chapters, the Property Guide offers up-to-the-minute information about the current performance of each region's property market, with comparative price charts and profiles of the hotspots, as well as property price guides highlighting the types of homes available in each area.

Part Three: Buyer's Reference
The Buyer's Reference offers a swathe of useful information and contacts to help you in the conveyancing procedure.

Price Matrices
To enable you to calculate potential outlay and rental return, there are three price matrices offering a clear comparison between all 42 hotspots. The House Price matrix (see page 166) lists average 'for sale' prices for two to six–bedroomed properties, while the Apartments matrix (see page 167) offers prices for one to four–bedroomed apartments and condos. The Lettings matrix similarly covers all 42 hotspots and gives the average monthly figures you can expect to achieve for a one to six–bed property. Compiled from extensive research at the time of going to print, these prices reflected the current market situation.

Directory of Useful Contacts
A listing of professionals and organisations, from architects and real estate agents to visa lawyers, with addresses, telephone numbers and website details.

Index to Agents and Index
All the contact details for the estate agents featured in the Price Guides are listed on page 179, while a comprehensive general index begins on page 181.

FINDING ANSWERS TO YOUR QUESTIONS

The way you use this book will depend on your priorities when choosing a property. The major priorities are as follows:

■ Investment and, as is the case with most people, your budget is limited: use the cross-Florida property price matrix on page 208 to see how much you can afford in which areas, then use the index to locate the profiles of your chosen area.

■ To find the right property for a private residence in a given area; turn straight to the chapter on your chosen region and use the property price matrix, profiles and fact boxes of the area's hotspots to find out which particular area suits you and where you can find the best value for money.

■ To find the right property for a private residence in a choice of areas read through all the profiles to see which may suit you. The index will help you find profiles for areas that meet your needs, for instance a property near the sea, near a major city or in the mountains.

■ Buying to let: turn to the letting property price matrix on page 212 to see where you can hope for the best return on your investment, then use the index to locate the profiles of your chosen area.

■ Exchange Rate: An average exchange rate of 0.55 dollars to the £1 is used.

Every practical aspect of successfully living and working in Florida is covered in detail

There is nothing minimalist about our website

14000 properties in all the main overseas property markets and many emerging ones. PLUS 1000 articles on the buying process

newskys.co.uk
The overseas property search experts

Open 7 days a week 0845 330 1449

■ BUYER'S GUIDE INTRO

BUYER'S GUIDE

BUYER'S GUIDE INTRO

Buyer's Guide

Follow the buyer's guide and you could soon be looking at beautiful sunsets like this…

Property market in 2005 — 20
Economic overview 2005 — 22
Buying and selling in 2005 — 24
Letting in 2005 — 26
Choosing your home in 2005 — 28
Florida transport 2005 — 30

STEPS TO BUYING

Taking initial advice: Step 1 — 33
Appointing a lawyer: Step 2 — 35
Choosing an agent: Step 3 — 37
Finding the right home: Step 4 — 38
Steps to take in Florida: Step 5 — 39
The contract: Step 6 — 41
Securing a mortgage: Step 7 — 43
Home inspection: Step 8 — 44
Contract follow-up: Step 9 — 46
Title services: Step 10 — 46
Closing the sale: Step 11 — 47
Things to be aware of: Step 12 — 49
Relocating to Florida: Step 13 — 51

We did it… Buying in Florida — 52
We did it… Buying to let — 54

LIVING AND WORKING

Work permits and visas — 56
Taxation in Florida — 61
Securing a social security number — 66
Education — 66
Healthcare — 66
Car insurance and driving licences — 67
Banking and credit — 67
Renovating a property — 69

We did it… Relocation — 72
We did it… A few years on — 74

■ BUYER'S GUIDE

The property market 2005

Identifying the location and type of home that best suits you will save considerable time and energy in your Florida property search

As with virtually every property market in the world, location is always the most important criteria when deciding where to buy. This is true whether it's a holiday home for personal use, for the purpose of letting, or if it's a commercial property.

Geographically, Florida is about the same size as England and its diverse landscape provides the opportunity for many different lifestyles. The south is warmer but its tropical climate ensures that it's much wetter than the north in the summer months. Central Florida – the best of both worlds – is rapidly becoming the most popular choice of location for many people who decide to buy a holiday home in the state. Property is still relatively affordable in comparison with some of the more expensive coastal areas, and the healthy exchange rate at present between the pound and the euro against the US dollar is encouraging overseas buyers to invest.

The area is close to all the main attractions such as the Walt Disney World Resort, Universal Studios and SeaWorld, and it's within a short drive of the Kennedy Space Center at Cape Canaveral. For sporting enthusiasts and particularly golfers, the region is a paradise. Tennis, water sports and horse riding are among many other sports catered for. It is estimated that more than 40 million people visit the Orlando region every year, considerably more than any other part in the state.

Prices are increasing on an almost weekly basis at the moment because the demand is much greater than supply for quality holiday homes. Developments often sell out even when the completion dates are up to a year away. Many new bulk-buying investors have been attracted recently, particularly to Central Florida, and it only takes a few of them to buy up large sections of new gated developments and condominiums. Some of them even sell the properties on as soon as the new-builds are complete because the prices are rising during the intervening months. Although the strength of the pound has made the UK housing market extremely strong, houses tend to be much cheaper per square foot in the US. Much of this comes down to the fact that land is less expensive because there is much more of it. An average four-bedroom, two-bathroom home of around 2,000 square feet with a private swimming pool can cost as little as $250,000, which is not dissimilar to the price of a one-bedroom apartment in one of the major UK towns or cities.

> Garrett Kenny entered the property business 13 years ago and has been involved in developing both domestic and commercial real estate. In 2002, he established the Coldwell Banker Team Realty franchise in Davenport. A fully licensed real estate company, it has secured over $100 million in sales in its first 18 months of operation.

Additional costs

Florida has always been popular with American buyers and in recent years, many people from the northern states have been buying holiday properties or retirement homes which they can use or let over the years until they retire. Both single family homes (most of them come with pools) and condominiums have

AVERAGE REGIONAL PROPERTY PRICES

Region	Property Market	Average Property Prices
The Panhandle	The median property price is 12% below the state average	$124,600
The North East	The median property price is 17% below the state average	$117,800
The Gulf Coast	The median property price is 2% above the state average	$143,200
Central Florida	The median property price is 16% below the state average	$119,200
The South East	The median property price is 37% above the state average	$193,400
Miami	The median property price is 5% below the state average	$133,800
The Florida Keys	The median property price is 46% above the state average	$221,889

BUYER'S GUIDE

A four-bedroom home with around 2,000 square feet and a private pool can cost just $250,000, not dissimilar to the price of a flat in the UK

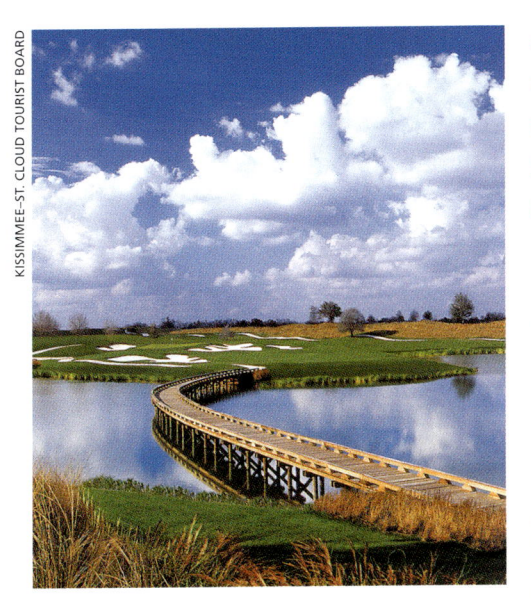

With 1,300 courses, golf attracts hundreds of buyers to Florida's many golfing developments

been increasing very strongly in value in the past 12 months, with homes going up on average 12 per cent and condos as much as 17 per cent. Many large investors look on property as a much safer investment compared to the often volatile stock market.

The climate is a great attraction when it comes to buying in Florida – there are more than 300 days of sunshine every year. There is virtually no winter in terms of how you would perceive it in the UK, and increasing numbers of northern Europeans have recognised this. Over here, winter is more commonly known as the golfing season! Millions of golfers from all over the world arrive in Florida during the winter for days filled with sunshine and golf on some of the finest courses in the world, of which there are almost 1,300, many of professional standing.

Having made the decision to purchase a property,

the first step should be to contact a reputable real estate agency, and you must ensure that is fully licensed. Florida is a 'user friendly' state when it comes to purchasing a property, even though each county has its own laws. And this is where your real estate agency comes into the picture because they should be completely au fait with the requirements of each county. Having your own real estate agency is even more important if you are planning to rent the property because short-term rentals are not permitted in certain areas.

If the property is going to be rented, whether this is to cover mortgage and running costs or simply as investment income, decide on the size of property you want. The most popular sizes for rental purposes are four/five bedrooms with two/three bathrooms. This is because often two families decide to go on a Florida holiday together and it makes it more cost effective to rent one house, or a number of golfers decide to rent one house for the duration of their stay.

Additional costs

Your real estate agency will identify a number of properties which match your requirements and arrange for you to view them – with no obligation. If you decide on a new home, a small deposit of usually around $1,000 is all that is required to secure the site, and a further $5,000 is often necessary to book a home. If a mortgage is required it's simply a matter of choice whether you secure one from a bank or building society in the UK, or choose a local bank in Florida. In the US, fixed and variable rate mortgages are available for between five and 30 years and for up to 80 per cent of the purchase price, with no age restrictions. Remember that with all such purchases there are additional costs to cover the transaction, and these usually amount to about four per cent of the total purchase price.

With a strong pound and great value still to be found even in some of the state's most popular regions, it's an excellent time to buy in Florida. ●

PROPERTY MARKET FACTS

- Fixed and variable rate mortgages are available for between five and 30 years, for up to 80 per cent of the purchase price
- The most popular size of property for rental purposes are four/five-bed, two/three-bath homes
- An average four-bed home, with 2,000 sq.ft. and a private pool can cost as little as $250,000. This would only buy a decent one-bedroom apartment in most major UK towns and cities

■ COMPANY CONTACTS

Garrett Kenny, Coldwell Banker Team Realty
Tel: 00 1 (863) 420 9404, or visit their website at www.coldwellbankerteamrealty.com

■ BUYER'S GUIDE

Economic overview 2005

With an annual economic output of over half a trillion dollars, Florida has one of the world's largest and most dynamic market economies

RANKING EIGHTH IN THE AMERICAS, AND 15TH worldwide, with a population of over 17 million and an annual economic output upwards of half a trillion dollars, Florida has combined international trade and inward foreign direct investment (FDI) of more than $100 billion a year to create an economic powerhouse matched by only a few countries.

Internationally renowned for its magnificent beaches and tourist attractions, Florida is also rapidly gaining in visibility as a global business destination. Its strategic location, economic and political stability, extensive transport and communications infrastructure, multilingual workforce, and highly competitive cost of doing business, have led to hundreds of multinational firms establishing their operations in Florida.

Over the past decade or so, Florida has made tremendous strides in diversifying its economic base and produced one of the fastest growing economies among US states. Driven by a combination of rapid population growth, capital inflows from overseas, expanding international trade and tourism, most sectors of Florida's economy, from construction and real estate to high-tech and healthcare, are booming. With more new jobs created over the last few years than in any other state, these trends will continue.

Driving forces

Florida's strengths lie in the following industries: life sciences (including biotechnology, pharmaceuticals, medical device manufacturing, and healthcare); information technology (including: IT products and services, software development, modelling/simulation/training, photonics/lasers/optics, microelectronics, and telecommunications); aviation/aerospace; homeland security/defence; and financial services.

Florida's life-sciences cluster is blossoming and future growth is predicted due to the arrival of Scripps – a major biomedical research centre – and continued capital funding. The state's medical technology companies, healthcare system, research capabilities and pro-business climate have created an environment where biotech, pharmaceutical and medical device companies can enjoy rapid development, and thrive.

Birthplace of the PC

Information technology is another driver of economic growth in Florida – it was the birthplace of IBM's personal computer (PC) in the early 1980s. Florida leads the south-east in high-tech employment, with

As the Senior Director for Strategic and Market Analysis, Z. Joe Kulenovic heads up Enterprise Florida's research team. Since joining the organisation in 1999, Joe has taken part in a wide variety of Florida's statewide economic and business development initiatives.

284,800 workers in 2002, and ranks fourth among states. Especially strong in photonics, simulation technology and telecommunications, Florida has multiple internet switching stations and a host of internet companies, and has been dubbed the 'Internet Gateway' to Latin America. Florida has been the geographic focal point for modelling, simulation and training (MST) development since the 1960s. In addition, it is home to some of the largest photonics integrators and users; it's among the top four optics regions in the US, and will continue to play an important role in the advancement of this industry.

Florida is also a premier global location for space technologies. Organisations such as the Florida Space Authority and the Cape Canaveral Space Partnership aim to ensure that Florida remains the leader in space innovations. Florida has one of the largest shares of US businesses in the aviation industry. Together, these companies have developed a pool of scientific, technical and management talent that is providing the foundation for the state's expanding aviation industry.

The emerging homeland security business sector includes a broad spectrum of Florida's world-leading industries: aviation; IT; modelling; simulation and training; medical technologies; photonics, and a host of high value-added services. Florida is ideally positioned for developing these breakthrough innovations and sourcing the quality products and services crucial to preventing, responding to, and recovering from any international threat to public safety.

Florida has a more service-intensive economy than the US as a whole, with over 70 per cent of its total economic output arising from service-producing sectors, which have in recent years accounted for a large share of the state's total job growth. Florida's highly diversified economic structure has enabled the state to be a global player in the provision of high value-added services, such as financial services (banking, trade finance, insurance) and other

BUYER'S GUIDE

professional services (legal, accounting, consulting, engineering, distribution).

In terms of international business, Florida truly is THE place to be. Consistently among the top states in attracting foreign direct investment, Florida is host to nearly 2,000 international companies, including some 300 regional corporate headquarters of multinational firms. The state also has one of the largest concentrations of international banks, consulates, and bi-national chambers of commerce in the US.

Six million visitors

Florida is one of the world's leading trading entities, with international merchandise trade of over $70 billion annually flowing through its airports and seaports. In its role of trade gateway, Florida is unique: for many years, it has held a commanding share of US trade with Latin America and the Caribbean, as well as with the rest of the world. Keen to cement its status as the commercial capital of the Americas, Florida is now bidding to become the home of the Permanent Secretariat of the Free Trade Area of the Americas.

Florida is also a premier global travel destination, with people from all over the world visiting for both business and pleasure. The number one destination state for overseas visitors to the United States (excluding those from Canada and Mexico), Florida accounts for over six million visitors, or more than a quarter of the total number of overseas visitors to the US. Following the disruption to international travel in the aftermath of the September 11 attacks, Florida's tourism industry is now undergoing a strong revival.

Regional information

Florida is made up of eight, highly diverse regions, each with a mix of demographic characteristics, business advantages and lifestyle options. Florida's north-west, home to the state capital of Tallahassee, offers abundant land and competitive utility and labour rates. The region's key industries include aviation/aerospace/defence, and IT.

North-central Florida is booming with innovative ideas, anchored by the world-renowned University of Florida in Gainesville – the birthplace of Gatorade. Industries experiencing significant growth include; healthcare, manufacturing, distribution and biotech.

Booming north-east Florida is home to over one million people, including the port city of Jacksonville and the oldest European settlement in the US – St. Augustine. The economy is strong in distribution/logistics, manufacturing, financial services, biomedical technology, and aviation/aerospace.

The central Florida 'Space Coast' region accounts for a significant portion of the technological advances in the state, especially in photonics and simulation. The region, which includes Orlando and Cape Canaveral, is experiencing sizzling growth across virtually all sectors.

Home to the state capital, the Panhandle is experiencing rapid economic growth

VISIT FLORIDA

ECONOMIC FACTS

- Florida's annual economic output exceeds more than half a trillion US dollars
- Over 70% of the economic output comes from service-producing sectors
- Florida is the fourth largest state in terms of its numbers of high-tech employees
- More than a quarter of overseas tourists visit Florida, over six million every year

Also bustling with explosive growth, the Tampa Bay area on Florida's west coast is emerging as a hotspot for the global financial services. Including the bustling cities of Tampa, St. Petersburg and Clearwater, the area offers an environment conducive to high-tech company growth, as evidenced by numerous area companies specialising in medical devices and information technology. Southwest Florida offers the sparkling blue waters of the Gulf of Mexico and charming towns like Naples and Fort Myers. With a population approaching one million, its international profile is ascendant.

In the state's interior, adjacent to the Everglades, Florida's heartland region offers a wealth of land in which businesses can build structures to specifically fit their needs and ensure room for future growth.

South-east Florida has a population base close to six million, and is home to more than one in three Floridians. One of the largest metropolitan areas in the US, global companies find this region the perfect location for their businesses. Multilingual Miami is regarded as the business capital of Latin America, and seen as the likely future home of the Permanent Secretariat of the Free Trade Area of the Americas. ●

■ COMPANY CONTACTS

Joe Kulenovic, Enterprise Florida, +1 407 316 4690, www.eflorida.com

■ BUYER'S GUIDE

Buying and selling a home

Getting the right mortgage advice and a qualified estate agent is essential when buying a property in the United States…

As GEORGE BERNARD SHAW PUT IT SO WELL: "England and America are two countries separated by a common language." Nowhere is this more true than for UK residents buying villas and other investment properties in Florida, where surveys are 'appraisals', completions are 'closings' and no one is quite sure what an 'escrow' is!

It is important, therefore, that British property buyers in Florida not only understand 'both languages' but also keep abreast of the differences in US and UK property law as well as the often very different buying and selling procedures in both countries. Keeping up-to-date with new ways to find, evaluate, purchase and finance property is an absolute cornerstone of successful property investing in the Sunshine State of Florida.

That is why it's important that UK property investors secure the assistance of companies or individuals expert in trans-Atlantic real estate and finance practices. Protected with this expertise UK purchasers will minimise the risks and maximise the personal and financial returns on their investment in Florida property. And these returns can be significant indeed. As the Central Florida Business Journal magazine announced in June: "Florida's median existing-home price rises 70 per cent in five years."

Legal documentation

The most stark difference in the property buying and selling process in the US versus the UK is the large amount of legal documentation required by the various US Federal, State and local regulatory authorities involved. Though this can be quite daunting to UK property investors, this documentation does provide a high level of safety to buyer and seller alike – particularly for UK investors who often complete the purchase by post from over 4,000 miles away.

Additionally, the almost universal use of an independent US 'Closing Agent' or 'Title Company' dramatically simplifies the process and allows many UK purchasers to complete the entire villa purchase and/or sale from the comfort of their home in the UK. Consequently it is now possible, under the right circumstances, for UK investors to find, evaluate, purchase and finance a Florida villa without even visiting the state itself.

Lee Weaver served four years with the British Army before coming to the US to pursue a career in real estate and finance. As Director of Operations for the Mid-Atlantic Group in Orlando, Lee specialises in assisting UK residents identify and acquire investment properties throughout the state of Florida.

What's new this year?

The 9/11 attacks resulted in increased security and occasional delays in trans-Atlantic travel – but there is nothing new that affects the fundamental benefits of investing in Florida property.

FIRPTA withholding tax

US tax specialists Swart Baumruk & Company, LLP (www.sbc-cpa.com/) advise that the only US legislative change this year affecting UK property owners in Florida relates to the temporary withholding of sales proceeds when the property is sold. The Foreign Investment in Real Property Tax Act (FIRPTA) requires 10 per cent of the selling price be withheld until the seller's tax liability with the US government is determined.

The buyer cooperates with the seller's obligation by providing a notarised copy of their passport and a completed application for a US Individual Taxpayer Identification Number (ITIN) called a 'W7'. W7s are issued by the US Internal Revenue Service (IRS) and are given to the seller's accountant prior to their completion. The authorisation enables the Title Company to hold the 10 per cent in escrow while the seller's tax liability is assessed. And having the Title Company, rather than the US government's IRS, withhold and disburse the retained sales proceeds can speed up the whole process, as well as help prepare the new buyer for when they sell the property at some time in the future. To read the complete rules and regulations relating to FIRPTA go to the US government's IRS website (www.irs.gov/) and search 'ITIN Guidance' to find the posting captioned 'ITIN Guidance for Foreign Property Buyer/Sellers'.

A survey indicated that 72% of homebuyers are regularly using the internet as part of the purchasing process…

24

BUYER'S GUIDE

New British sterling mortgages

A new development on the mortgage front this year is the expanded availability of British currency mortgages specifically designed for UK property owners in Florida. These UK sterling mortgages are offered to qualifying UK residents by British Mortgages Abroad, a GE company based in Harrow.

The major benefit of a sterling mortgage for UK owners in Florida is that it removes any currency exchange risk from monthly mortgage payments. Many UK property buyers in Florida have selected an American '30-Year Fixed-Rate Mortgage' in the mistaken belief that it will 'fix' their monthly payment. All it fixes, however, is the interest rate and not what is perhaps the most critical variable in international finance: the currency exchange rate.

Let's say, for example, that the UK borrower takes out a US loan with a 'fixed' monthly payment of $1,700, and that at the time the first dollar mortgage payment is due the exchange rate is $1.70 to the pound. The UK borrower, therefore, needs £1,000 to 'buy' $1,700 for his or her first US monthly mortgage payment.

Further, let's assume that either the US dollar strengthens, or the UK pound weakens against it, over the next few months (as many industry observers think may happen) and that the exchange rate moves to $1.60. The UK borrower will now need £1,062.50 to meet the same $1,700 US mortgage obligation.

Although the increase in the monthly mortgage payment may not overly concern some borrowers, it's the uncertainty of what the next monthly payment will be that has them worried – and accounts for the huge popularity of the new BMA sterling mortgage facility and the reason so many UK residents are refinancing their US home loans with a more predictable UK currency one.

These British home loans are secured by the Florida property rather than the home in the UK and assuming that the Florida villa is rented out for at least part of the year, the sterling mortgage payments to British Mortgages Abroad in the UK are deductible from any rental income in the US, thus reducing the UK property owner's US tax obligation, if any.

Internet property search

A recent market research study indicated that 72 per cent of homebuyers in Florida used the internet as part of their purchasing process. The internet can dramatically increase the efficiency of a UK buyer's search for properties in Florida by eliminating non-starters with little effort and no expense.

And that is why, unlike in the UK, it is only necessary to deal with one estate agent in Florida, who has access to information about all of these properties rather than working with several in various locations, some of whom you may not know, care for, or, perhaps most importantly, trust.

The Multiple Listing Service (MLS) was developed by the leading US professional estate agency organisation, the National Association of Realtors (www.realtor.org). In this context it's important to understand that although all US realtors are estate agents, conversely, not all US estate agents are realtors. Ensure you work with a fully licensed and accredited realtor; this will ensure you're working with a professional agent who meets the stringent academic and financial requirements of the National Association of Realtors, and that you'll have access to the MLS.

One-stop shop

Buying and selling property in Florida is a multifaceted venture and it can be somewhat complex and time-consuming. Hence the growing popularity of a convenient 'one-stop shop' company that can offer, or has access to, all the services necessary to facilitate a hassle-free purchase in Florida. The new one-stop shop concept allows UK investors to integrate and coordinate the entire property acquisition and mortgaging process under one roof – often saving considerable time and expense.

One such company is the British Homes Group (www.BritishHomesGroup.com) based in Orlando. Using a one-stop shop such as the British Homes Group brings a new level of convenience to villa purchases in Florida and can both simplify and significantly reduce the cost of buying and selling investment properties in the Sunshine State. ●

BUYING AND SELLING FACTS

■ Florida villa prices currently range from a median high of $389,100 in Naples to a low of $101,000 in the Lakeland/Winter Haven area

■ Areas most popular with UK owners have shown healthy appreciation over the past 12 months

■ The most popular vehicle for internet property searches is the US real estate industry's Multiple Listing Service (MLS)

■ The MLS provides information on thousands of different properties for sale in every location in Florida and the US

■ COMPANY CONTACTS

Mid-Atlantic Group East Orlando, FL Tel: +1 407 396 9914 or by e-mail, leemweaver@earthlink.net, www.BritishMortgagesAbroad.com

BUYER'S GUIDE

Florida letting in 2005

Investors are pouring into Florida's lucrative buy-to-let market. Many are buying here as an alternative to a pension

THE INVESTORS' BUY-TO-LET CONCEPT IN ORLANDO has completely taken off over the past two years, probably beyond almost any agent's expectations. Having realised steady growth over the past 20 years, the market has seen anything but steady activity recently. The supply of quality vacation homes in the districts known to provide a healthy rental income due to the presence of Disney World has reduced dramatically. It's reached the point where many new developments, without even having the roads laid, already have waiting lists with deposits from eager purchasers wanting to take advantage of the fantastic prices that this area has to offer.

Buying now could save you a fortune. As little as two years ago, it was possible to choose an off-plan, custom-designed home with its own pool, and have the whole process completed – with the home built from scratch – in a little under six months. In the current market, such a process is rare to find within a year; indeed, many developments are not guaranteeing the delivery of a home for at least 18 months. This doesn't seem to deter investors, who take the view that the longer the build time is, the greater the chance of being able to make significant capital growth before even receiving the keys to their investment.

In this area of Orlando, short-term lets seem to be the way that almost all investors head toward. Long-term lets are available from a number of local management companies. This is likely to gain you a tenant from the local area, perhaps a worker from one of the many theme parks, and could save you the cost of furnishing a home because a local tenant would more than likely have some of their own furniture, particularly if they are in the process of moving from another home.

Short-term lets are easy to obtain. Many of the management companies specialising in the vacation home rentals industry will be able to supply, through their own advertising, overseas or even domestic US families who are looking to holiday in the region.

With Disney World no more than a 20 minute car ride away from the majority of these homes, this is the easiest market to aim at, particularly bearing in mind that more than 40 million people visit the Orlando region every year. The larger management companies in the area, generally the longer established ones, also work with tour operators from around the world, specialist villa companies and travel agencies, and are generally able to provide a higher volume of bookings.

Although the rates obtained by travel agencies and tour companies who contract to larger management companies are not the highest available, many owners take the view that a large volume of bookings, even at a lower rate, is the way forward to covering costs. Higher rates are generally obtained by owners who organise their own lettings. As much as 20-25 per cent more money can be obtained this way, mainly due to

> Nick Thake has been the UK sales director of Florida Choice Realty for the last six years. He has dealt with well over 500 clients who have purchased buy-to-let properties in Florida.

> In Orlando, £150,000 buys you a great piece of real estate, a four-bed, three-bath detached villa with a private swimming pool

THE FLORIDA LETTINGS MARKET

City	Rental prospects	Average weekly rentals
Clearwater	Not a huge rental area, predominantly a local market	$818
Miami	Good rental prospects but expensive	$1,418
Orlando	Excellent rental prospects for investors	$525
Sarasota	Good prospects, but restricted rentals	$605
West Palm Beach	Expensive rental market, very exclusive area	$1,576

BUYER'S GUIDE

the fact there is no middle man. A safe bet may be to do a bit of both and try to maximise the lets as a team.

So why has the buy-to-let market for this area gone so crazy of late? First of all, the exchange rate has been extremely favourable for buyers from Britain. Not so long ago, you were lucky to scrape $1.40 for your UK pound, yet the rate has been fluctuating around the $1.80 mark for a while. When looking at healthy sums of money, this 40 cents in the pound makes a huge difference to the price of a home. If interest rates sustain the strength of the UK pound, then the market is sure to continue to surge.

Next, you need to look at general property prices in the UK. Ask yourself this question: "If I were to buy a home for rentals in the area in which I reside, say a basic three-bedroom home, how much would I pay?" In Orlando, £150,000 buys you a great piece of real estate, a detached villa with four/five bedrooms, three bathrooms – probably over 2,000 square feet in total. It would have a fully-fitted kitchen with a vast choice of tiling and carpets if bought as a custom–built, off-plan home. The icing on the cake would be the screen-enclosed swimming pool at the back of the home with decking for soaking up the sun.

Television has undoubtedly helped the boom in Florida. Programmes featuring property abroad are incredibly popular and it has become such a key interest that they are gaining prime time slots. Florida has been the focal point on a number of occasions, and this has sparked a huge awareness of what is available and how inexpensive it is.

Finally, the arrival of bulk investors has also contributed to sending this market crazy. Investors in general seem to want to build up a portfolio of homes in a variety of locations. The majority are almost certain to already own homes in the UK, which are probably let out on a long term basis. A large percentage of them probably also own property in the popular areas of southern Europe, too. These people seem to have identified Florida as the latest region in which to invest their money. Investors have a habit of buying multiple homes in a market they have confidence in. It takes just a handful of these people to eat up an entire phase of homes within a development. This has helped drive prices up and at the same time cut supply down.

Tax awareness

Owners of a home in Florida will need a US-based accountant (or UK-based specialising in US law). Just as in the UK, you will need to produce a tax return for the IRS (Internal Revenue Services). You can offset virtually all costs incurred on a home against US income tax. Interest on the mortgage, associated management fees with the ongoing maintenance and care for the home, and your utility bills and insurances are a few of the costs incurred that you can offset. You

RENTAL ZONING

- Rental zoning varies from county to county and there is no rule of thumb by which to judge it
- In Orlando you have to apply for zoning in Polk County, Lake County has no zoning policy, and Orange County allows short-term rentals
- Along the Gulf Coast, Sarasota has no policy on rentals, Naples has some developments zoned for short-term rentals, and Clearwater has banned all short-term rentals
- Some areas are even restricted to letting for only one week every seven months. For example, Daytona Beach

also receive an allowance on your own costs to visit your home to monitor the maintenance of it. Even bearing all this in mind, you still get a tax-free allowance before reaching the threshold to pay US taxes. In the last calendar year, this threshold was around $3,000. Most owners who borrow against their property find that they don't end up having any tax to pay at the end of each financial year. Those who have a very small mortgage (or no mortgage) can find themselves paying a small sum of income tax.

When owners of Florida homes decide to let short term instead of long term, this gives them the facility to use the home as a holiday home while it continues to work as an investment.

Pension scheme

Most purchasers in the Orlando area are buying almost as a pension scheme. Instead of calculating percentage investment returns, this type of purchase works slightly differently. Buyers can place a minimum downpayment of 20 per cent and obtain funds for a capital and interest mortgage either in the US or in the UK which is secured against the home in Florida.

The idea is that with the correct management company and advice on purchasing, the income can cover the running costs inclusive of the mortgage to present the buyer with a self-funding home that doubles up as a holiday home. Given recent price rises it would be realistic to expect the value of the home to double over the next 10–15 years, providing buyers with an excellent addition to their existing pension. ●

■ COMPANY CONTACTS

Florida Choice Realty, 542 Rayleigh Road, Eastwood, Leigh-on-Sea, Essex, SS9 5HX, Tel: 01702 529600, www.choice-properties.net

BUYER'S GUIDE

Choosing a home in 2005

Finding the right home for your budget and future financial requirements is not always quite as simple as it sounds…

THE LAWS REGARDING REAL ESTATE ARE DIFFERENT in Florida from those in the UK and it's dangerous to assume you can rely on your knowledge of purchasing a property in the UK when buying a home in Florida.

The hole into which foreign buyers fall most often is the financial one. Everyone has their own financial circumstances and so each case is obviously different. Outlined here are a number of guidelines so that you can ensure you don't over-stretch your budget or purchase the wrong type of property for your needs.

As a foreign national in Florida, you must pre-qualify your financial arrangements. In the first instance, advice should be sought from either British or Florida licensed mortgage lenders or brokers.

Do not fall into the trap of choosing a home that's too expensive for your budget; it won't always bring you a greater return on your investment. In many cases, the number of bedrooms will determine rental value. However, don't necessarily be tempted to buy the cheapest home available, particularly if it is resale. This can prove to be a false economy and more than likely will not attract ongoing rentals into your home.

Resale homes can initially appear to be a good buy, but due to the 'appraisal' system, you really only get what you pay for and you may not be aware why that house seemed to be a 'bargain'.

Real estate law

In July 2003, the real estate laws changed dramatically and most brokers in Florida opted to operate as a transaction broker only, a role that gives the client limited protection. According to Florida real estate law, the 'selling agent' does not have a duty to answer the questions you ask as honestly as he could. He is not obliged to tell you everything about the property: his duty is to the seller/builder, not to you. On the other hand, a buyer's agent has a fiduciary duty to represent you and to disclose any defects.

Homes in Florida are zoned into short-term rental and residential areas, although some developments are mixed. Coastal areas are largely zoned as residential with varying degrees of rental restrictions. They range from no rentals, rent for 30 days minimum 12 times a year, 30 day minimum three times a year, to a few areas with no rental restrictions. The restricted areas should provide a good return on your investment.

Janette Thorne set up Homes of America Ltd with her husband and daughter after spending years visiting and planning to buy a home in Florida. The company helps people to buy homes in US and their sister management company looks after the properties when the owners are in the UK.

However, Central Florida and in particular south of Orlando, is still an area that allows daily rentals. This attracts not only the family looking to buy a holiday home with the intention that it will self-finance itself, but also those who buy for investment purposes. You can optimise the return on your investment in this area more than any other region in the state.

The amount you deposit is an essential aspect of the purchase; the ratio of loan-to-value is important if you want for the rental to pay for all your outgoings.

As a foreign national, you have to put a minimum of 20 per cent down. If you put 30 per cent or more down, you are eligible for a 'No Doc' mortgage. This is a mortgage where you don't need to detail your income or assets. On production of your passport and the requisite deposit, an American lender will offer you a 'No Doc' mortgage of up to 30 years.

If you are thinking of taking a slice of the equity from your UK home to buy your property in Florida then you really should reconsider. A 100 per cent mortgaged property is difficult to maintain and could result in you losing both your home in Florida and in the UK unless you have the means to pay all the money back. You need to be aware that the overheads when selling a home in Florida are much higher than when you buy it – you pay around six per cent in fees. However, capital gains tax, currently at 15 per cent in Florida, is not as high as it is in the UK.

Every community will have its own deeds and restrictions, so do not assume anything until you have looked through them. Make sure that you can use your home for the purpose that you intend to, and that if you are seeking a property to rent short term,

> Many people want to buy a property to replace their pension and to run as a business, and if you obtain the correct advice, this can be a very fruitful option

BUYER'S GUIDE

you are not mistakenly sold a residential property. It may be that you are simply not allowed to park your car on the road or that children are not allowed in the community. These community rules can affect your return. If you are buying your home as an investment, ensure it is a solid prospect.

Never assume that the term 'conservation area' means that the area is protected from further development unless stated in the deeds of the community; always check with the county planning office. You need to be aware that something could be built in that so-called 'conserved' space in Florida at some point. When choosing your property, it may be safer to choose one where there is already something acceptable at the foot of your garden rather than, for example, commercial buildings.

Buying with friends

You may wish to consider pooling your capital and buying a home with friends or members of your family – this is a common occurrence. In this event you will all put your name on the house deeds, but one person will assume the mortgage with a document drawn up by a solicitor to state that all members are responsible for it. This will then enable you to buy more properties in the future. The system works exceptionally well, not only from the financial aspect, but also from the marketing angle: the more people there are to market the property, the better the rental result.

The disadvantage is that it's human nature to want a home all to yourself and this can cause conflict. Many couples have come forward and said that initially they had been too scared to purchase alone. But with hindsight, once they realised how simple a process it was, they wished that they had bought their own home, and they often go on to buy a further property to achieve a home each.

The legal aspect of purchasing a property is very simple in Florida. It is the duty of the title company to ensure that all papers are assembled correctly and legally by Florida real estate law – you will receive a certificate of 'title insurance'. Solicitors are rarely used and often unnecessary. There is the option though of using an attorney in the transaction if you are not comfortable with the process. However, while a buyer's agent will offer his services for free, an attorney will charge you a fee.

Many people want to buy property to replace their pension and to run as a business. With the correct advice this can be very fruitful. Buying the right property in the first place is important, but it is equally important to choose a reputable management company for your home; this can make or break your investment. You should beware of 'guaranteed' rental promises, though. If you choose to buy a property under this promise, you may be best advised to ask to have it notarised to protect yourself and your investment, and to prevent any misunderstanding.

FLORIDA FACTS

- Only five states in the US have a lower tax burden than Florida

- Florida receives around 60 million overseas visitors every year and the economic impact of this on the state is around $50 billion

- Almost 900,000 people in the state are employed in tourism

- 40% of all US exports to South America pass through Florida

Live and let

It is often asked: "Can I buy a home in Florida and spend my retirement there?" The simple answer is that buying a home in Florida does not give you any rights to live in the US on a permanent basis. Do not be misled by the oft-used term "retirement community". You can, however, buy a home in the US, but the longest time that you can spend in it without a visa is six months, or 183 consecutive days. If you are found to be abusing this rule you will be deported. It is common for families to buy a home and use it for six months, and then rent it out for the time that they are not using it.

There are many ways that you can legally relocate to Florida but you must get the correct visa. The most common ones are the E2 and the L1 visas, both of which require you to either invest into/buy an existing business in the US or open another branch of a business that you run in the UK, while leaving the UK business running. Both these routes are simple if you follow the criteria – lots of families choose this method and are now living and working in Florida.

■ TRANSPORT

Florida transport 2005

The transport infrastructure in the Sunshine State has to cope with millions of people who travel by air, sea, rail and road

WITH FLORIDA'S POPULATION INCREASING AT A RAPID rate and more than 70 million people visiting the state annually, the transport infrastructure requires constant upgrading and expansion to cope with demand.

Airports

Florida's airports are currently undergoing a lot of development in order to deal more efficiently with the influx of tourists and new residents. Miami International has the most extensive plans; the airport has more take-offs and landings per runway than any other US airport resulting in delays at peak times. New plans to expand and modernise the airport include improvements to North and South terminals. North Terminal will gain 47 gates, increasing the Federal Inspection Capacity to 3,600 passengers per hour, while South will gain 15, increasing the capacity to 2,000 passengers per hour. Other improvements for 2005 include new navigation aids and taxiways.

South West Florida Airport's new terminal is due to open in the spring of 2005. The 798,000 square foot terminal will have 28 gates and a baggage handling system with more space and checkpoints, and will be accompanied by a three-storey garage and taxiway.

Another new terminal will be opening at Tampa International in April. It will have 16 gates, as well as new passenger areas. Tampa Airport is currently acquiring property in the Drew Park area for future expansion. The boundaries of this area are West Crest Avenue (North), Dazzo Avenue (South), Hesperides Street (East) and Westshore Boulevard (West).

Expansions are taking place at Pensacola and Fort Lauderdale airports. Both are extending existing runways. In Pensacola this will mean the relocation of Jerry Maygarden Road and disruption for months. The extension of runway 9R/27L in Fort Lauderdale will stay within the confines of NE 7th Avenue.

Leesburg Regional Airport in Orlando is also expanding; it has grown from a military training field to a regional airport designed to support general aviation needs. In-bound traffic to the area will increase when international flights can land.

Miami International Airport has more take-offs and landings per runway than any other airport in the whole of the United States

FLORIDA TRANSPORT FACTS

■ Orlando International Airport carries around 30 million passengers every year

■ The three busiest cruise ports in the world are in Florida, and there are seven sea ports in total

■ The railroad arrived in Key West in 1912 but was devastated by a series of hurricanes

■ It's 792 miles by road from Pensacola in the north of the state to Key West at the southern tip

A lot of new routes are being planned for 2005. American Airlines is introducing flights from Miami to Vail, St George's Bermuda, St Lucia, Manchester and St Kitts. Orlando Airport will provide services to Ottawa and Halifax (Air Canada), Toronto and Calgary (West Jet), and Virgin Atlantic is increasing their flights to six per week to Manchester and 17 per week to Gatwick.

Sea ports

Florida's ports sit along the Atlantic and Gulf coasts and provide passenger and cargo services. The world's three busiest cruise ports, Canaveral, Everglades and Miami-Dade, are situated on the Atlantic Coast. They served in excess of 10 million passengers last year and cover extensive routes including Trans-Atlantic, Panama Canal, Gulf Coast, Caribbean, South American and many others worldwide. Miami-Dade is in the process of building two new terminals which are due to open in 2005.

In addition, there are seven other ports which provide passenger services. The newest of these is

TRANSPORT

Miami-Dade port is not only the world's busiest cruise port, it's the cargo gateway to South America

Jacksonville, which began services with Celebrity Cruises and Carnival Cruise Lines in July 2004. Tampa is one of the fastest growing cruise ports and is adding new cruise lines and routes. Radisson Seven Seas Navigator has joined the fleet along with Carnival Cruise Line, Holland America Line, Royal Caribbean Cruise Line and Celebrity Cruises. The Tampa Port Authority is building the facilities necessary to accommodate further passengers.

Pensacola is also building a cruise terminal, which will open the port to a new business segment and could generate as many as 100,000 new visitors annually. Manatee and Panama City ports offer seasonal cruises, St Petersburg specialises in one-day cruises and unique diving cruises to Mexico, and Key West also has a passenger cruise fleet.

Florida's ports also provide an important service for the arrival and departure of many goods from the country. Tampa is the largest port by tonnage in the state of Florida, handling almost as much as the rest of the state's ports combined. Other cargo ports in Florida such as Palm Beach, Fernandina, St Joe and Pensacola have good road and rail connections to the north, making the dispersal of goods easier. Cargo also goes through Manatee, Panama City, Fort Pierce, Miami-Dade and Jacksonville ports.

Railways

Rail company Amtrak has two main routes which serve Florida. The Silver Service/Palmetto route runs daily from New York south to Jacksonville, Orlando, Tampa, West Palm Beach, Fort Lauderdale and Miami. The Sunset Limited route runs three times per week from Los Angeles to Tallahassee, Jacksonville and Orlando, and daily between Tallahassee and Orlando. Amtrak also organises Thruway connecting bus services to many towns in Florida which do not have rail connections. Long distance trains in Florida are often infrequent and services have suffered due to the emphasis placed on motor vehicles.

However, one route which is improving is the tri-rail service in South East Florida. This route runs south from Mangonia Park along the coast to Miami via West Palm Beach, Lake Worth, Boca Raton, Fort Lauderdale and Hialeah, through Palm Beach, Broward and Miami-Dade counties. Two new trains were added to this route in August 2004 and after some work on the tracks, two more will be added in January 2005. Currently, the tri-rail trains share a single set of tracks with CSX freight trains and Amtrak passenger trains, which means that delays are often caused when trains have to pull over. Double tracking has already been completed on the track between Deerfield Beach and Lake Worth and by December 2005, 30 more miles should have been completed, which means that trains will be able to run every 20 minutes. Despite the current delays, record numbers of passengers are choosing to use this rapidly improving service because the roads are often congested and fuel prices are high.

The Metro Rail, which connects with the tri-rail service and serves the city of Miami, stopping at Hialeah, Brickell, Coconut Grove and South Miami among other stations, is also a popular service.

Roads

Due to the huge number of people visiting Florida, even some of the major arteries are very congested. For this reason, there is work being done on many roads to accommodate the increase in traffic. One of the main East-West roads, the I4 from Tampa to Daytona Beach, is undergoing improvements which are expected to continue until 2012. The areas affected in 2005 are between Polk County and US192, which is being widened to six lanes, and between Saxon Boulevard and SR 472 which, again, is being widened to six lanes.

The I95, which runs from Miami up the east coast of Florida, is also being widened. Other areas soon to be affected are Delray Beach (CR 782) to Lake Worth, and from Riviera Beach (FL 708) to Palm Beach Gardens. Major work is being undertaken around south east Jacksonville. The I295 is being extended around the city and this will increase accessibility to Jacksonville and decrease congestion when it is completed. ●

Your **life in the sun** starts here

The Daily Telegraph

DESTINATIONS
THE HOLIDAY & TRAVEL SHOW

LONDON EARLS COURT 3–6 FEBRUARY 2005

PRESENTS

DESTINATION HOLIDAY HOMES ABROAD

in association with

HOMES WORLDWIDE

Turn your overseas property dreams into reality at Britain's favourite live holiday event. You'll find everything you need to locate your perfect place in the sun, plus thousands of the hottest holiday ideas.

Book in advance and save ££s at **DestinationsShow.com**

BUYER'S GUIDE

Steps to buying

Everything you need to know about buying a home in Florida is contained within this easily digestible, step-by-step guide

DECIDING TO BUY A PROPERTY IN FLORIDA IS AN EASY decision but navigating the Florida legal system can sometimes be difficult, and it differs drastically from that of the UK. With the Florida property market currently booming and demand for property continuously growing, it is becoming increasingly important to be aware of, and wherever possible, avoid the possible pitfalls associated with buying a property in the Sunshine State. As title insurance companies (normally selected by the seller) handle the conveyancing aspect of a Florida property purchase and a buyer's lawyer is not legally required, issues are further complicated for the British buyer who is accustomed to buying property with a lawyer's aid. On top of this, there are no restrictions placed upon a British buyer purchasing a second or investment property, and this further adds to the wealth of choices available. In order to help make those choices and ensure the decision-making and buying process progress smoothly, this chapter strives to give a clear and detailed analysis of the mechanics of buying a home in Florida. It isn't necessary that the following steps are always taken in the order below, but it's suggested that it would be in your interests to do so.

Step 1: Taking initial advice
Having decided that you would like to purchase a property in Florida, you should take preliminary advice about the basics prior to a visit to the States.

Before you sign anything, you should secure the services of a specialist lawyer who can advise with regard to both the relevant Florida and UK issues when purchasing property abroad

a) Preliminary tax and legal advice
It's recommended that one of the first things you should do is speak to a lawyer, preferably one who is qualified in, and can advise on, both UK and Florida law. Your lawyer should inform you at this early stage of the various types and roles of Florida estate agents you may deal with.

This advice should also include the setting up of a US bank account, relevant tax implications resulting from purchasing a property in Florida, general international estate planning and, perhaps most significantly, the best way a buyer from the United Kingdom might seek to purchase a property: for example, whether through sole ownership, joint tenancy, tenancy in common, or through a company, trust or other entity. The way in which you hold the property can potentially save you thousands of pounds and also can have implications for estate or

GB Pound to US Dollar

[Line chart showing GB Pound to US Dollar exchange rate from Dec '99 to Jun '04, ranging from approximately £1.40 to £1.90]

THE 4LESS GROUP PLC

33

BUYER'S GUIDE

Florida is a state that allows transactional brokers who, by their very definition, act on behalf of neither the buyer nor the seller and do not actually owe any loyalty or confidentiality to either of the parties involved

inheritance taxes when you come to passing your estate on to a spouse or to children.

Being for US tax purposes a 'non-resident alien', as a UK buyer you're not in the same tax position as a US citizen. Most Florida property sellers and estate agents would not be aware of this as they deal mainly with US buyers. It is only the lawyer or tax advisor you retain who will assess your potential exposure to US and UK taxes and what may need to be done to minimise, or in some instances, eliminate such tax exposure. Advice taken regarding taxes and how best to hold title may require decisions to be made and action taken before you even sign a purchase contract. As it's a seller's market, many Florida sellers take the position that they will allow no amendments, changes or assignments of the contract.

You may also wish to talk to a tax advisor about your financial circumstances to give you a tailored view of your tax exposure in both the US and UK in purchasing a Florida property. Financial assessment is a wise move given that you are considering a financial outlay which could jeopardise your future position.

b) Preliminary financing advice

Before even attempting to fulfil your dream of buying a property in Florida, it's crucial to establish whether or not you (or any entity you might use to hold title) are a financially viable buyer. It is absolutely essential that before you make any commitments you ensure that you can afford the expenditure involved in buying your Floridian home, and be certain that by doing so you won't jeopardise your assets in the UK. Secondly, before even putting in a bid for your property, you should make sure you are prequalified for a mortgage, as there is nothing worse than finding your potential new home, putting in a bid and then failing to qualify for a mortgage.

With regard to financing a property purchase through a mortgage, it's even more critical to get preapproval where there is no mortgage contingency clause in the purchase contract (as is the case with condominium purchases). A mortgage contingency clause allows the buyer to be released from the contract where a satisfactory mortgage could not be obtained within an agreed period of time.

As a buyer, securing mortgage preapproval prior to entering a commitment is essential

Mortgage preapproval

The first step is to get preapproved for a mortgage before entertaining the idea of buying a home, and you have the option of borrowing from US or UK lenders. With some UK lenders, you may now have the option to borrow against your UK assets or against the property you intend to purchase in Florida, whether you choose to borrow in sterling or dollars. Whichever you choose, getting preapproved allows you to safely make an offer on a property with the knowledge that you have financial backing before ever becoming contractually obliged to purchase.

Where possible, it's preferable to be preapproved for your maximum home mortgage amount in writing by an actual lender and not just prequalified by a mortgage broker (where no lender has yet made a loan commitment to you). Getting preapproval also gives you peace of mind, establishes your price bracket and avoids problems of over-commitment beyond your own personal budget. Please note that you need to inform the lender or mortgage broker if you intend to purchase the property through an entity rather than in your own name(s), as the available terms and rates do differ. Also, notwithstanding what some mortgage brokers may state, lenders do exist (although admittedly not many) who will lend in sterling or dollars to companies or other entities buying Florida properties.

It is important to remember that there are lots of outgoings to cover when buying a home in Florida beyond the purchase price itself. There are the closing costs, mortgage costs, furnishing costs, payments in escrow (which non-residents are obliged to pay covering three to six months worth of mortgage payments), home or condominium owners association assessments (fees) and in some instances, special assessments (for items agreed by the majority of owners and benefiting them such as new sewer lines, improved roads, pavements etc.), property tax and insurance premiums. Also, the day-to-day running costs of a property need to be calculated by the potential buyer.

Tax deductions

If you were planning on making a cash purchase, you may want to take note that in financing your purchase, you would be able to offset mortgage interest paid during the year against income from rentals secured in the US. By paying mortgage interest, the amount of which is listed on 'Form 1098', you're entitled to deductions on your US income tax. Any UK lender lending against Florida property in dollars should be asked (like a US lender)

A condo is a 'box in the sky' (like a UK apartment) although such a property will often have resort facilities available within the community such as a clubhouse, a communal swimming pool, a gymnasium and barbecue area

for the same US 1098 form which will entitle you to deductions on your US income tax return for the dollar equivalents of such mortgage payments.

Also, the 'points' you would pay to a lender on the completion of a Florida property purchase can usually be deducted as a prepayment of interest. These points are also described on the relevant closing (completion) statement as:

- Loan origination fees
- Maximum loan charges
- Loan discount
- Discount points

Step 2: Appointing a lawyer

Whether you have taken preliminary legal advice or not, it is advised that once you have decided to go ahead and purchase in Florida – and before you sign anything – you secure the services of a specialist lawyer who can advise you with regard to both the relevant Florida and UK issues to purchasing property abroad. Your lawyer is there to help guide you through the legal issues involved in buying your home, to make you feel secure, and to seek to secure for you an advantageous and less risky contract. If you have not already taken preliminary legal advice, your lawyer should advise you of the various estate agent roles, the relevant tax implications (both US and UK), your options in holding title, and perhaps discuss arrangements for appropriate wills where you buy in an individual capacity.

If you're buying the Florida property together with family members, friends or other associates, please note that you should have an agreement drafted up beforehand, setting out in black and white who is responsible for arranging lettings, how and when time spent in the property is allotted, and how taxes are paid. Your lawyer can assist in drafting an agreement. These decisions should be made before you enter into a contract with friends or associates to alleviate any problems which could occur later.

BUYER'S GUIDE

At an early stage in the purchase process you'll be presented with a Florida property purchase contract for your signature. By retaining the services of a UK resident lawyer who normally would have been appointed before you visit Florida, you'll be in a position to fax the contract to the lawyer for his or her advice before signing.

Once you are in a position to sign the contract, the lawyer will consider the terms concerning the deposit, terms and conditions addressing breaches of the contract and all other terms generally. You will need to be advised as to your own, and the seller's contractual obligations. Each purchase contract has a Liquidated Damages clause, which normally states that the deposits received up to a certain percentage of the cost of the property are due to the builder should you cause the sale to fall through. On a new build, builders usually claim as 'liquidated damages' 10 per cent or more of the overall purchase price should you pull out of the sale. They may also seek deposits agreed but as yet unpaid, charges for options (such as swimming pools, etc.), and/or lot premiums.

Lawyer-free purchases?

It's possible in Florida to purchase a property without the services of a lawyer, and in that instance you rely solely on the relevant real estate agents, brokers and the title-closing agents. Always remember that unless you have something in writing to the contrary, you should assume that these individuals do not represent you. Indeed, when navigating the Florida property market, some Floridian estate agents may tell you that the property purchase process is lawyer-free. However, with a new build the seller will use a lawyer as their lawyer is responsible for drafting the purchase contract (unlike the UK, there is no such thing in Florida as a 'standard contract') and the seller selects their lawyer's title insurance company to handle the closing.

As estate agents in Florida deal mainly with local purchasers and some UK buyers, they are usually unaware of all the additional requirements faced by, and the options available to, an overseas buyer, and consequently do not recommend the services of a lawyer which could potentially save the buyer thousands of pounds.

While the benefits of having a lawyer come at a cost, those buying without a lawyer may run the risk of being faced with far higher costs or penalties if obliged to comply with terms or sign a contract they do not fully understand. If a breach of contract does occur and you have not had the contract checked by a lawyer then you will be faced with the expense of litigation as opposed to preventive law, which is less expensive. The legal fees paid to a buyer's lawyer to advise the buyer before signing or to check over closing documents on a contract are much less than this. Given that you are buying abroad, it is the most sensible course of action to take.

If buying a business, consult a business broker and identify any competition in the field

VISIT FLORIDA

BUYER'S GUIDE

Make sure you speak directly to people who have actually bought houses in Florida and have experienced the buying process, because you can learn a lot from their experiences and mistakes

While many Floridians may not use a lawyer when they purchase a residential property, you as a UK buyer should remember that you would never consider buying a property in the UK without a lawyer, so why would you not use one in a foreign country? If you want to protect yourself, you should engage a lawyer to represent you. Otherwise, there is really no one legally on the buyer's side.

Step 3: Choosing an agent

If you want to take advantage of the option to use a Florida buyer's estate agent (who under Florida law is loyal to and owes confidentiality to you), always choose and retain your agent before even starting to look at any properties, so that the seller is obliged to pay your buyer's agent a share of the sales commission.

Be aware that in walking through the door of a model home (or a showhome in the UK) you have effectively waived your option to use an unbiased agent as you have bound yourself to the seller's agent by dealing with them directly rather than retaining your own agent. You can still retain the services of a buyer's agent but you will be responsible for their fees. It is therefore of value to consider carefully the types of estate agents you may be dealing with at an early stage in the process.

The differences between estate agents in Florida and the United Kingdom lie not just with who they represent, but also who they are loyal to. Florida is a state that allows transactional brokers who, by definition, act on behalf of neither the buyer nor the seller and owe no loyalty or confidentiality to either one, yet are still obliged to bring about the sale of the property. Transactional brokerage is basically a means of providing neutral third-party real estate services to buyers and sellers with reduced liability to the broker. Agents act for either the buyer or the seller at any given stage of the conveyancing, but never both at the same time. Transactional brokers are not actually agents as they do not represent either party.

An alternative choice of broker is a buyer's broker or agent who works exclusively for you. While a buyer's agent may be a good option, you may, especially when dealing with agents in the UK, want to balance the benefit of using such an agent against any discounts or reduced purchase prices sometimes available with a seller's agent.

There are numerous estate agents touting for business, so if you're looking for an agent located in the UK, you may want to check to ensure that it's a registered member of FOPDAC (the Federation of Overseas Property Developers, Agents and Consultants; www.fopdac.com). Member agents have been vetted and approved, and offer unbiased advice for the buyer. The common aim of FOPDAC members is to conduct their activities in a manner which seeks to protect the interests of those who have decided to buy or sell a property overseas.

Membership of the federation is restricted to UK resident companies or individuals whose probity is beyond reasonable question. The individual principals must have the experience and professional expertise to meet the strict criteria set in their Code of Ethics.

BIGGEST BANKS AND CONTACT DETAILS

- **Barnett Bank**, 80 S Flamingo Road, Pembroke Pines, FL 33027, Tel: +1 954 327 5600, www.bnett.com
- **AmSouth Bank of Florida**, 1042 Main Street, Dunedin FL 34698-5200, Tel: +1 727 736 1995, www.amsouth.com
- **Sun Bank**, Western Way Office, 13137 Cortez Boulevard, Brooksville, FL 34613, Tel: +1 352 597 7300, www.suntrust.com
- **Capital Bank**, 800 S Jefferson Tallahassee, FL 32301, Tel: +1 850 671 0589
- **Intercontinental Bank**, 5722 SW 8th Street, West Miami, Miami-Dade County 33144, Tel: +1 305 441 2401
- **Washington Mutual**. Washington Mutual, 8851 Glades Road, Boca Raton, FL 33434, Tel: +1 561 488 0406.
- **Bank of America** Search for a branch on www.bankofamerica.com

BUYER'S GUIDE

You will note that FOPDAC's members also include sellers, developers, consultants and lawyers.

Licensed realtor

Alternatively you may want to secure the services of an estate agent in Florida, but you must make certain that the agent is an experienced realtor licensed with the Florida Real Estate Commission. A realtor you retain has your best interests at heart and it's a powerful statement to view a home with a realtor, thus giving forth the message that you will see, and have seen, a large portfolio of homes. It is a common misconception that dealing directly with a builder saves money. This simply isn't true because the independent broker gives unbiased advice and is only paid their share of the seller's commission once the deal is completed or, in the case of a new build, the build is completed.

There are many estate agents based in the UK and Florida who are willing to handle the process from start to finish, but it's well worth shopping around, especially when it comes to finding the property of your dreams. Whatever you choose to do, always assume that unless you have a written agreement with an agent, they do not instruct you and cannot keep confidential information about you. In the absence of a written disclosure always ask for a written 'notice of non-representation'.

Step 4: Find the right home

As with every country the dynamics of buying a second home are down to the personality of the buyer; however, there are certain fundamental rules to bear in mind before launching into the buying process. Florida is a land of plenty, boasting everything from coastal properties to the ideal investment homes of bustling Orlando and the swampy Everglades, but this choice can be problematic for the buyer.

Research is the key word here and it's best to first visit the intended destination on holiday before deciding to search for a home there. It's crucial to study the potential location of your property as there are many counties or individual developments with rental restrictions in place.

If you're buying with rental in mind it's vital for you to receive written confirmation that the area or development in which you buy has an unlimited rental season. The term used in Florida is 'short-term rentals', and where they're allowed you should have no problem letting the property. However, where short-term lettings are not allowed you will not be permitted to let, or be limited to no more than four lettings, for a minimum of 30 days.

Don't simply be tempted by glossy brochures and unrealistic projected rental offers. You should be safe if you do your homework and investigate by talking to others who've bought

Buying a condominium

A condo is a 'box in the sky' (like a UK apartment) although such a property will often have resort facilities available within the community such as a clubhouse, swimming pool, gym and so on. Your purchase will provide you with a title similar to freehold because you should have ownership of your individual condo plus shared ownership of common areas and facilities in the entire development.

In a condominium, only the interior space is individually owned. Most homes, whether residential or vacation, will be located within a community where there will be an operating condominium association. This will control the maintenance of the communal community areas, building hallways, private roads, lawn care and so on. Typical monthly costs can range from $100 up to as much as $400, depending on the specification of amenities provided, such as a golf course. The association is normally owned and controlled jointly by the owners themselves, though there will be a separate management firm involved which will administrate it.

If you use a property management agency, you may also be paying to cover the maintenance of your own condominium. Expect to pay a monthly sum that reflects the cost of the entire package and any maintenance work required. An older condominium will demand a much higher cost than that of a new one. Typical monthly maintenance costs can range from around $200 to $600.

With regard to condominiums, you need to ensure that your prospective neighbours are like-minded in terms of short-term rentals; recent cases in the Florida courts have stated that associations may vote to change such policies. As of May 2005, a bill is expected to be passed allowing current condominium unit owners to keep any rental rights that existed at the time of purchase, in case they are later removed or restricted by an association board or vote. Such rights would be preserved only for as long as the owner owned the unit.

Buy-to-let
If you are seeking to let a property you need to ensure that the property is located within the correct rental zone. Has the land been zoned or not? With escalating property prices comes another risk worthy of serious consideration: what are the prospects of the property you wish to purchase meeting your rental income expectation? Are the rents rising in line with property price increases? Your choice of location, size and price will help determine this. Don't simply be tempted by glossy brochures and unrealistic projected rental offers. You should be safe if you do your homework and investigate by talking to others who have already bought homes in the area.

The future management of your home is critical. Try to ensure that you obtain truly independent advice from someone who is in the know prior to employing any firm. Capable owners who can control rental bookings themselves will obtain the best results; they will control their own lets and therefore any achievable rental income. You may want to speak to a lawyer to prepare suitable terms for letting, and all terms and conditions. With the internet and effective networking, this should not be difficult to achieve and there is nothing to prevent a management firm from being employed to work with an owner on bookings, and to create an operating agreement, stating the first booking obtained is the one accepted.

Buying off-plan
This type of purchase method is extremely common due to an unprecedented demand for new homes, and many excellent opportunities exist for potential capital appreciation during the build time. Different developments will have varying payment structures, although it's wise to consider whether or not the building works are in advance of any payments, prior to any possible agreement to purchase being implemented. We recommend that you should be most wary of buying off-plan purely in reliance of any capital gain, for there can be no guarantee of this occurring.

Buying a business
Your first action should be to take advice from a US immigration lawyer. Be wary of immigration 'consultants' who are not lawyers, as they normally carry no insurance, nor can they legally represent you. Ensure that all persons you deal with (including the seller) are genuine. Employ a qualified business broker to find a proposal that will suit your requirements and look carefully at any competition. Be particularly careful if you seek to purchase or lease a business as part of any 'E-2' non-immigration visa application; you will need to ensure that this will be regarded as a qualifying business and any such purchase will need to have a contract that is conditional on this visa being obtained. You should not assume that an approval for any subsequent change of business will automatically be approved.

Step 5: Steps to take in Florida
Opening a bank account
Once you've established the feasibility of purchasing your home in Florida, the next step is to open a bank account in order to allow the transfer of currency. If you don't do this while in Florida then you will more than likely be required to send your passport and utility bills from Britain to the States in order to open an account, so the most practical procedure is to do this while holidaying there. Having your own US bank account also avoids the complexity of worrying about ongoing currency exchange issues and the exchange rate, and allows for payment of bills such as utility deposits and any administrative expenses. It also removes the stress of worrying about meeting the deadline for final payments, which is the buyer's responsibility and generally occurs over two to three days and can be a very stressful process.

If you don't have a US bank account then it may be very difficult to purchase your dream home. The first thing to be wary of is whether or not the bank is covered by FDIC insurance (which covers up to $100,000 per account), which protects against bank failures and guarantees deposits: never deposit money in a bank which isn't insured by the FDIC (the Federal Deposit Insurance Corporation; check out the website at www.fdic.gov).

Commercial and savings banks
America has two types of banks: 'commercial' banks that offer a very wide range of services, and 'savings' banks, which offer a better rate of interest and are granted government charters to hold half of all mortgage loans and are licenced collect deposits and make home loans.

In addition to banks there are also loan associations known simply as 'thrifts', although these have fallen drastically in number over recent years from 4,000 to 1,000. When choosing a bank you need to realise that Florida's banks, of which there are 250, are regularly competing for customers and offer comprehensive packages detailing their services and the variety of accounts they offer. An initial deposit of $50 will be enough to open an account once you have the paperwork in place.

BUYER'S GUIDE

All mortgage applicants must be homeowners in the UK; some lenders will allow potential rental income to be taken into account when deciding the size of the loan, but not if you remortgage

ITIN number

An ITIN number is required when an individual who is not eligible to obtain a Social Security Number (for example, a foreign national) does any one of the following:

- Opens an account with a US financial institution
- Sells a US real property interest (the seller needs an identification number so the purchaser can withhold and remit the required US withholding tax, FIRPTA see page 48
- Is subject to reporting and withholding on investments in US partnerships and rental properties.

Until December 2003, an ITIN could be obtained by sending a completed Form W-7 (application for IRS Individual Taxpayer Identification Number) to an IRS (Internal Revenue Service) office, along with an original passport, or two or more original documents that verified the owner's foreign identity and non-US status. However, the laws regarding ITINs have been changed recently and the IRS may, *subject to certain exceptions*, require you to have an income tax return ready to be filed before you will be permitted to apply for an ITIN.

One of the exceptions to the rule is where you can provide evidence that you have already opened up a US bank account. However, many banks require the ITIN number before permitting you to open an account. You may need to explain that you cannot yet get an ITIN number to a bank (or branch of a bank) which does not deal often with foreign nationals opening accounts and is unfamiliar with the recent changes in the law.

The rules keep changing but you can get the most up-to-date information and look at the recent list of exceptions at www.irs.gov/pub/irs-pdf/p1915.pdf. However, should you wish to wait until such time as you're ready to file your first US income tax return, it's advisable to obtain this ITIN when in Florida or in the UK at the US embassy in London; it can be risky and costly to post your passport and relevant documents to the IRS in the US, or to visit an approved IRS acceptance agent in the UK who may charge in excess of £400.

To apply while in the United States, you need to visit your nearest IRS office. You will be required to produce your passport or other identification documents. The application will be done for you completely free of charge and will require you to complete a W7 form. You can visit the IRS website at www.irs.gov for further information, or call the IRS at +1 800 829 1040.

TYPICAL BILL OF COSTS

Paid for by the borrower

Cost of property	$184,000.00
Closing costs	$7,923.00
Community costs (only relevant if buying in a development/community/condo)	$610.00
Transfer fees (typically cost of deed)	$100.00

Paid for by the lender

Deposit	$1,782.50
Loan amount (mortgage)	$128,800.00
10% escrow deposit (good faith deposit)	$18,400.00
Closing costs credit (credited to the buyer for using an affiliate of the lender)	$5,924.90
County taxes	$596.01

Total paid for the borrower by the lender	**$155,503.41**
Total due from the borrower to the lender	**$192,935.04**

Data supplied by Bennett & Co. Solicitors

BUYER'S GUIDE

TYPES OF MORTGAGE AVAILABLE

● Fixed rate mortgage
This type of mortgage has an interest that is fixed from the time of the loan, and it remains constant for the duration of the mortgage repayment. Lenders generally demand a higher rate of interest on a fixed loan of this type and consequently monthly mortgage repayments are higher than on an adjustable or balloon mortgage.

● Adjustable rate mortgage
Known as an ARM, this mortgage offers a fixed interest rate, and a fixed initial monthly repayment. These are only fixed for a period of between six months and five years, rather than the life of the loan. After the initial fixed period, both the interest rates and monthly repayments adjust to reflect the current market interest rates. Most ARMs do carry a cap, the upper limit that a homeowner can be charged. For example, if the initial rate on your loan is six per cent and the cap is 11 per cent, if interest rates climbed to 15 per cent the interest on the loan would not climb past the cap of 11 per cent.

● Balloon mortgage
A balloon mortgage has a fixed interest rate and fixed monthly repayment. For example, after a fixed period of five years the entire balance of the loan becomes due for repayment. This can obviously create problems and can mean if the buyer cannot repay, they have to organise another mortgage. This is not a hugely practical mortgage unless the buyer cannot get a standard fixed or adjustable rate mortgage.

Bear in mind that whether you choose a fixed or flexible rate mortgage, it's essential to get expert advice on the current state of the economy and its impact upon your mortgage. Before signing your final purchase contract it is recommended you sign a 40-day provisional contract in order to allow you to close your mortgage and meet the financial requirements of the final contract which is based upon financial backing.

Finding a property management agency
Although many estate agents also act as property management agencies for their clients, it's advocated that as a buyer seeking to let your property, you consider the services of an independent property management agency. Something to be aware of is that as estate agents may earn between six and seven per cent commission from selling a home, there is always some concern that they may in time neglect the management of your property in the hope that you may resell with them in the future. This of course would apply to only a small percentage of estate agents/management agents, but it's worth bearing in mind when considering what type of management agency you seek to employ.

Independent advice
It is important that you ensure you get independent advice and references from previous buyers. If you're planning a viewing trip to Florida, it's suggested that you organise a number of interviews and viewings with estate agents and management agents, thus making your time in Florida as productive as possible. Make sure you speak directly to people who have actually bought in Florida and have experienced the buying process, because you can learn a lot from their experiences and mistakes.

Step 6: The contract
Nowhere in the Florida conveyancing process is there a 'subject to contract' period. This means that you must ensure you are happy to buy the property before signing the contract because there are very few ways of getting out of it. As everything hinges on the signing of the contract, it is suggested that you should consider including contingencies and protections against any possible problems that should arise, thus protecting your investment and safeguarding your interests. Caution is urged when dealing with a developer's contract, as contracts vary from seller to seller and are personalised by the seller's attorneys to suit the seller's needs and circumstances.

With regard to resales, the contract used is usually (but not always) one of two basic forms: the FAR/BAR (drafted by the Florida Association of Realtors and The Florida Bar) or the FAR contract (drafted by the Florida Association of Realtors only). While these contracts are generally more reasonable than developers contracts, it's very useful to have further contingencies or addenda made to these contracts. Where possible, every contract should incorporate the 'legal' description of the property (which is not the street address as it is in the UK).

The purchase price, payment dates and terms should, however, be in every contract. It's important that the contract details or addenda also include any additional extras and options that have been agreed by the seller, such as the inclusion of furniture, closing costs contribution and an agreed closing date. You may want to condition your purchase on certain contingencies such as the approval of a mortgage, the approval of your lawyer, a satisfactory valuation

■ BUYER'S GUIDE

KEY CHECKS TO MAKE

- Bulging walls
- Cracks in the wall, both inside and out
- Lead water pipes
- Asbestos
- Unsafe electrical wiring
- Lead-based paint (which is now illegal to use)
- Poor plumbing and drainage
- Rising damp
- Dry and wet rot
- Mould
- Unlevel floors
- Subsidence
- Exposure to radon (a radioactive gas that is carcinogenic)

of the property, a satisfactory inspection/survey of the property, the receipt of completed disclosure documents or questionnaires from the seller, or on the seller's approval of your right to assign the contract to any entity you may need to establish before closing for tax purposes. You may likewise want to stipulate the deadline by which the seller should have approved the buyer's offer and contract. When you're buying a condominium, you are given a 15 day period of grace in which to decide whether you want to revoke the contract or not.

Good faith deposit

Payments to the seller usually start with the payment of a 'holding deposit' or 'good-faith deposit', which normally refers to the amount you put down to reserve the property when you are first provided with the real estate contract before signing. There is often no set amount for a true good faith deposit but these may range between $100 and $5,000, and sometimes even more.

You should secure in writing whether or not the seller will refund your holding deposit in case you decide not to go ahead with the purchase. In that event, never part with more money than you're willing to lose. If the seller wants a large good faith deposit, you may be able to negotiate a two-part payment where you pay the larger half of the deposit upon the signing of the contract, or after any agreed contingencies are met.

With all deposits totalled, including any good faith deposit, you will normally have paid between 10 to 30 per cent of the purchase price. A 20 per cent deposit of the property's full price is often asked for with new builds, and usually during the period of signing the contract. The usual size of deposit requested for a resale or renovation home is 10 per cent. Under Florida state law, deposits paid of up to 10 per cent of the purchase price may not be used by the seller towards construction costs, and must be held in escrow until completion/closing, (see page 35) unless you waive your rights in the contract. It is, however, fairly common for sellers and developers to ask you to waive this right.

Contingency clauses

The contingency clause can be very significant, in so far as it may be your only means of ensuring the property meets your requirements. Such a clause may allow you to withdraw from the purchase without penalty. Contingencies can also be used by the seller and may range from time scales for payment, to proof that the funds can be raised. Essentially, contingency clauses contain deadlines, and permit either party to enter into the sale without being sure he can meet the terms of the contract: for example, secure a mortgage, or if certain procedures such as the home inspection will not be carried out until later on. Common clauses include a satisfactory appraisal, which gives the value of the property to be no less than the price paid by the buyer. Arranging for two appraisals is sometimes done to alleviate the worries of the mortgage lender.

Appraisal costs

The cost of such appraisals (up to $300) is usually met by the buyer. Approval by third parties, such as the agreement by a lender to issue a mortgage, can be made a contingency making the sale reliant on the ability of the buyer to gain third party support. Another contingency clause is where the buyer seeks to make the purchase contingent on the sale of another property (this is not particularly common in Florida however), or where the buyer seeks the approval of a family member in order to go ahead with the purchase.

Some contracts also hold a mortgage contingency clause which states that the buyer should ensure they apply for a mortgage within a week of signing the final contract, and the contract may contain a loophole which states that if the buyer cannot get a loan commitment within 30 days of signing a contract, they may back out of the sale (or the seller may likewise cancel the sale). However, some sellers refuse to write this into the contract.

BUYER'S GUIDE

Step 7: Securing a mortgage

As discussed in Step 1 (page 28) it is recommended that your first action should be to get preapproved for a mortgage as this defines your price bracket and allows you to safely put your name to a contract. It is also advised that you look into securing both a dollar and sterling mortgage as there are variables such as currency exchange that could cause problems.

Mortgages from US lenders are available from a number of different sources, with savings and loan associations providing over half the mortgages in the US. Non-residents will be lent no more than 70 to 80 per cent of the market value of their property, while a resident can secure up to 95 per cent.

When you're purchasing your Florida property through a company or other such entity, you will normally have to put down 20 per cent and you'll find that the rates are not as favourable. Therefore, if the value of your home is $100,000 you will have to cover at least $20,000 of the cost with your own money. However, if for some reason you have already secured residency before you buy, you also have to ensure that you have enough credit to be entitled to a US mortgage.

If you buy as a non-resident then no credit check is necessary and you're immediately entitled to apply for a US mortgage. If you pay less than 20 per cent of the value of the property, mortgage lenders will insist that you have private mortgage insurance, or a mortgage life insurance policy. This pays off the outstanding balance of the mortgage should you die before payment completion.

Credit rating

In order to qualify for a mortgage, an assessment is carried out through evaluation of the property in order to confirm its value, and your credit rating is then checked; it will have to be perfect in order to qualify for a home loan. As in the UK, the amount the mortgage company will lend you is determined

CONSTRUCTION PERMITS

Some counties in Florida demand a permit for specific constructions. These include:

- New constructions, including additions and remodelling of any building
- Demolition work
- Any new roof covering or replacement
- Stucco or siding work over 500 square feet
- Any work associated with changing the occupancy size of the building
- Residential accessory buildings or residential driveways over 150 square feet
- Any gas work
- Any mechanical work, except for self-contained air conditioning units less than three tons
- Plumbing work on any building, water/sewer lines, septic tanks, wells and fire lines
- Any electrical work
- Removal of trees deemed protected, grade/fill work, and site clearance greater than 500 square feet

Consequently, ensure you have an inspection to check that all changes or constructions carried out by the vendor are legally permissible.

BUYER'S GUIDE

CLOSING COSTS

Generally, most of a buyer's closing costs are related to any loan they take out (if any). These lender costs, or fees which would be listed on the HUD closing statement, may include the following: Mortgage Origination Fee, Mortgage Discount Points, Wood Destroying Organism Report, Appraisal Fee, Tax Service, Document Preparation Fee, Mortgagee (or Lender) Title Insurance Policy, Title Insurance Endorsements, and Flood Certification Fee. The buyer also usually pays the Florida Documentary Stamp Tax on the mortgage note. If the buyer is utilising other services such as their own lawyer, home inspector, or termite inspector, the buyer must pay those fees as well.

The seller pays for costs such as securing and delivering a good and marketable title that fulfils the terms and conditions of the contract. This includes the title search, owner's title insurance policy, survey, recording fees and any other services chosen to be carried out by the seller. A rough rule of thumb for the buyer to take into account is that you should only be paying around five per cent of the purchase price if you are using a mortgage lender, and two to three per cent if purchasing your home by cash. The seller may also pay the Florida Intangible Property Tax and Florida Documentary Stamp Tax on the deed.

At the current time, however, because it remains a seller's market, when you're buying from a builder, the treatment of closing costs may be very different. The builder, for example, may refuse to pay any closing costs at all, or where you are using a 'preferred lender', make only a contribution to the closing costs (which are all yours) or place a cap on the amount you would pay, with them paying the difference.

---

by your income and it's limited to no more than three times your income. It's also possible to take out a non-income status mortgage which will loan you between 60 to 70 per cent of the cost of your home without proof of income.

You should note that it's much more difficult to finance a home in Florida than in the UK and it takes quite a lot longer to secure a mortgage – usually between 30 to 90 days and sometimes even longer. All mortgage applicants must be home-owners in the UK, and some lenders will allow potential rental income to be taken into account when deciding on the size of the loan, but not if you remortgage your UK home. You can also obtain an interest-only mortgage as well as a repayment mortgage. Lenders can charge a fee for supplying you with a mortgage and these charges are known as 'points', which are equal to one per cent of the total mortgage provided. As the mortgage market is extremely competitive some loans can be offered with no points, but it's important to check.

Types of mortgage

You can take out a mortgage for a period of 10, 15 or 30 years, and you can opt for a fixed rate mortgage or an adjustable rate mortgage, which is slightly more risky and only recommended for those who believe that their income will increase enough to offset a rise in repayments. Bear in mind that as little as a one per cent increase could enlarge the cost of repayments by $75 a month. It is also possible to secure a mortgage which is repaid weekly.

Alternatively, you can apply for a two-step mortgage, which has an adjustable rate that changes just once in its 30-year lifespan. A minimum loan size would be £30,000 or $50,000. The maximum loan is £1,000,000 or $1,000,000, although the average loan is fixed at 4.65 per cent, with a maximum LTV (Loan To Value ratio) of 80 per cent. You would be well advised to gain preapproval for your mortgage before you sign any binding contract.

Step 8: Home inspection

You need to note that there is a fundamental difference between a home inspection and a walkthrough, both of which are equally significant and both can be a crucial part of the purchase process. The walkthrough is where the seller invites you to inspect the property so that you can both agree a punchlist of any items to be repaired or replaced, and this is generally done before the closing. In the home inspection, you arrange with a professional to inspect the property, normally before your walkthrough.

Professional qualifications

You should request to have written into the contract your right to arrange for a home inspection, as some sellers will not agree to this. Where the property is being purchased 'as is', which is now how some new homes are sold, a home inspection may be critical – you will have the opportunity to bring defects to the seller's attention prior to completion. The home inspection is focused on taking in the actual state of repair of the home. Take note that anyone can call themselves a home inspector as it requires no professional qualification.

If possible, you should use someone with professional qualifications such as an engineer, architect or licensed contractor. Alternatively, it's advisable to secure an inspector through an organisation such as the American Society of Home Inspectors (ASHI) which has developed formal inspection guidelines and a professional code of ethics for its members. Membership to ASHI is not automatic for inspectors: proven field experience and technical knowledge of structures and their various systems and appliances are a prerequisite. Also, you should ensure that the inspector has 'errors and omissions' insurance coverage.

Hurricane protection

New builds should also be checked to ensure that they are hurricane proof if located in an area prone to hurricanes – and many parts of Florida are. It's also beneficial (where the sellers will agree to it) to write the builder's responsibilities into the contract, thus reducing the chances of shoddy and irresponsible workmanship. Where this is not permitted by the seller, you may want to arrange for a home and termite inspection to be performed immediately after the sale. The importance of securing a home inspection is further enhanced by Florida's building laws and regulations, which vary from state to state. In Tampa it is law that a potential buyer be made aware of the possibility of flooding in the area, thus avoiding hidden costs in the future. It also counters construction in areas that are prone to flooding. Specific details of the Florida building code can be found at www.floridabuilding.org. In order to ensure the checks are properly carried out make sure you ask the home inspector to check for these specifics.

The walkthrough is where the seller invites the buyer to inspect the property so that you can both agree a punchlist of any items to be repaired or replaced and this is generally done before closing

You may need to instruct a separate individual or firm to carry out the termite or other desired inspections. In any event, securing such an inspection is hugely necessary in Florida given that one of its most problematic residents is the wood-gauging termite which causes thousands of dollars' worth of damage. If buying a resale or renovation property then the termite inspection is the first port of call; although sellers are legally bound to make a buyer aware of any problems with the property that aren't visually obvious, they can easily plead ignorance once the transaction has been made. In fact, it's a good idea to ask them in writing to disclose whether the property was ever inspected for termites, the results of those inspections, whether any repairs were ever made, whether the property been regularly treated and when it was last treated against termites (which is a good thing). Following the expansion and boom of the property market in the 1980s there were many rush jobs and dodgy properties constructed, so there is a need to be vigilant with resale properties.

The walkthrough

A walkthrough is different to the home inspection in that the seller provides you with an opportunity to inspect the property yourself before the final closing.

WHAT IS AN ESCROW AGENT?

An escrow agent is a person or company that acts as a neutral third party and holds property or money involved in a transaction until certain conditions are met. With a Florida property purchase, the escrow agent holds the deposits until the legal title to the land can be proven. The escrow agent (who may be a lawyer, or closing agent, or other entity approved under Florida law) will:
1) Look after the down payment on your property until the closing is complete.
2) Receive the amount of loan from the lender.
3) Transfer the down payment and mortgage money to the seller on confirmation of closing.
The purchase contract should spell out the terms of the escrow agreement (or direct the buyer to where they may be found) and if a dispute arises between the parties, the escrow agent is bound to follow the terms of the contract. Where a disagreement cannot be resolved amicably in a reasonable time, the escrow agent may have to file the deposits with the court or other entity pending a decision.

BUYER'S GUIDE

Before closing, check your contract for errors that could jeopardise your purchase

The walkthrough is sometimes your only means of checking and ensuring that the seller has completed the construction to your liking. If you have already had a home inspection performed, it gives you an opportunity to ensure the repairs suggested by the home inspector are listed on the punchlist. If a copy of the inspector's report was already provided to the seller, some of the items found by the inspector may have already been repaired. If you cannot attend the walkthrough and the seller will not accept the home inspector as your agent for purposes of the walkthrough, be aware that you should not simply agree to the reference provided by a real estate agent. The buyer should have an agreed proxy and take the home inspector's report with them to check whether recommendations against the property have been implemented, and the buyer and seller then, as discussed above, agree a punchlist of things that the seller will agree to repair or change. However, most, if not all, developer contracts, will not allow the buyer to withhold any payment at the closing if these changes are not made before the closing. Such repairs may have to be made shortly after closing.

Step 9: Contract follow-up
Between signing your contract and closing the sale there may well be a number of deadlines to be met. If you have bought a preconstruction property then throughout the period of construction there will often be a schedule of payments to be met: for example, five per cent of the sale price may be due on the laying of the foundations. This is something the buyer needs to be aware of, ensuring their lawyer checks the contract and flags this up.

Resale
If the property is resale (and even more so where under the contract the property is sold 'as is') you should have ensured that an inspection or home survey is carried out before closing the sale, so that any repairs that need to be made are carried out and written into the contract. The buyer may also be responsible for guaranteeing that certain documents are returned to the lender or seller within this period to ensure the smooth transfer of property.

The most important part of this period is to make certain that payment of funds for your deposit reach the seller's broker by the deadline set in the terms of the contract. If this doesn't happen then the contract may well be terminated and you could lose your deposit. This can be problematic if you're wiring money from the UK and it is vital that this is done with time to spare. You should also check with your bank as to how long this procedure may take because it varies from between one and seven days to reach the States, so it's vital to ensure that this reaches Florida before your deadline because you can be liable for huge, ongoing financial penalties. These can range from anything between $200 and $3,000 depending on the terms of the contract. Remember also that closing is not just about the documents, but just as importantly about securing the financial backing.

A significant part of setting the closing date is the issuing of the certificate of occupancy (the 'C.O.') which has to be issued by the local government, stating that the property is in a fit state for habitation. It is not until this is issued that a date for closing the sale can be set.

Step 10: Title services
This is one of the final stages and one which you as the buyer will not be aware of normally until long after the contract is signed and returned to the sellers, if at all. The title insurance agents will research the county title records and prepare the relevant documents, thus enabling the process to reach a satisfactory conclusion.

Where you use a lender, they will also prepare their own documents for your signature before a notary. The title work, known as the conveyancing to UK buyers, is defined as the transfer of the deeds of ownership of the property from the vendor to the purchaser. Also, you need to be aware that as the title insurance agents are normally seller's lawyers or agents, or in the case of resales, independent of either party, you will not be advised as to the meaning of the title documents, and are unlikely to speak to the agents. The essence of this part of the transaction is the proving of the 'title', or registered ownership, of the vendor in the public records and consequently, the right of the vendor to actually sell the property. The process will involve the certification of the title, the preparing of the relevant documents to declare you as

BUYER'S GUIDE

WHAT IS THE ROLE OF THE NOTARY?

A notary may be required to witness the signing of the closing contract and 'notarise' it. They will charge a fee to do so. It is normally only where you have an American mortgage lender that a notary will be required to witness your signing of the documents, and if this will be done in the UK, it's best to acquire one through your solicitor. Please note that a commissioner for oaths or solicitor will not suffice as notaries fall into a separate category of lawyer other than solicitor or barrister (although a solicitor or barrister could also be a notary). This is very different from the concept of a public notary in Florida where notaries are (save for Florida's new civil law notaries) not required to be lawyers or professionals at all. In Florida, public notary charges may not exceed $10 and commonly are one or two dollars, whereas the UK notary charges frequently range between £40 and £60. Public notaries are very common in Florida and are in most lawyer, bank, and real estate agents' offices.

In America, public notaries are normally non-professionals who have no knowledge at all of the law but are granted the right when within Florida's state boundaries to certify documents they witness being signed. Florida has recently created a new form of notary, 'civil law notaries' who, like UK notaries, are lawyers, and who may notarise documents when outside Florida. In the UK, you will need to use a UK-resident Florida civil law notary, a US public notary at the US embassy in London, or find a UK public notary by searching for your local town at www.thenotariessociety.org.uk or looking at the US embassy's list of notaries in London.

the new owner of the property (upon payment of the purchase price) and the payment of the closing and/or notary costs.

Boundary survey

During this process the title company will undertake title research to ensure that there are no problems, outstanding debts or costs recorded in the county records that could come with your new home. The more often a property has been sold and the more complex its ownership history, the more necessary it is to make certain these checks are made. It's also essential, especially where lenders are involved, to check that the boundaries documented tally with the property's boundaries by carrying out a boundary survey. This is not to be confused with a home inspection which is the equivalent of a UK survey. As a rule boundary surveys are not normally prepared for condominium purchases.

Step 11: Closing the sale

This is the final stage of the conveyancing process, with the date being agreed in the purchase contract. It's also where the title-closing agent should be getting ready to record the deed of title and to distribute the funds to the relevant party. Where you are represented by a lawyer, your lawyer will either have requested a copy of the closing documents, or have arranged for you to attend his or her offices before the closing date with the documents to review them. A review of the documents is crucial as the deed can quite often contain errors in your names or in the technical legal description of the property. The 'HUD closing statement' should be reviewed to ensure that the seller is making the agreed contributions to the closing costs, and to ensure you are generally paying no more in closing costs than is reasonably acceptable. A review of the 'title commitment' is necessary to ensure that the property is insured and that there are no exceptions to the title insurance coverage which can be removed, thus providing you with the broadest possible coverage. If you choose not to have a lawyer, be sure you carefully examine the closing documents.

Transfer of ownership

Your final deposit or the balance of the purchase price will, of course, be due before the closing and should normally be payable to the title-closing agent. Be wary of paying your deposit directly into the builder's funds unless it is confirmed in writing that this is delivered to the title-closing agent or escrow agent. For the buyer, the signing of the deed confirms the sale. The closing includes the signing of the deed of sale and transferring legal ownership of a property and the payment of the balance of the purchase price (the total amount of the mortgage minus the deposit), plus any other outstanding costs such as closing costs, taxes and insurance. Both the buyer and seller are then issued with a closing statement, which details all the costs and any fees that each party is to be responsible for. Before the deed of sale is signed the closing agent must ensure that all the conditions detailed in the preliminary contract have been fulfilled, with any

BUYER'S GUIDE

OTHER TAXES TO LOOK OUT FOR

Florida imposes a sales or 'use' tax of six per cent which is levied on each retail sale, admission charge, storage, use or rental (including the letting of your property). If you are the lessor and do not have a property management agent handling this and collecting the tax, then you are subject to pay it yourself. As the owner of the property to be let, you're required to register each such property separately. You can register to collect and/or report this tax via the Florida Department of Revenue's website at www.myflorida.com/dor and click on e-Services.

- Out-of-State Purchases are subject to the use tax within six months of being brought into the state of Florida.
- Documentary Stamp Tax: this is levied on documents on deed, such as stocks and bonds, notes, and any written obligations to pay money, mortgages and any evidence of indebtedness. The tax rate for property transfer documents is $0.70 per $100 (or portion thereof) of the total consideration paid, or to be paid, for the transfer. The contract should set out who pays this fee.
- Tourist Development Tax Application: if you're letting your property for 180 days or less, this is a tax that's levied at six to seven per cent depending on the county.

costs due being collected. The agent then witnesses the signing of the deed and arranges for the name of the new owner to be listed in the local property registry. However, one relevant point of note is that the closing agent does not verify or guarantee the accuracy of any statements in the closing contract, or guarantee either party against fraud.

It is common practice for both the buyer and seller to attend the closing, where a Florida public notary would be present to witness the signing of the contract. There is also the 'mail-away closing' where all the documents are posted to the out-of-state buyer by the closing agents in Florida, ready for the buyer's signature. If you have your own lawyer in the UK, he or she will review the documents (as set out above) and inform you when they have been corrected or approved. You may have already taken the documents to a UK notary for their signing and notarisation so that the documents can then be sent back to the closing agent in Florida. Once the closing agent has received the documents, followed the title insurance company's requirements and confirmed all is set, the original deed is forwarded for registration at the local county court's official property records department. You are now the owner of your Florida home.

Title insurance

The first thing to be aware of as the buyer is that the title insurance policy is probably more valuable than your deed, as it's the insurance company who protect you against a claim concerning ownership of your property. Title insurance can be taken out by both the mortgage company and the buyer (and you should always insist on getting your own policy) and it insures against a number of occurrences. Firstly, a lender can take it out to protect themselves against failure to meet any mortgage repayments and thus protect their title. Whether you finance your purchase or not, you should always ensure you have obtained title insurance. This protects you, the buyer, against any problems that may occur following the purchase such as problems regarding legal ownership, or anything that was not discovered during the title service prior to the contract being signed. For instance, if the deed was forged, or part of the land sold to you with the property actually belongs to someone other than the last owner, then you as the new owner are protected.

If you have to defend your title, the title insurance will cover attorney fees and all other costs incurred in defending the title. It should be noted that title problems are infrequent but they can lead to the loss of your home should they arise.

Title insurance does not cover all instances that may jeopardise the ownership of your home. Any problems that arise which are not listed in the county real estate records, such as unpaid utility bills or other sundry community fees, cannot be dealt with and resolved through the title insurance.

FIRPTA

If the seller is a foreigner and not a US resident, the closing agent is obliged to withhold 10 per cent of the purchase price (credited to the seller's income taxes on the capital gain) when the property is sold. This is a legal obligation which falls under federal law rather than state or county law, and is known as FIRPTA (the Foreign Investment in Real Property Tax Act). The only exception to this rule is where the buyer is a resident who is buying to permanently relocate, and if the property is sold for less than $300,000. This is obviously only a concern for a buyer when they come to sell their property, if they are not US residents. In certain appropriate circumstances, your accountant or lawyer may be able to assist you in avoiding this or seeking a refund.

BUYER'S GUIDE

Step 12: Things to be aware of

Letting your home

If you are planning on letting your Florida property you're required to have a State Hotel Licence from the Florida Department of Business and Professional Regulations. You can contact them at: Department of Business and Professional Regulations, Division of Hotel & Restaurant, 941 W Morrison Blvd, Suite 290, Winter Park, FL 32789; website, www.myfloridalicense.com; Tel: +1 (850) 487-1395.

You will require a county occupational licence and also in some cities in Florida a city occupational licence. You should inquire with the appropriate municipality about licences; you'll need to provide them with a copy of your State Hotel Licence. As a non-resident alien you would be required to pay 30 per cent of your gross rental income to the state. There is a way around this: if a buyer fills out a 'W8ECI' form and passes it to their withholding or property management agency, their rental income would be treated as business income and as a consequence of this, they would be subject to the standard income tax rates only on net proceeds, with deductions being possible for business expenses and losses. This form is available from the IRS website, www.irs.gov.

Property tax

As a non-resident alien in Florida you may be subject to US federal, Florida, and UK income, capital gains and estate/inheritance taxes on your property. If you let out the property, income tax will be charged on an annual basis, and if you die while still holding the property, you may be subject to US inheritance tax if the value of your US assets (the property) is in excess of the exempt or threshold amount of $60,000. In certain circumstances, you may be entitled to an election to use the US/UK inheritance tax treaty, or otherwise have options to minimise or eliminate an exposure to US inheritance taxes.

If you gift the property to a relative or friend, you may also be subject to US gift taxes. If you own the property through an entity, such as a corporation or a partnership, there are US corporation and partnership forms which must be filed annually.

With a partnership, you may have flow-through amounts to you which may have to be reported in the US or the UK depending on the circumstances. You should consult an accountant (preferably one who is knowledgeable on both US and UK taxes) to determine which forms need to be filed for your entity and how these flow through to your personal US and UK tax returns.

Anyone earning income from their property through rentals is liable for tangible personal property tax. You should keep receipts for any purchases made for the the tangible tax return

There are three types of property tax in existence in Florida: a real property tax for home owners, a tangible tax on business assets, which includes tax on rental income, and an intangible tax on stocks, bonds, mutual funds and money market funds.

Ad valorem tax

Real estate taxes are known as 'ad valorem' taxes, which simply means they are taxes based on the value of your home. If you are purchasing a home in Florida, whether you are legally a Florida resident, or merely a non-resident, you will still be liable to pay ad valorem tax. However, there are differences on the amount you have to pay depending on the functionality of the property: for example, a farm owner would pay much less property tax than a city centre property owner.

Retirement buyers will be faced with smaller payments than a working couple. Ad valorem payments are calculated per thousand dollars and usually range from between one and two per cent of the property's value. These are based upon the assessed value of the property and the non-ad valorem assessments, including costs such as providing fire protection and rubbish collection.

Millage rates

The Board of County Commissioners, School Board, municipalities and other ad valorem taxing bodies set the 'millage rates' for properties within their boundaries. The millage rate is the dollar amount to be paid in taxes for every $1,000 of their appraised value. For instance, if your property is valued at $100,000 and the millage rate is $15, you would pay $1,500 a year.

Assessments for the payment of ad valorem tax begin in November of each year, as soon as the tax roll has been certified, with tax notices mailed on October 31. Florida state law requires property owners to be responsible for paying their property taxes and ensuring that they pay them before the due date of April 1.

BUYER'S GUIDE

Tangible personal property tax
Tangible personal property tax is an ad valorem tax that is assessed against:
- Any equipment, fixtures or furniture used for a business or commercial purpose
- Leased equipment: for example, articles contained in properties that are rented, such as furniture, washing machines and computers
- Furnishings and appliances in a rental property that are owned by the real property owner
- Any attachments made to a mobile home or manufactured housing in a rental park

Any person, firm or corporation is required to complete and file an annual return with a Property Appraiser if they in any way own tangible personal property such as that described above. Anyone earning income from their property through rentals is liable for tangible personal property tax. If you own a home which you rent out, then any purchases you make should have receipts kept in order to file your tangible tax return. Household goods or personal items used by the homeowner in their own home are exempt from this.

Filed returns
All returns are to be filed between January 1 and April 1 of each year to avoid any financial penalties, which rise by five per cent each month after the deadline of April 1. If no return is filed a 25 per cent penalty is enforced and an assessment made on the property. The payment amount is based on an estimate by the Property Appraiser and taxes are assessed at the same rate as ad valorem tax, although payment differs from county to county, with some assessments based on the length of time you rent the property out for every year. The definitive, most concise answer regarding state taxes will come from the Florida Department of Revenue.

Returns that are filed early are subject to a discount:
- 4 per cent if paid in November
- 3 per cent if paid in December
- 2 per cent if paid in January
- 1 per cent if paid in February

Intangible tax
Intangible tax applies to the calendar year in which the assets are valued, unlike income tax, which is levied on the previous financial year. Recent changes in Florida law mean that individuals will pay no tax on the first $250,000 of their assets, and couples will pay no tax on the first $500,000. Businesses, similarly, will pay no tax on the first $250,000 of their assets and no tax will be paid if they owe less than $60 in tax. For instance, if a couple owned less than $560,000 in intangible property, they would not be liable to pay any tax.

Intangible tax is a state wealth tax levied on an individual's intangible assets costing $20,000 or more, and couples' assets totalling more than $40,000. Intangible assets include bonds, stocks, mutual funds, accounts, loans receivable, annuities and real estate outside Florida. It does not apply to cash assets such as bank deposits or a retirement savings plan. The intangible tax rate is $1,000,000 ($1 of $1,000) and is assessed on the value of your assets on January 1 of every year. No tax is due to be paid if your liability is less than $5, but a return must still be filed. There is a discount of four per cent if tax is paid in January or February, three per cent in March, two per cent in April and one per cent in May. Bills are mailed in the first week of January and your returns are due in by June 30.

Your will
While Florida law generally provides that the Florida courts should accept and attempt to follow valid foreign wills, there may be administrative difficulties in some instances. Wills prepared under Florida law provide for a 'proof of execution' form to be signed contemporaneously with the will, and which generally avoids any requirement that the witnesses be brought before a court on a challenge to prove the execution of the will. Another very relevant point is that as there is no spousal exemption for US

CHECKLIST

If you are in fact emigrating to Florida country there are a lot of things to be aware of:
- Make sure your, and your families visas and passports are up to date and all above board
- If you are shipping your pet to Florida make sure it has been given an Official certificate of vet Inspection which clears your pet of rabies
- Look into accessing your UK bank account from Florida
- Check that your mail is to be forwarded and that all credit card bills are up to date
- Cancel all utility bills
- Ensure that yourself and your family all have health insurance and stock up on any prescription medicines as these are very expensive in the States

BUYER'S GUIDE

Unless you take the necessary steps, your spouse will be liable to pay inheritance tax

inheritance taxes for 'non-resident aliens', there is the possibility of including a qualified domestic trust (or 'QDOT' trust) in a will, so that any such inheritance tax liability may be deferred until the death of the surviving spouse, or the sale of the property. Also, there is a very useful will substitute in Florida, ideal for foreign owners of Florida property. A lawyer can set up a revocable living trust where, unlike a will, your estate may avoid the delays and costs to your estate of a probate in Florida.

Step 13: Relocating to Florida

Once you have bought your Florida home, unless you are purchasing furniture out there or have a furniture package provided to you from your seller, you may wish to ship items to Florida. This will take anything from between four and eight weeks to ship your furniture and other personal effects from the UK and it's advisable to approach a number of companies and get a selection of written quotes before committing yourself to any one removal company.

Air freight

You could also consider air freight which is certainly swifter and easier than waiting up to two months for your personal effects to reach your new home. The first thing to check is whether or not the quote you secure includes insurance and the packaging of your furniture and effects. The second thing to be aware of is clearing your freight through customs. There are two ways of doing this: the first is to pay for 'Custody in-bond' where a third party clears your effects through customs; the second way is to fill out form 3299 to ensure your effects can be cleared by customs, but this does take longer. Also, bear in mind the possibility of having to pay duty and internal revenue tax on importing your items, although in most instances you won't have to.

In general, international moves are best commissioned to a removal company that is a member of the International Federation of Furniture Removal (FIDI), the Overseas Moving Network Inc (OMNI), or the Association of International Removers Ltd. (see page 218 for contact details). Companies associated with these bodies usually subscribe to a payment guarantee or bond scheme, so that if your contract is not fulfilled by your chosen mover, the contract will be completed at the agreed cost by another company, or your money will be refunded. Ensure you make a complete list of all items to be shipped be made so that you can prove if something is missing. TVs, 220V electrical items and wardrobes should be left behind, as Florida homes have walk-in wardrobes and operate off an 120V electrical system.

Once you take possession of your new home, if not before, one of the first and most valuable tasks is to make an inventory of all fittings and furnishings and check it against the terms of your contract, thus ensuring the previous owner hasn't absconded with anything promised to you. Thus, the ideal scenario is for the buyer to obtain written instructions regarding the appliances from the previous owner to ensure they can operate the utilities. Check with your town hall to ensure all the regulations are adhered to regarding recycling, parking and home maintenance. ●

■ REAL LIFE

We did it … Buying a home

The relaxed lifestyle and quality of life encouraged Neil Marshall and his wife Katrina to seek their own holiday home in central Florida…

MEET THE BUYER…
Neil & Katrina Marshall

Neil and Katrina Marshall are from Twickenham and have been married for seven years. Both thirty-somethings, they work in the financial services industry, Neil as an Investment Consultant, and Katrina as an Associate Director at Legal & General Investment Management. They were drawn to buying a property in Florida after holidaying there. They now own a villa in Orlando which they enjoy with their family and friends.

THE SUNSHINE OF ORLANDO PROVED AN IRRESISTIBLE draw when the Marshalls decided to buy a home in Florida. "My wife Katrina and I both love the US and had holidayed in Florida several times," explains Neil. "We've always enjoyed the lifestyle and range of activities available; theme parks, beaches, shopping malls, restaurants, and of course, the weather." Neil and Katrina initially bought the house as a holiday home but also as a future investment. "As we have family and friends living north of Orlando, we were drawn to the area, but we realised that if we wanted to rent the property out we'd need to purchase in an area zoned for short-term rental. We decided to look for a new-build within 20 minutes drive of Disney World, which is what we ended up buying."

Neil's advice is to carry out extensive research on buying in Florida, and ensure that you know exactly what you're getting into. As part of their research they went to various overseas property exhibitions where they met agents from F I Grey, an established Florida realtor. When they visited Orlando to find a property, they were put in touch with a buyer's agent who spent two days showing them a huge range. "Having an agent working for you, the buyer, is a much superior system to that in the UK, where agents work only for the seller," says Neil. "It affords you personal representation which is invaluable when you are effecting an expensive purchase in an unfamiliar market. We did not have to pay for the agent's services, as he was remunerated by his commission."

Points system

Their agent recommended a mortgage broker to the couple, who proved very useful. "The legal system itself is no more complex than that in the UK," reckons Neil. "However, we found that, when taking out a mortgage it's worth spending time getting to grips with the 'points' system, as this affects which mortgage is best for each borrower. Also, as a non-US resident, proof of credit worthiness is required, so we spent some time getting letters from banks, employers and our UK mortgage lender as evidence of this." The process took Neil more than three months, longer than anticipated, and the first set of letters was time-barred and had to be redone. "You need to be prepared to respond to queries quickly, and to send documents backwards and forwards by UPS/Fed-Ex in order to keep to the timeline. We used the notarial services at the US Embassy in London to get copies of documents officially authenticated."

The Marshalls' new-build home is just a 20-minute drive from Walt Disney World

REAL LIFE

Homes in Orlando are popular due to the excellent transport links and the great climate

Management company

Throughout the building process their agent kept the couple up-to-date with the construction, and undertook the final walkthrough with the developer, so there was no need for them to fly out especially, and the final closing took place nine months after selecting their plot. As they also rent their home, they have a company called AHN Management, which looks after the house for them and arranges bookings. "This is our second management company after having had an appalling experience with the first, and I would advise any potential buyers to secure a personal recommendation, rather than choosing a name from the internet or an agent. There are a large number of companies in this market, and their quality varies."

Owning and running a home in Florida costs more than many people would estimate. Neil and Katrina purchased their house on a 'turn key' basis (i.e. a furniture package was included in the price) although there were some items which were not included. "We had to purchase a pool heater, buy patio furniture, install ceiling fans – we would recommend these as they help to reduce air conditioning bills – and add some extra touches to make the house more homely. In addition, there are fixed costs such as; the mortgage, insurances property taxes, home-owner association and utility bills, which you incur irrespective of whether the property is occupied."

Extra costs

If you are planning on letting your property there are also the variable costs, which mainly result from the inevitable wear and tear on the property. These include things such as; carpet cleaning, replacing linen/towels and other household items as and when

> "We've always enjoyed the lifestyle and range of activities; theme parks, beaches, malls, and of course, the weather"

required. Also, whether you rent the property or not, you need someone to manage and maintain it for you. Management companies generally make a monthly charge in the region of $250 for this service. "Our rental generates some revenue to offset the expenses, but be sure to factor in the cost of cleaning between renters, commissions, local county and state taxes in your total budget."

There are also taxes to take into account. "The tax system in the US is complicated to the outsider," asserts Neil. "We use an Orlando-based accountant to file an annual federal tax return and a Tangible Personal Property Tax return on our behalf. It only takes a few hours each year to compile the information needed for these. On the British side, be prepared to complete additional pages for your tax return, because you derive income from an overseas property." However, on the plus side, the Marshalls have no visa implications to consider. "As we spend less than 90 days a year in Orlando, we never go above the limit of 90 days, and consequently we simply use the visa waiver I-94W form." During those 90 days Neil and Katrina use their house for all their holidays and often invite family and friends to join them. "We typically spend four weeks there each year, and we often go off for a few days at a time to explore other parts of Florida; we went up to St Augustine last year and to Key West at Easter. In addition, my mother spends about a month there each year so she can spend time with her friends who live in Orlando."

In future, Neil and Katrina hope to spend even more time in Florida. "We love our home," enthuses Neil. "We get great enjoyment from it and would never change the decision we made to buy." ●

NEIL'S TOP FIVE TIPS

- Go into it with your eyes open and ensure you research and visit the area before making any commitment
- Overseas property exhibitions are useful for information as well as the Florida Brits Club
- You need to decide whether to buy a resale property or a new-build
- There are hundreds of properties being built in Orlando, so new houses and apartments abound
- If you intend to let the property for short-term rentals, be aware of the strict zoning regulations

■ REAL LIFE

We did it… Buying to let

For the price of an apartment in the UK, John Chauhan bought a five-bed villa in Florida which generates enough rental income to pay for itself

MEET THE BUYER…
John Chauhan

John Chauhan is married with two children and lives in the West Midlands. In 2001 he invested in his Florida villa, which was finished in 2002. "I enjoy owning a property here in Orlando and, of course, visiting Florida with friends and family," says John. He became so involved that, following classes and state exams, he applied and gained his Real Estate Licence in the US. John now has many friends, business connections and colleagues there, and although running the business is hard work, he says it remains an enjoyable experience.

If you're buying a property to let, a swimming pool is an excellent selling point when it comes to attracting visitors. You must ensure it's regularly cleaned, though

In 2000 John began looking for a holiday home and future retirement retreat, initially searching in Spain, Portugal and the South of France. Before he bought his home in Florida, John purchased an apartment in Cannes, and despite an appreciation in the price of the apartment, he experienced difficulties. "Despite night schools and several self-help books, I still struggled to communicate with the French rental agents, management companies and all the various post that inevitably comes with property ownership here," he explains. It wasn't until a golfing holiday in Florida that John was given the opportunity to investigate the Florida property market. "When I looked at how the homes are managed and how sophisticated the system was, I was sold." Compared with France, John has found the Florida market much easier to deal with. "The Americans are very helpful: the special relationship that people say exists between Americans and the Brits is clearly evident." With excellent weather and a high but cheap standard of living, John and his family never get tired of visiting their Orlando home. That said, there are one or two drawbacks to Florida that a potential buyer needs to be aware of. "There were so many other concerns, like distance and flight time, and the care of my home in our absence," says John. To counter these concerns he contacted other British buyers in Florida and asked for a recommended management company to look after his home in his absence, something he would strongly urge every buyer to consider.

The buying process

In 2001 Calabay Homes, an established British firm that deals purely with Florida real estate, began the construction of John's five-bedroom villa to his specified requirements. The property was completed without hitch in January 2002, its value increasing massively in the past couple of years. "When I initially bought my home, appreciation was not a factor. We assumed we would get about a three per cent growth, but due to the current popularity of Florida and the exchange rate, we have seen our house appreciate by 40 per cent since purchase." The similarity of the US tax regime with that of the UK benefits the British buyer, and John describes the IRS as treating his home "generously". Bills such as gas, electricity and the telephone, can be settled any time of day or night via the internet, eliminating concerns of being UK-based. In terms of the costs involved, John says: "The important point to remember with any holiday home is that even if you don't rent it out, you will have fixed costs to meet throughout the year, such as air conditioning, general maintenance, pool cleaning and taxes." There are also mortgage repayments to think about. John is currently repaying a $200,000 mortgage, but his rental income covers this and most other expenditure. "Our current position is that we have a lovely home, which pays for itself: we secure 20 to 25 weeks of rentals a year at £650 a week."

Letting your home

As Florida is such a tourist magnet, potential rental returns on your investment are huge. However, before you buy a home to let, you need to be aware of the rental restrictions. If your property is not zoned for short-term rentals, you may only be entitled to rent your home once a month.

As is advocated by any expert, John found his property management company through personal recommendations, and even set up his own website to promote holiday rentals, which has encouraged business. His home is within 20 minutes of Disney World and set in an executive development zoned for short-term rentals, a hugely popular area for villa

> " When we first bought our Florida property we thought it would appreciate by 3%, but this has been closer to 40% "

rentals, due to it's proximity to Orlando's theme parks. The villa also has a swimming pool, an important facility for anyone seeking to buy-to-let. Demand for the property has been huge and led to John being forced to turn down potential bookings. "The rentals we budgeted for have been achieved easily by networking and our own website, and the whole process has been straightforward, especially when compared with my experiences in France."

If you're seeking to rent your home, it's necessary to register it with the Florida State Department and the Department of Revenue for tax purposes. It is also important to install a number of necessary extras in order to bring your property up to scratch; for example, installing fire extinguishers and patio door alarms. An owner will also have to apply for a Tax ID number in order to allow them to file a tax return, because income from your lettings is tax deductible. "The legislature requirements were straightforward and the licensing is easy," states John. "In most cases the management company appointed to look after the house will deal with these things for you." As John bought a property in a short-term rental community, the house was fully geared-up to meet all legislative standards, and he registered the property himself,

John's five-bedroom villa is ideally positioned for Florida's wealth of fantastic theme parks. Disney World attracts millions of visitors every year

finding it an easy process, given that he had bought a home zoned for short-term lets. To secure state licensing, John completed the relevant form and payed a subscription, then for IRS purposes, he applied online for a tax ID number, which was issued quickly once the form was processed.

John believes that the rental income from his property is so great that once the mortgage repayments have been completed, the property should produce a minimum pension of £1,000 a month to help fund his retirement years. He has now obtained a real estate licence and assists others in purchasing their dream home. "I enjoyed the process of purchasing and letting a property in Florida so much that I am now a licensed realtor. I can offer all the expertise, but from a British owner's perspective with an empathy that you can only impart as an owner yourself." ●

TOP TIPS FOR BUYING-TO-LET

- Contact current owners to find a recommended management company
- Remember you still have fixed costs to meet throughout the year, such as air conditioning, general maintenance and property taxes
- Before you buy, you must check with your agent whether the property is zoned for short-term lets, or else your annual letting periods will be restricted
- Ensure you register your property with the Florida State Department and Department of Revenue for tax purposes – lettings income is taxed
- Choose a home with a pool that is close to all amenities and theme parks

■ BUYER'S GUIDE

Living and working in Florida

Understanding the essentials of the rules in the United States should ensure that the transition to your Florida home is a smooth one…

WORK PERMITS AND VISAS

Under the Visa Waiver Programme (VWP), UK citizens don't require a visa to enter the US. However, if you wish to stay for longer than 90 days, or work or study for an indefinite period then you will need one.

Generally speaking, a citizen of a foreign country who wishes to enter the US is required to obtain a visa: either a non-immigrant visa for a temporary stay, or an immigrant visa for permanent residence. Immigration officials are very stringent and visa applications are subject to much more intense scrutiny than previously.

Secondly, the INS (Immigration and Naturalization Services) no longer exists and applications are now made to the Bureau of Citizenship and Immigration Services. Visa applications now have longer processing times (except for some business and investment visas) and it's recommended that you apply early, especially as an interview will be included in the process.

Types of visa

1) Family-based residency

If any members of your immediate family are residents or citizens in the US, you may be entitled to permanent residency, and issued with a green card. There are two immediate categories into which the US authorities divide applicants. Firstly, immediate relatives: this includes parents, children and spouses, and there is no waiting period for someone who is marrying, or has married a US citizen, or for children, although processing can take up to 12 months. These applicants are entitled to permanent residence and there are no limitations upon the number of applicants who are entitled to receive these visas.

Secondly, there are also returning residents who were previously US-lawful, and permanent residents who are returning after a stay of more than one year abroad (not in the US).

2) B Visa (For tourists or business)

This is a non-immigrant visa for people who desire to enter temporarily for business (B-1), for pleasure, or for medical treatment (B-2). Most UK citizens travel without a visa and are not entitled to apply for one for such a temporary stay. B visas allow you to stay for up to six months at a time. To apply for a visitor visa you need to have:

MAIN TYPES OF VISAS

Non-immigrant, temporary visas which require ongoing renewal

B-1	Business
B-2	Tourist
E-1	Treaty trader
E-2	Treaty investor
H-1B	Speciality occupations and professionals, at least a Bachelor's Degree
H-2A	Temporary or seasonal workers
H-3	Temporary trainees
H-4	Immediate family of H visa holders
K-1	Finances of US citizens
L-1	Inter-company transferee
L-2	Dependant of L-1 visa holders
O-1	Extraordinary ability
P	International artists
R	Religious workers

If any other members of your immediate family are residents or citizens in the US, you may be entitled to permanent residency and issued with a green card

● A Non-immigrant Visa Application (Form DA-156).
● A Supplemental Non-immigrant Visa Application (Form DS-157), which provides additional information about your travel plans, and this is required for all males between the age of 16 and 45, and for all applicants from certain designated countries.
● A passport valid for travel to the US with a validity that extends to at least six months the applicant's period of time in the US.
● One 2 × 2 photograph of the applicant.
The cost is $100 for the processing of a non-immigrant application, and there is an additional visa issuance fee which is applicable for some applicants.

See www.travel.state.gov for more details.

BUYER'S GUIDE

Applications for visas are now made to the BCIS who have lengthy processing times

THOSE ENTITLED TO PERMANENT RESIDENCE

Family sponsored immigrants (Note: as used herein 'sons and daughters' refers to individuals who are over 21 years old. Only the term 'children' refers to those who are under 21).

The number of family sponsored immigrants are restricted to 675,000 persons a year entitled to receive a visa. These are based on family preference categories:

- **First Preference:** Unmarried sons and daughters of US citizens, and their children (23,400). The current processing time is approximately three years.
- **Second Preference:** Spouses, children and unmarried sons and daughters of lawful permanent resident aliens (114,200). The current processing times is four-and-a-half years for spouses and children, and nine years for unmarried sons and daughters.
- **Third Preference:** Married sons and daughters of US citizens and their spouses and children (23,400). The current processing time is approximately seven years.
- **Fourth Preference:** Brothers and sisters of US citizens, and their spouses and children, provided that the US citizens are over 20 (65,000). The waiting period is up to 12 years.

BUYER'S GUIDE

3) Student Visas (F-1 visa)
Applications for a student visa allow you to remain for the duration of your study time. The school/university handles the details of the visa application so you don't have to pay for the cost of an attorney. You still have to prove that you can afford the cost of living and tuition fees. Retirees with academic interests prefer to apply for this as it allows them to remain all year round and covers everything from nuclear physics to many artistic pursuits.

4) Employment based
These fall into three categories:

i) E Visa – for entrepreneurs
Under the US-UK Treaty, any British citizen is entitled to an indefinite visa for the purpose of setting up a business. There is no minimum investment figure but your type of business and the potential for it to sustain yourself and your family will be examined. You're required to prove that you are starting an enterprise and not merely investing, and in practice this means that you should be investing no less than £50,000 to prove the growth potential.

When looking at business visas there are two golden rules. Firstly, there is an industry of sharks ready to capitalise on your desire to enter the US by selling you a poor and sometimes doomed business. Secondly, particularly at the lower priced end, businesses with a high ratio of profit-to-turnover sell very quickly. Your offer on an American business is subject to the granting of a visa, so many sellers will prefer to sell to a legal US resident who has no such visa complications.

As a property owner you're entitled to have your US real estate investments taken into consideration as an investment, but this must mean you're purchasing more than one property. It's essential that when applying for this visa you ensure you have the support and backing of an experienced US immigration lawyer, especially if you're keen to prove that your real estate investments are an enterprise. This is another area where there are a number of creative and often dishonest practitioners capitalising on the desires of would-be immigrants, so separate legal advice is critical.

- The E-1 Visa. This refers to the treaty country conducting trade with America, and E-1 covers trade which is frequent, long-term and continuous, creating enough revenue to sustain the trader and their family. To qualify, the company must be planning to establish a US-based office, and be generating 50 per cent of its revenue through trade with the US.

> **Immigration officials have become more stringent and visa applications are now subject to much more scrutiny than they were in previous years**

VISA CASE STUDY

Jan Leather is originally from Scunthorpe where she trained as a registered nurse (RN) until 1978 when she moved to Saudi Arabia to work for an American company. In 1980, she moved with friends to America and visited Florida and fell in love with it. "The people, climate, opportunities – they were all wonderful. I had to do a six week midwifery course so that I could apply to sit an RN exam but I couldn't find a hospital to sponsor me. I had sent off my immigration papers, but as I had no sponsor I was asked to leave America. I desperately wanted to live in Florida, and from the UK I contacted Lakeland Hospital who agreed to sponsor me." Jan did everything US Immigration asked of her, one step at a time. "I ended up at the US Embassy in London where everything was passed and I applied for a H1 visa. However, I hadn't enlisted the help of a lawyer and I ran into big problems. Consequently, I was forced to hire an immigration lawyer at a cost of £700." Jan recommends that anyone seeking to gain visa entry into Florida should just keep going.

"Do whatever it takes to make your dream come true and keep plodding on, even during those times immigration becomes difficult. Read through everything thoroughly, photocopy every document and letter you send to the INS, and establish an 'I'm going to live in America' file." In 1995 she became a citizen, having decided she could never see herself living in England again. Jan now lives full time in Englewood on the Gulf Coast and has set up her own real estate venture, TheTalkingHome.com. She buys property and mortgages and is about to launch as a mortgage broker. Jan offers British buyers advice on relocating to the States, gleaned from her own experiences. For more details about Jan's services, check out www.myUSALoan.com

BUYER'S GUIDE

FREQUENTLY ASKED QUESTIONS ABOUT VISAS

Who is covered by the visa?
The applicant and his or her spouse are both covered by the visa, as are any dependant children under 21. A couple who are not married can apply under a discretionary provision, but it is more complex.

Can anyone apart from the applicant work in the US?
If you have an L (executive visa) or an E (entrepreneur) visa your spouse will be automatically granted a work permit and entitled to work in any field of employment in the US.

What is the cost?
With the exception of tourist and student visas, it's extremely unwise to apply for any of the other visas on your own. This is because many of the actual requirements are not listed on the forms' instructions. As such, you will at best end up taking three or four times as long to process the visas, and at worst, your application will be denied, creating a permanent stain on your immigration record and making it more difficult to obtain a visa in the future. Legal fees for these services range from about £3,000 for the L and E visas to £2,500 for the H visa. The government's fee is $130, except for the H visa which carries a government fee of $1,130. In each case, the normal processing time is about four to six months, unless you pay the government an expedite fee of $1,000.

• The E-2 Visa. This refers to a company involved in substantial investment within the US. E-2 visas are granted only to key employees or the principal owner of a company, and that company must be deemed to have invested a substantial amount of money in the US. There is no defined amount and it depends on the type of business, with a safe sum being $100,000 or more, although they have been granted for as little as $50,000 and sometimes less.

There can be problems finding businesses for these relatively modest sums that can return the necessary profit margins to qualify for entry. The business can be jointly owned with a spouse or partner (who can also be a US citizen). The E-2 visa is only granted if the investment is likely to create jobs for American workers, and the investment therefore can't be for the investor and their family alone. A case can also be made sometimes for a new franchise.

Both E-1 and E-2 visas are initially granted for five years and can be extended for up to five years at a time. The E visa, however, only remains valid if the company continues to operate and be viable, and while you remain employed with the company.

The spouse and children of the E visa holder are also entitled to an E visa, and the spouse is additionally entitled to full work authorisation but may not work in the US unless they work as a co-investor or co-trader. Children are entitled to attend an American school until the age of 21, and then they must apply for a visa in their own right. The E-2 visa is indefinite and allows multiple entries into the United States.

The US government are happy to provide long-term visas for any skilled workers who are offered employment. Generally, the requirements for securing such a visa are that you have at least four years of university studies

ii) H Visa – for professional and skilled workers
The US government are happy to provide long-term visas for any skilled workers who are offered employment. Generally, the requirements for securing such a visa are that you have at least four years of university studies or its equivalent in experience, and most importantly, that you have a specialist skill, your employer requires your skills, and has the money to pay you a salary at least equal to, or higher than, any other US citizen with the same skills. However, if your employer is a new company you don't need to show the financial documentation, and consequently it would be easier to obtain a H visa by applying through a new company.

Initially, the visa will last for three years. At the end of this time, the company who employed you have to prove they can afford to pay your salary to entitle you to remain on your H visa in the States. Professionals may also obtain a Permanent Residency H visa if they

BUYER'S GUIDE

prove that there is a shortage of specialist workers in their field, but this process can last for up to three years so many people obtain a H visa and work for three years while waiting for a Work-Based Permanent Residency Application.

There are four types of H visa:
- H-1B Visas: These are issued to specialist workers, occupations and professions such as doctors of medicine, a worker with a college degree or the equivalent experience/degree.

As most professions in the US are licensed it may be necessary for the applicant to take the licensing exam relevant to the profession, allowing you to be licensed by the state to practise. To obtain a H-1B visa you must be made a job offer by an American company who will then file a petition with the local INS office. The employer must fill out a Labour Condition Attestation (LCA) before he can sponsor you to apply for a H-1B visa, and as a H-1B visa holder you may be entitled to adjust your status to that of a permanent resident.

- H-2A Visas: These are for temporary agricultural workers filling positions for which there is a shortage recognised by the Department of Agriculture.
- H-2B Visas: Issued to workers who are temporary, skilled, non-skilled and agricultural workers who are in short supply, or jobs which cannot be filled by American workers. No educational or qualification restrictions apply and any job offers are strictly temporary. In many cases this employee would be a skilled technician employed by a foreign company to install machinery or train staff in America. They are issued initially for two years and may be extended for one year at a time.
- H-3 Visas: This is issued for temporary workers and trainees entering the country in order to carry out on-the-job training or work experience in a particular field (for example, commerce, communications, finance, transportation and government work).

There must be a specific reason as to why the training cannot be carried out in the employee's own country, the employee must carry out less than 50 per cent of the workload, and any employment must be incidental to the training. This visa is issued for a maximum of 18 months and extensions are very difficult to secure.

iii) L Visa – for executives, business owners and multinational operations
This visa relates to inter-company transfers, for persons who are employed abroad and transferred from their native branch to a US-based branch.

Professors, researchers, athletes and artists of extraordinary ability are also entitled to immediate residency and to be able to take advantage of this, it is necessary to have extensive documentation to prove it

The employee's company must generally own at least 50 per cent of the American-based associate office, and to qualify, the employee must have been employed abroad (outside the US) by the company for at least one of the last three years. You're also required to have served in a managerial or executive capacity, or possess specialised business knowledge.

Although Labour certification is not required, an American employer must file a petition with the INS regional service centre. Large multinationals benefit from a blanket L-1 rule, and needn't file a separate petition for every employee. The L visa is initially issued for up to three years and may be extended for two years at a time for a person with specialised knowledge, and four years at a time for an executive or manager.

As a manager you can qualify for a Green Card for yourself and your family and an L-2 visa is granted to the L-1 visa holder's spouse and children, with full employment authorisation being granted to the L-1 holder's spouse, once they have qualified for their own work visa.

5) Immediate residency for those with extraordinary abilities
Demand for healthcare workers is high. Some doctors, nurses and healthcare workers are eligible for residency, provided they pass their professional examinations. Professors, researchers, artists of extraordinary ability and athletes are also entitled to immediate residency and to be able to take advantage of this it's necessary to have extensive documentation to prove it.

6) The Lottery
This is what the Americans refer to as the 'lottery'. To enter, applicants should contact the United States' consul and the winners will gain residency. There are a specific number of winners allocated per country. However, UK citizens are not permitted to enter, although Republic of Ireland citizens are.

TAXATION IN FLORIDA

If you own property in both the UK and Florida, you may be subject to US, Florida, and UK income and estate taxes. If you let out your property, income tax will be charged on an annual basis, and if you die while still holding a property in Florida, you may be subject to an inheritance tax if its value exceeds the inheritance threshold. If you give a property as a gift, you may also be subject to US gift taxes. Both of these can run into thousands of dollars and you need to be aware of the potential charges.

Confirming your residency status for tax purposes

Depending on what visa you have, you may be taxed as a resident or a non-resident. If you're a permanent resident of the US or a US citizen for tax purposes as confirmed by the physical presence test, you must file a tax return on your worldwide income, even if you did not spend any time in the US. If you're not a US citizen or permanent resident and do not meet a physical presence test, then you may file as a non-resident alien.

Working out your tax liability requires you to determine your residency status

The presence test

This complicated test confirms whether or not you qualify as a resident for tax purposes. Add 100 per cent of the current year's days spent in the US, $1/3$ of the previous year's days in the US, and $1/6$ of the second previous year's days together. If the total is 182

CORPORATE INCOME TAX RATES 2004

Taxable income over ($)	Not over ($)	Tax rate (%)
0	50,000	15
50,000	75,000	25
75,000	100,000	34
100,000	335,000	39
335,000	10,000,000	34
10,000,000	15,000,000	35
15,000,000	18,333,333	38
18,333,333	–	35

In addition to the above, the US charges 30 per cent branch profits tax on profits of foreign companies with US business activities. Most foreign companies set up US subsidiaries to avoid this tax. US source profits remitted outside the US are treated as dividends and are subject to a 30 per cent dividend withholding tax. This 30 per cent tax may be negated or greatly diminished further to the US/UK income tax treaty.

For properties not owned through an entity, income tax is withheld at 30 per cent of the gross rental income, unless you provide a TIN (Taxable Income Number). If you provide a TIN, you will need to file annual tax returns in the US. Tax will be charged in both countries on the rental income less expenses. As the property is located in the US, the US has first taxing rights. The tax is computed annually on a calendar year basis using form 1040NR. A separate form 1040NR is filed for each owner of the property. The net income may well be below the taxable threshold, as the US allows deductions for the value of the building, which results in a paper loss for most home owners in the first few years. The top US tax rate is currently 39 per cent.

Remember, if you don't rent out the property, you probably won't have enough US-source income to file US tax returns. US income tax is only due on US-source income.

BUYER'S GUIDE

US INCOME TAX RATES

Single Taxpayers 2004
Taxable income ($)

Over	But not over	Tax	+%	On amount over
0	7,150	0.00	10	0
7,150	29,050	715.00	15	7,150
29,050	70,350	4,000.00	25	29,050
70,350	146,750	14,325.00	28	70,350
146,750	319,100	35,717.00	33	146,750
319,100	–	92,592.50	35	319,100

Married Individuals Filing Joint 2004
Taxable income ($)

Over	But not over	Tax	+%	On amount over
0	14,300	0.00	10	0
14,300	58,100	1,430.00	15	14,300
58,100	117,250	8,000.00	25	58,100
117,250	178,650	22,787.50	28	117,250
178,650	319,100	39,979.50	33	178,650
319,100	–	86,328.00	35	319,100*

* Please note that married individuals who are not US citizens usually file separately. Their tax rates are the same, but on half of the taxable income in the married filing joint table.

days or less, the person files as a non-resident. If the total exceeds 182, the person files as resident. For example, Jane spent 100 days in 2004, 120 in 2003, and 60 in 2002. The total is 100 + 40 + 10 = 150, which is less than 182 days. In this instance, Jane file would now file her tax return as a non-resident.

There are a lot of treaty-based exceptions to the rule. If you have a student visa, you can be taxed as a non-resident for five full calendar years, plus your entry year. Depending on the particular country you are a national or resident of, and depending on if you come to the United States on a teaching or training visa, in the first two years you may be eligible to file as a non-resident. If you maintain a home in two countries, you may be able to make a treaty claim for closer ties and connections to another country, therefore enabling you to file as non-resident.

Non resident tax rates
Non-residents are taxed on US-source income only. Examples of US-source income are interest from a US bank account, dividends from US stocks and mutual funds, rental income from US property and wages from a US employer. Income not effectively connected with business, such as personal interest income and dividends from shares and stocks, is taxed at statutory tax rates. Income effectively connected with a business, such as wage income or self-employment, is taxed using graduated individual income tax rates.

Some things, like rental income, are considered not effectively connected, but you can elect to treat them as effectively connected. This allows you to take advantage of the lower graduated rates. Many rates are reduced or eliminated by various treaties. For example, the US/UK tax treaty allows dividends to be taxed at 15 per cent, and some dividends are eligible for even lower rates. The best solution is to have your taxes professionally prepared by an expert in taxation of foreign persons to ensure you are paying the lowest tax possible.

Resident tax rates
Residents and US citizens are taxed on their worldwide income. Any income from your home country, including income in 'tax-free' investment vehicles, will be subject to US taxes. Income that is tax-free in the UK but is taxable in the US includes gambling winnings, lottery earnings, unit trusts, investment trusts, OEICs, UK and offshore trusts,

lump sum pension payments, redundancy payments, ISAs, PEPs, current year contributions to and growth in foreign pension plans, film partnerships, Enterprise Investment Schemes, Venture Capital Trusts, and TESSAs. This is in addition to your usual taxable income. Investing outside the US does not lessen your tax burden.

How each item is taxed

Wages: Taxed at graduated income tax rates. You can get relief for foreign taxes paid on the wages if the workdays were outside the States. There are tax breaks for income earned prior to your becoming subject to US worldwide taxation that was paid after you arrived to the US. This would include back pay, redundancy, severance, and deferred compensation.

Interest: Taxed at graduated income tax rates. You can get relief for foreign taxes paid on foreign-sourced interest, but only if it's actually due. Most countries pay interest tax-free to non-residents, so be sure to notify your UK bank before you leave so that interest is no longer withheld.

Dividends: Some are taxed at the graduated income tax rates, but most dividends generated by publicly traded stocks that have been held for at least 60 days are eligible for a 15 per cent lower rate.

Foreign Investments: Any that generate from dividends, such as a stock or share, is taxed as dividends above. If the investment is in a wrapper

The aptly-named Seaside (as featured in *The Truman Show*) is one Florida's most idyllic towns

Income that is tax-free in the UK but is taxable in the US includes gambling winnings, lottery winnings, unit trusts, investment trusts, OEICs, UK and offshore trusts, redundancy payments, and lump sum pension payments

instrument, such as a Unit Trust or Investment Trust, it is probably subject to Passive Foreign Investment Company (PFIC) rules. PFICs are subject to onerous taxes in the US. It's best to divest yourself of these assets prior to moving to the US if you wish to avoid having to report the taxable income in the US. If you own any PFICs, you should consult a US Tax Advisor specialising in foreign taxation issues prior to your move.

Business: If you operate a business as a sole proprietor, you'll be taxed on the net income after deductions. You may also have to pay US social security taxes on the earnings. The US allows more deductions than the UK, so keep track of every expense. If you own more than 10 per cent of a foreign corporation or foreign partnership, there are additional forms you have to file in your initial year, and if you own more than 50 per cent of a foreign corporation or foreign partnership, there is an annual filing requirement. If the company earns more than five per cent of its income from passive investments, there may be tax to pay even if no distribution or dividend was paid. Seek advice about restructuring your business, prior to your move if possible. Penalties for not filing these forms are $10,000 per form.

Alimony: Taxable to the receiver.

Capital gains: Long-term capital gains (held more than one year) are taxed at 15 per cent. Short-term are taxed at the graduated income tax rates. PFICs are taxed at 35 per cent and can be subject to an additional interest charge of 10 per cent for each year owned, not to exceed 100 per cent of the gain from the sale.

Pensions and annuities: Taxed on an arising basis using the graduated income tax rates. Taxes on foreign-sourced pensions, including foreign social security pensions, can be reduced by foreign tax

BUYER'S GUIDE

credits. The US/UK treaty will allow you to pay tax just in the US. You will need to file a form to stop withholding in the UK.

Rents: Rental income is taxed on the net income after deductions, including a deduction for depreciation.

Trusts: If you're the beneficiary of a foreign trust, or a settlor or grantor of a foreign trust, there are a large number of annual forms you will have to file. Taxation on beneficiaries of foreign trusts can be as high as the taxes for PFICs. Penalties for not filing the forms can be as high as 35 per cent of the assets in the trust. Seek legal and tax advice prior to moving to the US to see if there is a way around the problem.

How are you taxed?
The US has annual filing requirements which are fairly easy to comply with, as everyone must file a return. There are many online and inexpensive local tax officials you can hire, but they will not be familiar with the foreign issues outlined earlier.

The US uses the calendar year, operating Jan 1–Dec 31 each year. The form you will file is either 1040 (if filing as US resident or citizen) or 1040NR (if non-resident). There can be numerous attachments to each form. Documentation from most US payers of interest, dividends, wages and so forth must be sent by January 31 of the following year. Your tax form is due on April 15 of the following year, but just because it's due on April 15 doesn't mean you DO it on the 15th. Fill in the forms early, as soon as you have all your documentation. That way, if you have a refund coming, you'll get it sooner; and if you owe money, you'll know exactly how much you need to pay on April 15. If you can't file by April 15, you can file an extension. This only buys you time to compute the taxes and file the form, not time to pay the taxes. You will need to send a cheque for the anticipated amount due.

Over half the people who file returns use a paid preparer to reduce the risk of error. Not all paid officials are licensed. You should hire someone with foreign tax experience if you still have income from a foreign country, or if you wish to make a tax treaty claim to reduce your US income tax. If you want to tackle the job yourself, the best starting point is www.irs.gov, the main web portal for IRS questions and issues.

Taxation for non-residents
The first consideration is to determine how the property is owned. Are you the sole owner? Do you co-own the property with friends? Do you own the property through a US or UK corporation or partnership? If you own the property through an entity, such as a corporation or a partnership, there are US corporation and partnership forms which must be filed annually.

These then may have flow-through amounts to you which may have to be reported in the US or the UK. You should consult a US tax accountant to determine which forms need to be filed for your entity and how these flow through to your personal United States and UK tax returns.

Income tax
Florida does not have a personal income tax, but it does have various business taxes, including Florida sales tax and in some counties tourist taxes which must be collected from tenants along with their rent and paid to the various state and local authorities. If you hire a management firm to arrange the lettings, they should also assist you with the collection of these taxes:

Florida Tax Rates
- Sales: 6–7 per cent
- City/County: 0–5 per cent
- Corporate: 5.5 per cent

Assuming you're domiciled in the UK, the UK then has second taxing rights. The rental income is computed under UK tax law, and a tax is computed. The top UK tax rate is 40 per cent, and any US tax on the property is subtracted from the UK tax. If you rent the property and also use it for personal use, you may have to declare the personal usage as income in the UK. Check with your UK tax advisor before using it for personal use.

Remember to keep track of all your expenses and receipts. If your return is selected for audit in the US or examination in the UK, you will need them to prove your deduction. Credit card and bank statements can be used as receipts.

Resident tax
Income Tax
You will be regarded as a resident in the United States if you spend more than 183 days in one calendar year in the country, or more than 121 days per year on average over any three consecutive years. If you become resident, you will have to file tax returns on your worldwide income, or else file a treaty claim if you can prove closer ties and connections with another country.

Capital Gains Tax

You may find yourself wanting to sell your Florida house some day. If you haven't got a TIN (see earlier in the chapter) by the time you sell, you will need one. There will be Foreign Investment in Real Property Tax Act of 1980 (FIRPTA) income tax withholding on the sale if you don't have a TIN, which is 10 per cent of the sale amount.

The withholding can make retiring a mortgage and paying closing costs difficult. The good news is that the amount that must be withheld from the disposition of a US real property interest can be adjusted pursuant to a FIRPTA withholding certificate issued by the IRS. This requires you begin the process of the sale at least three months in advance to allow time to process the form.

The actual tax you would owe in the US upon sale may be more or less than the withholding tax. It's computed as follows:

- Sale price
- Minus closing costs from the sale
- Minus purchase price
- Minus certain closing costs from the purchase
- Minus improvements made over the years
- Plus depreciation allowed or allowable during rental periods.

This last item means that you must add back the depreciation claimed on your return OR the minimum that could have been claimed, whichever is greater. In other words, if you don't claim any depreciation on a rental property in order to avoid having to add it back at the time of sale, you have to add back the minimum of what you should have claimed. As this effectively postpones income from a low tax year to a higher tax year, you may wish to deduct the minimum, not the maximum, depreciation allowable annually.

Capital gains are taxed in the US at 15 per cent currently. If you're UK domiciled, the sale is taxable in the UK, with the US tax allowed as a tax credit against UK tax due.

Estate and Gift Tax

Unfortunately, none of us live forever and it is therefore essential to make plans for our heirs, especially if you have to worry about foreign legislation taking a huge chunk from our loved ones' inheritance.

There are a number of different scenarios to consider when it comes to inheritance tax, depending on how you own your property. If you own the property through a corporation, then the shares of the corporation will pass to your heirs. The value of those shares will be close to the value of the underlying assets, less the underlying liabilities.

As the property did not change hands, no transfer deeds or titles will have to be dealt with. If the shares are in a US corporation, the shares will pass through your estate and a United States estate tax return will be required, as described in the section for owning property directly.

If you own the property through a partnership, this is similar to a corporation. There may be title transfers and deeds to be amended as technically a partnership is dissolved when one of the partners dies. It would be important to have a Florida property lawyer review the situation at that time. If the partnership is a US partnership, your percentage will pass through your estate and a US estate tax return will be needed, as described in the section for owning property directly.

If you own the property directly, your heirs will have to file US estate tax returns for the value of the property. US estate tax is due for non-resident aliens on the value of assets inherited (less the liabilities) in excess of just $60,000. There's no spousal exemption from inheritance taxation unless your spouse is a US citizen. There are many allowable deductions, including the option to tax the worldwide estate at the same rates as a US citizen, which could reduce or eliminate the tax. If you're domiciled for inheritance tax purposes, the UK taxes the estate, allowing a credit for US taxes paid.

If you've just got married and want to share everything you own 50/50 with your new spouse you will have to gift your assets. Gifting in the US is a taxable event, and if the value of the gift is in excess of $11,000 (or $112,000 to your non-US spouse), then a gift tax return must be filed. If the value of the gift results in a gift tax in excess of your Unified Credit Limit ($13,000), you will have to pay a gift tax. One way around the gift tax is to gift over a period of time, rather than all at once. The best way to reduce or eliminate gift taxes is to buy the property as joint tenants so that (a) you own the property together right at the start and (b) you avoid inheritance tax on it.

The UK does not tax gifts until you die, and at that point, any gift you made more than seven years ago is not taxed. Any gifts made within the last seven years are subject to a graduated tax based on how close the gift was made to your date of death.

The IRS has a helpful website, which covers many of these topics in greater detail:
Go to www.irs.gov/individuals/foreign/.

■ BUYER'S GUIDE

SECURING A SOCIAL SECURITY NUMBER

To begin with, it's easy to conduct life in the US without a social security number, but the more time you spend in the country, the more necessary it is to secure one because it can affect many aspects of your everyday existence. You will be required to have a number if you intend to open a bank account or go out to work, and it makes securing a driving licence a much easier process. If you are applying for a number for non-work purposes it's necessary to secure documentation from your county government/ relevant government division explaining your need for a number, and a letter from your bank manager. You will also need the name and number of a bank official who will verify your need.

EDUCATION

Florida's state schools vary considerably from county to county, but the best are pretty much as good as anything provided by the English state system.

Many people who have had first hand experience of schooling in the States say the choice of subjects offers something for everybody and very few students leave before the age of 18 – the High School Diploma is almost a minimum in career terms. Some parents have chosen to educate their children privately but it needs to be remembered that private schools are very different from the UK – often associated with the military or churches.

Parents who are moving to Florida or are moving to a new school district should spend some time researching the district and schools their children will attend. Initially, parents should determine the characteristics most important for meeting the needs of their children. For instance, some parents may be interested in the academic performance of students at the school, programmes for special needs of students, courses offered, teacher turnover rates, the availability of special resources, the size of the school population, the number of students per class, dropout rates, graduation rates, and other information. The best way to get guidance is by going through organisations such as FABB, and on www.fldoe.org.

HEALTHCARE

Although the US has some of the best healthcare in the world it does not operate through a national insurance scheme, and unless you're over 65 or disabled, you have to pay for healthcare. However, if you are over 65 and disabled you will have to pay unless you are a US citizen or a permanent resident who has made sufficient contributions to cover you for medical care – even then you may require top up insurance. An agreement does exist between the US and UK governments for you to use your social security credits in the US. Consequently, it's imperative that you secure health insurance cover when you enter Florida. If you are relocating through work then your company will, generally speaking, arrange healthcare cover for you; if not, you must obtain your own personal cover. Never depend on your British holiday cover as this will not be valid.

When you approach an insurance company for healthcare make sure that it's not merely a medical discount scheme – a 10 per cent discount will not go far when your bill runs into thousands of dollars. Sometimes there can be problems qualifying for health insurance; some will be entitled to immediate cover, some won't, but there are always options open to securing medical insurance. As every individual case is different it is recommended to contact the insurance company directly prior to leaving for the United States. Costs can vary from $100 for an X-ray to $300,000 for a hip fracture or heart attack, and if you fail to secure health insurance you will be left to foot the bill.

It is essential that you secure health insurance cover for peace of mind when you visit the US

VISIT FLORIDA

BUYER'S GUIDE

CAR INSURANCE AND DRIVING LICENCES

Obtaining car insurance can be extremely tricky during your first year of residence in Florida, but you need to have it securely in place before you can drive or buy any vehicle. It's worth making contact with an insurance company prior to moving to the United States to get advice on securing insurance, because if you convey incorrect details about the points on your driving licence, you're likely to be looking at an increase in the insurance premium. Getting a US licence is not easy.

The following documents will only be accepted with a supporting document, including but not limited to a passport, personal identification card, driving licence from any other state in the US, Employer Identification, Employment Authorisation Card, Identification from home country, Identification from school or college, and Social Security Card or other INS document.

Without a licence you cannot obtain vehicle insurance cover in Florida, and without your licence you won't be able to purchase your American car. For non US citizens, the law in Florida requires identification, proof of date of birth and a social security number (if issued) prior to the issue of a driving licence. Immigrants must submit their Green Card or identification card, and non-immigrants must provide an employment authorisation card or proof of their non-immigrant classification.

For the vast majority of those visiting Florida on the visa waiver programme, it's usual to bring your UK licence and use a rental car whilst in the US, obtaining insurance coverage in the UK as part of the rental package. For citizens from the United Kingdom seeking a Florida State licence, it is also necessary to take a theory test (usually at a local driving centre) and a short driving test which is less onerous than the UK driving test.

BANKING/CREDIT

Don't close your UK bank or credit card accounts before coming to the US. If you do not already have an American credit card, you will find them hard to obtain in the early days, as you will not have built up a credit rating. You will need a social security number in order to open a US bank account, and if you're planning on spending a lot of time in the States, it's recommended you open a US bank account to avoid problems with transferring money and paying bills.

Accessing your money and paying bills is made easier by opening a US bank account

QUICK CHECKLIST

Securing a social security number
- You need a number to open a bank account
- It will help you secure a driving licence
- You require one if you want to work

Education
- Few pupils leave before the age of 18
- Schools offer a wealth of subjects
- Private schools are often associated with the military or the church

Healthcare
- The US does not have the UK equivalent of the National Heath Service
- You must secure health insurance cover
- Ensure the cover is not limited to a discount scheme: 10% discount will not go far in the US

Car insurance and driving licences
- You need a licence before you can buy a car
- You cannot get insurance without a licence
- On a visa waiver programme, you can hire a car using your UK licence

Banking/credit
- Do not close your UK bank account
- Open a US bank account: it will help you to transfer money and pay bills

Wherever you want to go...
Merricks Media can take you there

The No.1 publisher in the travel and property sector

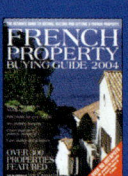

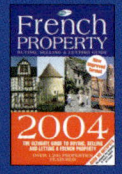

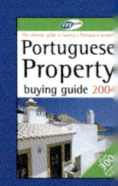

To subscribe call 01225 786850 or email subs@merricksmedia.co.uk
Merricks Media, Cambridge House South, Henry Street, Bath, BA1 1JT
www.merricksmedia.co.uk

Merricks Media Ltd

RENOVATING A PROPERTY

It's unusual for buyers in Florida to seek a renovation project. Unlike in European countries, Florida has never experienced a huge number of bargain hunters seeking a house to rebuild from scratch. The majority of properties in the state are well under 50 years old and new-builds have been quite easily affordable for such a long time, people are disinclined to take on hefty projects, particularly as many are taking on a second home and don't have the time or the energy.

With considerably fewer of what is usually termed 'period homes', Florida hasn't quite got the same culture of renovation that the Europeans have. In the UK, many properties from the Georgian, Victorian and Edwardian era are sought after and people want to preserve the character of the homes. Of course, many such buildings are grade listed and cannot be altered drastically. In Florida, in the main, homebuyers want to enjoy the outdoor lifestyle, the swimming pool in the back garden and all the modern conveniences that the 21st century has to offer. There are, of course, many beautiful old towns in the state such as St Augustine and Key West with protected historic districts, but buyers of homes in these areas are generally from the United States.

Rehabilitation

Renovation, or rehabilitation as it's known in Florida, focuses upon things such as timber treatment, installing a new kitchen, or updating air conditioning and faulty pipes. The most important thing to remember before you buy a house in the US is to have a home inspection carried out to establish just what exactly is wrong with the property.

It's also important to use the services of a good, exclusive buyer's broker to avoid any back-scratching for commission purposes between the home inspector and the buyer's broker.

The golden rule

When looking at buying a renovation property, never buy anything that isn't structurally sound as the bill will run into thousands and you may as well purchase a new property than fork out to rebuild from scratch. Secondly, all renovations and modifications must comply with the Floridian building code and any external alterations require planning permission and a building permit: for example, an extension.

Never start any building work without written permission, and if you are seeking to remodel a community property, for example a condo, you will need to check for any building restrictions listed by the condominium association.

Searching for a contractor

When searching for a contractor to carry out your renovations, ensure you gain written quotations from more than one contractor. It's essential that you draw up as thorough a list as you can, down to the last doorknob, in order to give yourself the most comprehensive idea possible regarding the final cost. A good way to find a reliable contractor is to ask a local resident for a recommendation, and once a contract is

CHECKLIST

- Always have a home inspection carried out before you buy
- Secure a renowned, exclusive buyer's broker
- Never buy anything that isn't structurally sound
- Always ensure you are complying with, and have written permission from, the Floridian building authorities
- Gain a written quotation from more than one contractor
- Have any contract drawn up with a contractor checked by your lawyer
- Never pay the contractor the whole sum up front
- Never secure a construction loan for renovation work yourself. Leave this to your contractor – if the company's reputable it will be able to do this
- Look at each property, new or resale, on its individual merits
- If you are buying a renovation property, be prepared to maintain and repair it

BUYER'S GUIDE

A great location can make a resale home a more appealing prospect than a new build

drawn up ensure it's checked by your lawyer. Check that your potential contractor is state licensed and never pay them the total amount for their work up front. Never seek to secure the construction loan yourself (i.e. the loan required to cover the cost of renovating the property), always let the builder do this. If they say they can't, then they are simply not reputable enough to be working on your property. Unfortunately, there's a significant number of poor quality building contractors in Florida, so it's worth consulting the Chamber of Commerce and Better Business Bureau prior to selecting a contractor. In Florida there is the added problem that even if you are dissatisfied with a contractor's work and withhold part of the payment, you can have this outstanding amount levied on your house by the contractor. In the worst case scenario this has led to people losing their property, so do be very careful.

New build versus resale

Given that the US offers cheap, newly built properties with numerous bathrooms, spacious bedrooms, swimming pools and patios, all fully furnished, it seems unbelievable that a buyer would plump for a resale home to renovate. However, if the property is in a great location, offering better value for money then why not? This is mainly down to cost and being able to move into the home quickly, but is it cheaper? There isn't a definitive answer to this question. You should look at each case on its individual merits. Generally, older homes may be located in more established neighbourhoods, offer more ambience, and have lower property tax rates. Some may include a few period features, although as mentioned, only the historic old towns have properties over 100 years old. Older homes built in the middle of the 20th century might have a little bit more land than houses on gated developments. Otherwise, there are few genuine benefits to buying resale houses.

People who buy older homes, however, should be willing to spend time maintaining and repairing their home. Newer homes tend to use more modern architecture and systems, they are usually easier to maintain and may be more energy-efficient. People who buy new homes often don't want to worry initially about upkeep and repairs. The main thing to be concerned about is the implications that can come from buying a property that may need a lot of work doing to it. In the UK, it's very rare that you buy a new property; it is nearly always a resale home.

A home inspection is essential, if not foolproof. It can be very expensive to replace below-par plumbing and electrics, so ensure that all the correct checks are in place before you commit to the purchase. ●

British Mortgages
FOR FLORIDA HOMES

Own your very own Florida dream villa!
Earn rental income when you are not using it.
Finance it with a *low-cost* British Sterling Mortgage!

THE BRITISH HOMES GROUP is the UK's favourite "one-stop shop" for British villa owners in Florida, the Sunshine State.

- Over 20,000 properties *throughout* Florida to choose from! *...one call does it all!*
- Low-cost fixed and flexible interest rate *British* mortgages!
- Loans repayable in pounds in the UK and secured by your villa in Florida!
- Repayment options include "Interest Only", no early settlement fees and "Payments Holidays". *...ideal for "Buy To Let" investment property owners!*
- *Refinance* your current US dollar mortgage with an affordable British home loan.
- *Eliminate monthly payment currency exchange worries!* Please call for more information - *it's free from the UK!*

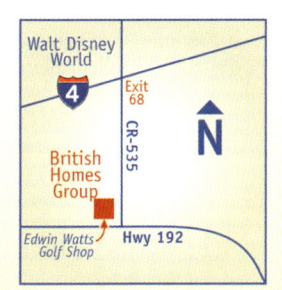

The British Homes Group
2960 Vineland Road, Kissimmee, FL 34746, USA
Telephone: **(407) 396-9914** (within Florida)
or Freephone from the UK – **0800-096-5989**
www.BritishHomesGroup.com

All enquiries are treated in the strictest of confidence and with absolutely no obligation.

Member: British-American Chamber of Commerce

REAL LIFE

We did it… Relocation

Just six years after relocating to Florida, Trina Simmons' real estate interests appreciated to the extent that she could retire from her day job

MEET THE BUYER…
Trina Simmons

Trina Simmons relocated to Sarasota six years ago when she married her American fiancé Pete, whom she met when he was based in the UK with the American Air Force. They purchased their first two-bedroom villa in a gated community in 1999. They have since bought some land and a three-bedroom home in Bradenton, both of which have appreciated to such an extent that they can now afford to give up their jobs and divide their time between the Caribbean and Florida.

Sarasota is one of Florida's most desirable locations. With fine restaurants, opera and ballet, plus miles of white, sandy beaches, prices have risen dramatically.

TRINA SIMMONS HAS NO DOUBTS THAT RELOCATING to Florida was the best decision she's ever made. Sitting by her swimming pool at home in Sarasota, she says that living the dream has exceeded all expectations. Originally from Bedfordshire, Trina arrived in Florida in late 1998 with her husband Pete. "We chose Sarasota on a whim, though its Gulf location was appealing," enthuses Trina. "As wildlife lovers, we longed to be close to some of the most fascinating nature in world. We wanted to swim with dolphins, watch turtles hatching and spot sharks in the ocean."

The buying process

When they first arrived they rented a property through REBB (Real Estate Broker & Buyers). "We thought this would allow us time to get our bearings," Trina continues. "Renting isn't cheap in Sarasota but many agents like REBB will offer an early release from the standard 12-month rental agreement if you purchase a property on their books." Their house was an old-style home, located in the heart of the quaint Southgate area of the city. Although it wasn't seen as a long-term solution, it proved an ideal base from which Trina and Pete could acquaint themselves with Sarasota and begin the search for their dream home. "With the help of REBB we found our house in Longwood Run in just a few weeks. US realtors are incredibly motivated and will work long and hard for their commission and, seeing that we were serious buyers, they pulled out all the stops." The house, a villa-style property with two bedrooms, two bathrooms, a large lounge, kitchen/diner and pool, is in a gated community in a desirable neighbourhood and had a competitive $132,000 price tag. Trina and Pete were delighted and felt sure they had snapped up a bargain. It turns out they were right, as their property was last valued at $200,000, with appreciation set to continue. Sarasota is a beautiful place with palm-lined streets, 35 miles of lovely beaches and a wealth of boat clubs and marinas. Known as Florida's Cultural Capital, it's home to a host of performing arts, museums and galleries, and despite having all the benefits of a big city it retains small-town charm, with a wonderful community spirit and a low crime rate.

Trina entertains no ideas about returning to the UK and ending her love affair with Florida. When asked why she would never leave the States she says: "I can't imagine ever tiring of waking each morning to blue skies and bright sunshine. It's so peaceful and I am still overawed at how beautiful it is."

REAL LIFE

Residents' fees

Trina acknowledges that there are plenty of extra costs for residents. "The downside is all the added extras. Residents' associations charge fees for communal maintenance and neighbourhood bylaws protect everything from exterior decor to the length of the lawn and cleanliness of the paths, and there are fines for residents that don't make the grade. Pools and air conditioning cost a lot, too." Gated communities often charge for communal areas such as gardens, basketball courts, lakes and a pool, as well as road maintenance.

However, Trina feels this is a small price to pay for living in such a healthy, relaxed environment. "Our neighbourhood is booming and prices are rising rapidly. In fact, Sarasota's healthy real estate market has encouraged Pete and I to take a keen interest in local property issues. Growth rates have been remarkable and many of the realtors we've befriended state that every sale they've handled in the last 10 years has generated a profit for the seller."

This solid economic base provides an appealing investment foundation for Trina and Pete who have since invested in more property. "Our latest buy – a three-bedroom, two-bathroom home with a shared pool, backing on to a conservation area and lake in Sabal Harbour, Bradenton – cost $130,500 in December 2002. Although we paid for extras such as white tile flooring and a covered patio for an extra $15,000, it's already realised a $50,000 profit."

The region's many boating clubs and marinas were a major selling point for Pete, who is a keen fishing and boating enthusiast

> "Trina and Pete were delighted with their $132,000 two-bedroom villa, and were certain they had snapped up a bargain. They were right; their home was last valued at $200,000"

Trina and Pete purchased the Sabal Harbour property specifically as an investment and always planned to use it for a rental income. Last year they placed an advertisement in the local newspaper, and within a couple of days had secured a long-term tenant at a monthly rental of $1,350 (£900), which is more than sufficient to cover the mortgage and maintenance costs. "This has given Pete and I the freedom to give up our jobs and enjoy more leisure time, and we plan to divide our time between Bastimentos, a Panamanian island in the Caribbean Sea, and Florida in the future. It's been a dream of ours to give up work and live a lazy tropical existence. Thanks to the buoyant Florida property market we have been able do this sooner than we thought."

Laidback lifestyle

Trina gets exasperated by people who assume that Florida is just beaches and theme parks, because it simply isn't the case. "To write a state the size of a small European country off as so one-dimensional is nothing short of a crime. Anyone who takes the trouble to explore Florida will soon discover a complex, fascinating and diverse destination of colourful, contrasting character. To be honest, while I'd love to spend all day on the beach, I rarely do. There's so much to do in Sarasota – fabulous bars, great restaurants, live music, absorbing culture and an endless list of leisure pursuits – that there just simply isn't enough time to do everything.

"We've taken to laidback Florida life well. The secret of getting the most from Florida living is not to try to accomplish too much. Despite our profitable dabbling in real estate, relaxation is the priority. If Pete has a hankering for a British pint and shepherd's pie, we'll head for the Coach & Horses, our local pub run by a British couple. It gives us a real taste of home and satisfies those moments of uncontrollable nostalgia." ●

■ REAL LIFE

We did it… A few years on

Six years ago Deborah Pira moved to Florida. Today she uses her experiences to help UK buyers turn their dreams in to a reality

MEET THE BUYER…
Deborah Pira

Deborah Pira is originally from Jersey but now lives in Deerfield Beach, Broward County. She moved to Florida in order to live with her American boyfriend (who she married four years ago) and is now a fully qualified realtor. Last year Deborah set up her own business, the British Real Estate Network, which consists of British agents operating throughout Florida, and she specialises in dealing with British buyers looking for property in the Sunshine State.

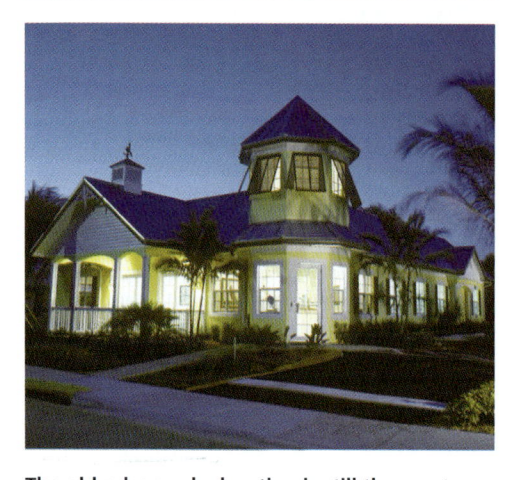

The old rules apply: location is still the most important aspect when investing

DEBORAH PIRA'S MOVE TO FLORIDA HAS PROVED more fruitful than she could have ever imagined. Successful in her chosen career as a realtor, Deborah is firm in the belief that the secret of success lies in loving what you do, and she certainly enjoys working in real estate and helping others realise their dreams.

One of the reasons she loves living and working in Florida is the international make–up of the community. "The United States is home to many foreigners who have come to start a new life, and a spirit of enthusiasm and will to succeed are very prevalent throughout the country," she enthuses. "I honestly still believe that it is possible to do very well here if you are willing to work hard and you believe in yourself all the way."

Deborah was able to train as a realtor before she became a permanent resident, but is keen to point out that there are strict visa regulations regarding employment. "You have to remember this still does not entitle you to work unless you have the correct visa. You really must ensure that you have a good immigration company working for you."

Once Deborah had secured her visa and finished (and passed!) her exams, she began working as a sales agent in Broward County. At the moment, her company organises her visa and insurance requirements and Deborah believes it is very important to get this handled by a knowledgeable and competent third-party, particularly as the regulations regarding visas are constantly changing.

Added value

When she first moved to Florida and before she became a permanent resident, Deborah purchased a two-bedroom beachside townhouse for $160,000. A year later she sold it for $200,000 and three years on it has doubled in value to $400,000. "Property here is an excellent investment, especially if you know where to buy, and mortgages are very easy to get whether you are an American or a foreign investor," she explains. "In fact, it's probably easier if you are a foreigner."

Deborah's second home is located on the waterfront: it cost her $365,000 but has since more than doubled in value to $850,000. As she was not a full US resident when she purchased her home, issues such as credit checks did not hamper the purchasing process. "Anyone can purchase a property here – it is no different whether you are an American citizen or not. However, the difference becomes apparent when you attempt to sell your property, and this is why it is essential you deal with a British realtor who knows the real estate laws of Florida and will enable you to go through the conveyancing process fully clued up."

Deborah recognises the importance of getting to grips with the Floridian lifestyle and assimilating into American society as quickly as possible. "It is important to be well integrated into the American system as this will make your future dealings and conveyancing process much easier." One of the main reasons why Deborah set up her business, was so she could educate other Brits on the differences between the British and American way of life.

Credit history

One of the first things you need to establish when you arrive in the US, is a line of credit and Deborah emphasises the importance of doing so. "A bank account is essential, and you need to procure a driving licence in order to secure a credit line," she says. Your credit history can be established in a number of ways, although Deborah recommends that it is done through a 'secured credit card' which your bank can

> "The United States is home to many foreigners who have come to start a new life, and a spirit of enthusiasm and a will to succeed are prevalent"

advise you about. "You should also look to establish two other lines of credit, maybe through leasing a car, a foreign investor's mortgage or a department store card." However, this may not be as straightforward as it first seems because some organisations will grant you these and others won't. Deborah herself went about setting up a bank account and securing credit in this way, but it took her longer to achieve as she had no real advice to fall back on, but would recommend to anyone that this is the easiest way to go about it. The best advice is to approach someone who has moved to the US and ask how they did it.

Citizenship

Deborah now works as an independent contractor for a real estate company called Balistreri, which she feels is the best way for her to conduct and enjoy her business. "Someone else takes care of all the headaches while I just get on with doing what I love and what I do best, which is helping British buyers realise their dreams." Deborah's husband, Frank, joined the company two years ago and consequently they now have a somewhat family-orientated company.

Deborah initially started out on a six month visa when she arrived in the country six years ago. "It was

By taking advice from those who have already bought, buying your home can be an easy ride

relatively easy to obtain at the time, but it isn't as easy now, I think," she says. Since she married, her visa has become permanent and she has a full Green Card, and intends to apply for citizenship next year. Now a permanent resident in Florida, she enjoys every minute of life in the Sunshine State. "I love living in Florida. The sun shines almost every day, the birds are exotic and colourful and most people love the British. I am constantly asked to 'just talk' so that they can listen to my accent."

Looking back, Deborah has no regrets about her move to Florida, although she does wish she had had more advice from people who had done it before her. On the positive side, Deborah's experience meant that she decided to set up a network of British realtors throughout the state, in order to give British buyers the benefit and security of her own and others' experiences. "People come to me and I refer them to someone who works in the area they want to buy. I guess I've come full circle, and now I'm helping other Brits find their own American dream." ●

DEBORAH'S TOP FIVE TIPS FOR BUYING-TO-LET

- It is essential to find an honest agent who knows the area you wish to buy in, intimately
- The old adage 'location, location, location' is very relevant when investing
- You must ensure you develop a good line of credit
- Ensure you purchase a property which will be a good investment, appreciate well, and provide enjoyment
- Try and get as much as possible of the preliminary work done prior to your permanent relocation, such as; securing a driving licence and opening a bank account

■ **PROPERTY GUIDE INTRO**

PROPERTY GUIDE INTRO

Sarasota Bay offers some of the most spectacular sunsets in the whole of Florida

Property Guide

Expert Market Analysis
Property Price Guides
Regional Profiles

VISIT FLORIDA

BUYER'S GUIDE

How to use this guide   **78**

Price Guide

The Panhandle   **81**
The North East   **93**
The Gulf Coast   **107**
Central Florida   **125**
The South East   **143**
The Everglades   **159**
Miami   **171**
Florida Keys   **189**

■ BUYER'S GUIDE

How to use the property guide

Florida's eight, distinct regions are profiled in detail and we've identified the state's latest hotspots and provided sample properties and prices

Hotspots

Our experts have identified the key 42 places in which to buy property in Florida. For the purposes of this guide a hotspot is classified as a place that's desirable both for its investment potential and quality of life, and that defines the property price bracket of both itself and the surrounding area.

Part Two: Property Guide

Divided into eight regional chapters, the Property Guide offers up-to-the-minute information about the current performance of each region's property market, with comparative price charts and profiles of the hotspots, as well as illustrated property price guides highlighting the types of homes available in each area.

Regional Profiles

An introduction to each region, including general information on the area and its main attractions, the state of the economy and housing market, and the main social groups living there and buying into it.

Property Price Chart

An at-a-glance snapshot of property values in the region, the price chart provides average sale prices for two, three, four and five-bedroom properties in each hotspot, wherever available. The prices are averaged from sale prices – that is, from the most recent sales prices achieved – supplied by a panel of property market specialists.

These will not always tally with the average property price listed in the hotspots profiles and key facts boxes, because the latter figures are the median property prices, averaged from the sale of houses throughout the hotspot area in the year 2000.

Regional Maps

For each listed region a map of the area is provided. A number on the map marks the location of each hotspot mentioned in the chapter, which corresponds to the number next to that hotspot's profile. Major ports, airports, roads and rivers are also marked on this map.

Hotspot Profiles

This section provides information on the cultural, economic and architectural identity of each hotspot, its popular residential areas and the dominant social groups. The profiles give an idea of the central focus of a community (for example, is it built around a bustling town centre or port?), and highlight the main characteristics of the hotspot (for example, is it rural, on the seafront, quiet?).

Discover all you need to know in our portraits of Florida's eight distinct regions	**Extensive property listings and price guides for a range of different budgets**

Check out the average seasonal temperatures and rainfall for all the regions in the state

BUYER'S GUIDE

Hotspot Key Facts Boxes

These key fact boxes detail each hotspot's pros and cons, population, airports, local taxes, etc. In some cases we have been rigorously selective, for reasons of space. References to the cost of living are based on the ACCRA cost of living index which rates the state average as 100. Anything below 100 and the property tends to be relatively cheap.

For each hotspot's rental market there is an indication of average rental prices both long and short-term. If this is short-term, details are provided regarding which months of the year you can expect to be able to let out your property. The 'Pros' and 'Cons' of each hotspot have been compiled in association with our panel of market experts, and include information, as appropriate, on employment prospects, potential tenants and current price trends.

Regional Price Guides

The regional price guides give a flavour of the type of property available in each area. They are not intended to be used as a sales brochure, as, given the nature of the Florida property market, it would be almost impossible to include properties that are still available to be purchased. However, they do offer comparisons between each region, for both prices and a wide range of architectural styles. The properties are divided into price bands which vary according to the market and the type of property on sale within each region.

The price is in dollars and the agent's three-letter code, e.g. COL, for Coldwell Banker, is listed at the top of the property details; these codes can be cross-referenced to the list of agent names and contact details, listed alphabetically with the codes in the Real Estate Agents Index. The next line details the town/area, followed by a brief description of the property and underneath, the price in £ sterling.

A selection of symbols indicate each property's number of bedrooms, whether it has a garden, if it's a town/city location, its proximity to a main road and whether there is parking, followed by a brief description or number. ●

GUIDE TO SYMBOLS

Bedrooms

followed by a number.

Garden

with the size in square metres, or a description, e.g. 'large garden'

Near shops/amenities

followed by a brief description of the distance from the property, or with the assumption that they are within five miles of the property.

Near a road

followed by a brief description of the location.

Parking

followed by a brief description of what is available, either a carport, room for parking, or a garage.

In-depth profiles of 42 property hotspots spread across the whole of the state

Succinct fact boxes provide you with each region's population growth and standard of living

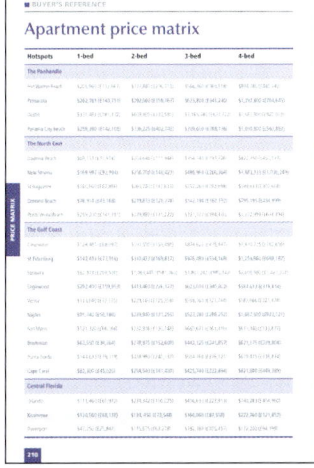

Comprehensive price matrices for houses, apartments and average letting rates

Absolutely irresistible!

Acclaimed as the "Number One Beach in the South" for 4 consecutive years!*

**Shocking White Sands...
Brilliant Green Waters...
Discover the 24 miles of
Northwest Florida's Emerald Coast!**

Discover what permanent residents know already – we live in paradise. 28 miles of natural beach bordering the Gulf of Mexico and 59 miles of inland waters. Okaloosa & Walton Counties span over 2300 square miles dotted with lakes, rivers, and streams. Natural, unspoiled beaches and woodlands thrive in over 2 dozen public parks. All this...dedicated to your enjoyment. Contact us for your place in the sun... with four offices, we cover the area.

*Southern Living Magazine, 2003

ERA REAL ESTATE

American Realty of Northwest Florida, Inc.
1270 N Eglin Parkway, Suite A-15, Shalimar, FL 32579
(850)651-2454 • www.era-american.com • mail@era-american.com

---

www.floridainvestmenthomesuk.com

- Finest quality luxury buy-to-let pool homes available in Kissimmee, Florida
- Close to all major attractions
- Unique UK $ mortgage facility with UK processing
- New build and resale available
- Tax and mortgage advise
- Management and rental
- Properties available from 20% deposit
- UK and Florida sales office – no pressure selling, just good honest advice to help you find the right home
- Thinking of selling?
We have clients on our waiting list ready to buy

Free Phone 0800 018 2442

Online information request and mortgage pre-approval
Exchange rate has never been so good —
buy now and actually save money

www.floridainvestmenthomesuk.com

Bella Homes

THE GUADELOUPE | THE DOMINICA
THE ARUBA | THE CURACAO

Buy you Florida home with Bellahomes...where quality of life comes to life

Offering you over 5,000 fully developed homesites in Port Charlotte Florida, located adjacent to the Gulf of Mexico halfway between Sarasota and Fort Myers

Call or visit our website to arrange your Florida trip today

T +44 7947 016 040
www.bellahomes.co.uk
sales@bellahomes.co.uk

THE PANHANDLE ■

The Panhandle

Historic cities, fine sandy beaches and warm gulf waters

VISIT FLORIDA

- **Population** 1.25 million
- **Population increase** Between 1992–2002 the population increased by 18.2% (193,000 people)
- **Migration** 21,000 people migrated to the Panhandle between 2000–2002, of whom 23% were international migrants
- **Median age** 35.2 years
- **Median home price** $124,600, which is 21% below the national average and 12% lower than the state average of $141,100
- **Cost of living** The ACCRA cost of living index rates the Panhandle as 97.9/100

Profile 82 ■
Hotspots 84 ■

Price Guide

$100,000–$300,000   87 ■
$300,000–$520,000   89 ■
$520,000–$775,000   90 ■
$775,000–$1,000,000   91 ■

THE PANHANDLE

GETTING THERE

AIR There are no direct flights from the UK into the Panhandle, and most flights will involve a detour to Panama City. **American Airlines** (0845 778 9789; www.aa.com) flies from Heathrow to Miami or Dallas, and on to Panama City or Pensacola. **British Airways** (0870 850 9850; www.ba.com) flies from Gatwick, via Tampa, Atlanta and Orlando and then on to Panama City. **Continental Airlines** (0845 607 6760; www.continental.com) flies from Gatwick, Manchester, Birmingham and Edinburgh via Newark, and then on to Panama City. **Virgin Atlantic** (0870 574 7747; www.virgin-atlantic.com) flies from Gatwick to Orlando and Heathrow to Miami, and from there offer transfers.

RAIL Amtrak (+1 800 872 7245; www.amtrak.com), the national rail service, offers trains to Pensacola, Tallahassee, Crestview and Lake City.

ROAD It is recommended that you hire a car if staying in the Panhandle. The roads are good with the I-10 running from Pensacola through Tallahassee, and all the way on to Jacksonville. The US 98 runs along the Panhandle coastline from Pensacola down to Apalachicola. **Greyhound** buses (+1 800 229 9424; www.greyhound.com) offer a comprehensive network of buses to Defunial Springs, Fort Walton Beach, Marianna, Panama City, Panama City Beach, Pensacola and Tallahassee.

Area profile

The Panhandle stretches for more than 200 miles below the southernmost borders of Alabama and Georgia. Its main cities are Pensacola – where Spain surrendered Florida to the US in 1821 – and the state capital, Tallahassee – a provincial city of around 150,000 inhabitants. The spectacular southern coast of the Panhandle is inundated with tourists, while Panama City Beach is renowned as the most popular spring-break destination in Florida. The idyllic seaside also lies on the coast, and this was the town that provided the backdrop for the movie *The Truman Show*.

Despite the region's vast number of condos and hotels, many areas are protected from property development, and the coast boasts some of the most attractive beaches and breath-taking scenery in Florida. The area is easy to navigate, and it's the only region in the state that extends east to west, eventually turning southward towards the tranquillity of Cedar Key. The coastal road (Highway 98) is linked by a spectacular network of bridges, and leads you to just south of Tallahassee from Pensacola, where it heads inland. Panhandle's small inland farming towns are warm and friendly; the inhabitants have a laidback attitude and a strong sense of the past. There are fine examples of Old South architecture on display, and a wealth of relaxing walks through pine forests, bubbling springs, hidden caverns, and the Apalachicola National Forest – a beautifully preserved wilderness area. Many rare animals exist in this region, including; the Peregrine Falcon, Eastern Chipmunk and Florida Black Bear, and locals are concerned that planned development could threaten the local wildlife.

The economy

Although the Panhandle gets little coverage in comparison to the well-established markets and world-renowned attractions of Orlando and Miami, this unspoilt and uncommercialised region has experienced a huge boost in investment recently. The state's largest private landowner – it owns around 825,00 acres of land, primarily in the north-west – the St Joe Company has poured a substantial amount of money into the area to aid

The idyllic Shell Island stretches for over seven miles, and remains an uninhibited natural preserve

THE PANHANDLE

the development of education, health, parks, recreation and art. Farming and agriculture are still the region's major economic forces, while the timber and fishing industries are thriving, too. One of the area's biggest employers is the huge Eglin Air Force Base which spans three county boundaries – it's even home to two championship-quality golf courses.

Property market

A strong economic forecast has been predicted, due to the concentrated development work and large-scale redevelopment projects underway, as well as a continued influx of visitors and retiring baby-boomers to the area's top-rated beaches. The strip of beach next to Panama City continues to develop into upscale, planned communities such as; Seaside, Rosemary Beach, Seacrest and Gulf Place. With a new airport recently built at the cost of $8 million, the area is increasingly easy to reach, and will undoubtedly bring in more property buyers. In Panama City there are 15 large-scale projects undergoing development, with four upmarket residential developments being built at Panama City Beach. Expansion along the coast is moving apace, and areas such as Fort Walton Beach and Niceville are experiencing huge sales.

With property values appreciating, it's an excellent time to buy in the Panhandle. Properties are cheaper than further south in Florida, but they vary across the region, with the cheapest being located in the north of Santa Rosa County, and the most expensive in the south of Walton, around Apalachicola. With Panama's facelift underway, there is a large pre-construction buyer's market. Waterfront properties with a view of the water retail at the highest prices, and also make the best rental properties. Condos are popular on the waterfront, and many more are being constructed.

Inhabitants and visitors

There has been incredible growth in the region, and the stretch from Pensacola to Panama City is becoming popular with outsiders. Construction has doubled, and prices are skyrocketing, though still affordable. It's a highly publicised area for holiday-makers and tourism is increasing every year. Buying property in the Panhandle is currently an excellent investment, and there has been a 20–25 per cent appreciation in prices throughout the region since 2000. Destin and Fort Walton have small, private airports which encourages wealthy visitors to invest in the region. In Panama City there is a lot of growth, but it's not quite as exclusive as Destin and Pensacola Beach. In the spring break, Panama City sees a lot of college students, whereas Destin sees more families and retirees and therefore its property market is much more stable. The planned developments are all focused around the tourist market and all have a similar architectural design. Primarily, locals and North Americans buy property in the Panhandle, although a growing proportion of Europeans – Germans in particular – are showing an increasing interest. ●

The Panhandle is home to some of Florida's best beaches

Primarily, Americans buy property in the Panhandle, although Europeans are now showing increasing interest

Average monthly temperature °C (Celsius)

PANHANDLE		LONDON	
12	Dec	7
16	Nov	10
21	Oct	14
26	Sept	19
28	Aug	21
28	July	22
27	June	20
24	May	17
19	April	13
16	March	10
13	Feb	7
11	Jan	6

Average monthly rainfall mm (millimetres)

PANHANDLE		LONDON	
101	Dec	81
113	Nov	78
105	Oct	70
146	Sept	65
174	Aug	62
204	July	59
162	June	58
112	May	57
99	April	56
162	March	64
119	Feb	72
136	Jan	77

Florida Climate Center (www.coaps.fsu.edu/climate_center)

AVERAGE HOUSE SALE PRICES

Hotspot	2-bed	3-bed	4-bed	5-bed
Fort Walton Beach	$196K (£107K)	$284K (£154K)	$482K (£263K)	$775K (£422K)
Pensacola	$143K (£78K)	$287K (£156K)	$441K (£240K)	$1.01M (£550K)
Destin	$567K (£310K)	$1.13M (£616K)	$1.47M (£801K)	$3.2M (£1.74M)
Panama City Beach	$494K (£269K)	$646K (£352K)	$1.06M (£577K)	$1.6M (£888K)

THE PANHANDLE

Property hotspots

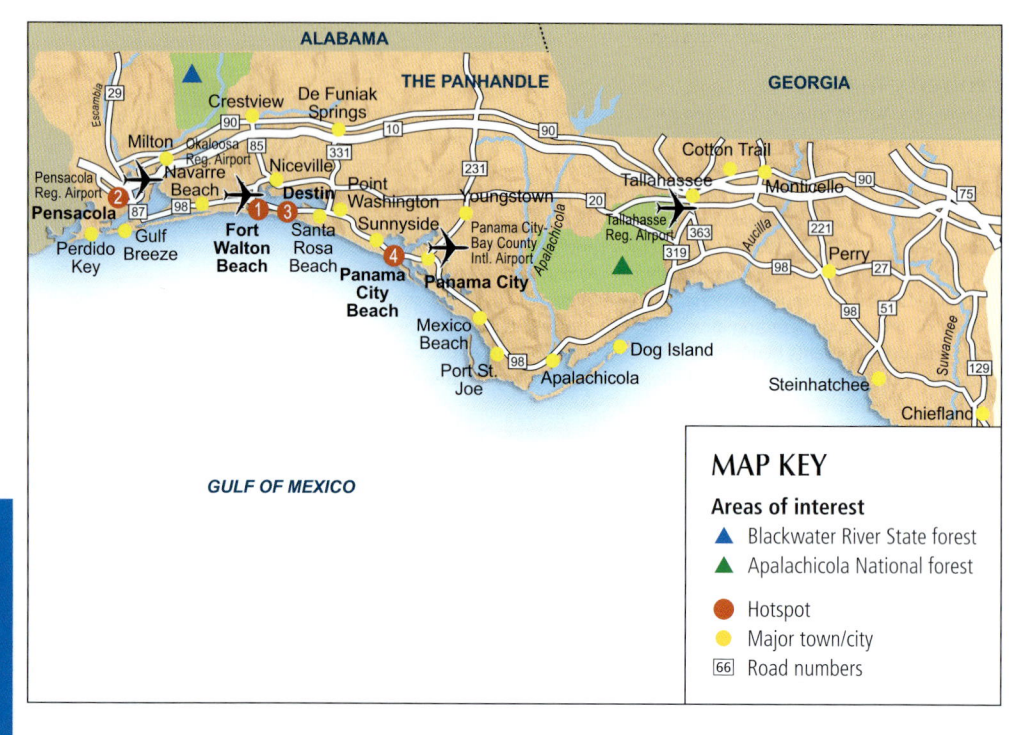

MAP KEY

Areas of interest
- ▲ Blackwater River State forest
- ▲ Apalachicola National forest
- ● Hotspot
- ● Major town/city
- 66 Road numbers

1. Fort Walton Beach

ESSENTIALS ■ **Pop** 22,000 ■ **Airport** Pensacola Regional Airport, 2430 Airport Blvd, Ste. 225, Pensacola, FL 32504, Tel: +1 850 436 5000 ■ **Tax** Property tax rate per $1,000: $15

KEY FACTS

■ **Schools** Fort Walton Beach High School, 400 Hollywood Boulevard S, Fort Walton Beach, FL 32548, Tel: +1 850 833-3300
■ **Medical** Fort Walton Beach Medical Ctr, 1000 Mar Walt Dr, Fort Walton Beach, FL 32547, Tel: +1 850 862-1111
■ **Rentals** The best rental properties in Fort Walton are those located on the waterfront ■ Fort Walton attracts many North Americans and a large number of German tourists, undergoing an enormous growth in tourism since the late 1970s ■ Weekly rental prices vary from $1,268 in spring, to $1,195 in summer, $767 in autumn and $547 in winter, for a beachfront condo sleeping 2-6 people, with a pool
■ **Pros** Being the most recently developed realty market, it is also the most overlooked by the international buyer and remains largely unsplolit ■ An ideal family-orientated resort, where you can enjoy the beaches of Okaloosa Island ■ The average property price is an affordable $117,800
■ **Cons** The Fort Walton area is predicted to see price hikes, and this makes it an ideal seller's market ■ An area which attracts a huge number of tourists, which means that the cost of living during the summer season can be high

Roughly twice the size of Destin, Fort Walton Beach is home to the Eglin Air Force Base. Primarily a beach and fishing resort, the area features some of the finest beaches in the US, the best of which are owned and maintained by the US Air Force. The region has undergone a lot of development in recent years, with condominiums springing up rapidly along the coastline and the many high-quality golf courses are a major attraction.

Fort Walton Beach residents have recently been attributed with having an excellent quality of life – among the best in the nation. Listed within the top fifty 'five-star communities', the affordability of it's housing was one of the criteria by which the town was judged.

The Eglin Air Force Base contributes significantly to the economy; electronic equipment is manufactured in Fort Walton Beach and military planes from all over the US are modified here. Housing prices are substantially lower in general than its neighbour, Destin. At the low end of the market, small two-bed homes and apartments can be picked up for just over $60,000, and three-bed homes with a pool can be bought for around $250,000. A one-bed apartment in an exclusive oceanfront condo on the Santa Rosa Boulevard setting sells for around $400,000, and prices can rise as high as $2 million. ●

84

THE PANHANDLE

2. Pensacola

ESSENTIALS ■ **Pop** 60,000 ■ **Airport** Pensacola Regional Airport, 2430 Airport Blvd, Ste. 225, Pensacola, FL 32504, Tel: 850 436-5000 ■ **Tax** Property tax rate per $1,000: $17

Pensacola's long and rich history stretches as far back as 1559 when Spanish sailors first landed in the bay. It is now a busy coastal city with a population of around 60,000, but its Hispanic connections are still evident in the architecture of the well-preserved old town, which underwent an extensive renovation programme in the 1960s. Still a community with an old-fashioned friendliness, Pensacola offers many types of homes for all budgets. Gulf Breeze – a peninsula in Pensacola Bay connected to the historic district by a three-mile bridge – is one of the most popular areas. Doctors, lawyers and other professionals populate this community, where it's still possible to buy an older home for $180,000. Five miles south-east of the city on the barrier island of Santa Rosa, lies Pensacola Beach. Home to the region's longest pier, it has a wealth of beach-facing houses and apartments.

Pensacola's two historic districts of East Hill and North Hill offer stunning renovation properties, ideal for those seeking to make a good investment. However, these properties do not come cheap and are quickly sold on, due to the high demand and limited availability.

The Pensacola economy is driven by the nearby Eglin Air Force Base which provides employment for many locals, and there is additional muscle from housing sales and a dynamic tourism industry. ●

KEY FACTS

■ **Schools** Brentwood Middle School, 201 Hancock Lane, Pensacola, FL 32503, Tel: +1 850 494-5640
■ **Medical** Gulf Coast Treatment Center, 1015 Mar Walt Drive, Fort Walton Beach, FL 32547, Tel: +1 850-863-4160
■ **Rentals** A popular hotspot for American vacationers, the area offers affordable holiday rentals ■ Weekly rental costs vary from $846 in winter, to $1,479 in summer ■ Its stunning beaches encourage those seeking holiday rentals
■ **Pros** Improved air links to Pensacola have resulted in a surge of overseas buyers and a 6% increase in prices ■ Gulf Breeze in Pensacola Bay is hugely popular, with many commuters for Pensacola City buying and living here ■ Pensacola is believed to offer the best value and growth potential of anywhere in Florida ■ Average prices are $116,400 for a single family home, and $162,939 generally
■ **Cons** Lacks a certain level of exclusivity in comparison with other parts of Florida ■ The city's busy dockyards and naval aviation school could be a turn off for some buyers ■ The beach apart, there are relatively few attractions in the centre

3. Destin

ESSENTIALS ■ **Pop** 12,000 ■ **Airport** Destin-Fort Walton Beach Airport, 1001 Airport Road, Destin, FL 32541-2807, Tel: +1 850 837-6135 ■ **Tax** Property tax rate per $1,000: $16

Described as an area of stunning natural beauty, the picturesque Emerald Bay in which Destin is situated, is home to some of the finest fishing waters in the region. There's an annual seafood festival and a bounty of great fish restaurants, and although the region is growing, it retains a certain homely, small-town charm. The development of the town in the past 20 years has attracted tourists and resulted in a switch of the major economic driving force from fishing to tourism. Newly-constructed condos line the shoreline and property prices have risen 10 per cent in the past year. These developments make investment prospects attractive for potential buyers, and local building contractors specialise in state-of-the-art home construction that includes individual, custom-built homes; Victorian, traditional or beach-style floor plans are but a few of the choices available. The newer resort town of San Destin draws a number of buyers, and there are an assortment of condos (from high-rise penthouse living, beachfront, or town homes) offering a great investment for additional rental income or personal use. Condos were selling from between $100,000 and $400,000 in March 2004. However, single family homes took the lead in the housing market at the beginning of 2004, accounting for 51 per cent of property sales. ●

KEY FACTS

■ **Schools** Destin Elementary School, 630 Kelly Street, Destin, FL 32541, Tel: +1 850 833-4360
■ **Medical** Fort Walton Beach Medical Center, 996 Airport Road, Destin, FL 32541, Tel: +1 850-837 9194
■ **Rentals** Destin is a hugely popular area for rentals and holiday-makers ■ The average price per week for a one-bedroom condo ranges from $448 in winter, $530 in autumn, $614 in spring and $788 in summer ■ Condominiums are the main rental properties available
■ **Pros** Property has accrued in value by 10 per cent ■ Voted the No.1 Beach in America and the Best Beach in the South, the sandy beaches offer great swimming and watersports facilities ■ There was a 7.7 per cent increase in realty sales, with condos accounting for 49 per cent of sales, while family homes accounted for 51 per cent
■ **Cons** Destin is a seller's market, with prices increasing by 10 per cent ■ Destin currently offers an average sale price of $368,100, while San Destin offers a cheaper $244,260 ■ There has been a 32.3 per cent decline in homes selling at an 'affordable' price; that is, $300,000 or below

HOTSPOTS

THE PANHANDLE

3. Panama City Beach

ESSENTIALS ■ **Pop** 6,000 ■ **Airport** Panama City-Bay County International Airport, 3173 Airport Road, Panama City, FL 32405, Tel: +1 850-763-6751, Fax 850-785-5674 ■ **Tax** Property tax rate per $1,000: $14

KEY FACTS

■ **Schools** Bay High School, 1204 Harrison Ave, Panama City, FL 32401-2433, Tel: +1 850 872-46
■ **Medical** Bay Medical Center, 615 N Bonita Av, Panama City, FL 32401-3623, Tel: +1 850 769-1511
■ **Rentals** Panama City Beach is a huge tourist and student spring-break destination, creating a large rentals market ■ Average weekly rentals for a one-bedroom condo vary from $520 for autumn, $556 for the winter, $610 for spring and $856 for summer
■ **Pros** There is an enormous amount of investment being undertaken in Panama City, with over 15 large-scale development projects, and an $8 million airport being constructed ■ This area is not as affluent as Destin and Fort Walton Beach, and remains affordable to the average buyer ■ With the market dominated by pre-construction property, now is a good time to invest as prices are predicted to double ■ There are plenty of resale properties available
■ **Cons** With recent investment and development, properties and the cost of living are destined to increase in price ■ Panama City is dominantly pre-construction with a growing waiting list for plots

Many years before Panama City Beach was officially founded in 1936, the area was home to Indians who fished the plentiful local waters. It was also a popular spot with pirates due to the coastal inlets and the many passing ships en route to Mexico and Spain, and a number of offshore wrecks testify to this. These days it's a tourist trap and every spring, thousands of students from across the US and Canada descend on the town. It's packed with shops, restaurants and amusement attractions, such as mini-golf and go–karting tracks. However, it is the endless miles of white, sandy beaches that are the main draw. Although it is undeniably commercial in nature, there are a number of religious retreats, so it's not just a party town.

Panama City Beach has seen a huge upturn in recent times. Three-bedroom condos range from $335,000 to $1,700,000 and a considerable number of old motels are being replaced by high-rises along the coast. Prices have soared in the last 18 months, with an average increase of 15 per cent across the board. Shops and restaurants are also being developed in conjunction with the residential areas. In property terms, Panama City Beach is 'up-and-coming' with predictions suggesting that waterfront condos may well triple in price over the next two years. Consequently, now is a good time to invest. ●

Panama City Beach is attracting many savvy investors

THE PANHANDLE

$100,000 – $300,000
(£55,000–£165,000)

The Panhandle is renowned for cheap properties that come with plenty of land

$19,900   CODE PAR

PONCE DE LEON
A bargain wood frame property, ideal for a rural retreat for those seeking solitude

£10,945

🛏 1   🌼 with a small garden   🏙 within driving distance of amenities   🚧 not located on a main road   🚗 room for parking

---

$79,999   CODE ERA

CRESTVIEW
Tucked away from city bustle, 40 minutes from the beach, an ideal investment home

£44,000

🛏 3   🌼 with a garden   🏙 close to the shops   🚧 not located on a main road   🚗 room for parking

---

$89,000   CODE PAR

PONCE DE LEON
A mobile home situated in a park with a well; excellent prospects for rental income

£48,950

🛏 2   🌼 in 2.5 acres   🏙 within easy reach of amenities   🚧 not located on a main road   🚗 room for parking

---

$103,500   CODE ERA

CHOCTAWHATCHEE BAY
This waterfront condo enjoys community amenities including a pool and tennis courts

£56,925

🛏 2   🌼 with a balcony and communal garden   🏙 amenities onsite   🚧 not located on a main road   🚗 room for parking

---

$114,900   CODE ERA

CRESTVIEW
Just 25 miles from the beautiful Gulf Coast, this is an ideal first investment in Florida

£63,195

🛏 3   🌼 with a large garden   🏙 within easy reach of the town centre   🚧 not located on a main road   🚗 room for parking

PRICE GUIDE

■ THE PANHANDLE

$165,000
CODE ERA
MARY ESTHER
Located close to the waterfront, a lovely property with light and spacious rooms
£90,750

🛏 4 | 🌸 with a garden | 🏬 close to amenities | 🛑 not located on a main road

🚗 room for parking, with a two-car garage

$228,000
CODE ERA
SHALIMAR
A well-decorated home set in a peaceful environment, ideal as a rural retreat
£125,400

🛏 4 | 🌸 with a large garden | 🏬 within easy reach of amenities | 🛑 not located on a main road

🚗 room for parking, with a two-car garage

$230,000
CODE PAR
PONCE DE LEON
A mobile home park, with three houses and seven trailers, ideal as an investment
£126,500

🛏 – | 🌸 with 4.5 acres | 🏬 situated close to amenities | 🛑 not located on a main road

🚗 room for parking, with a two-car garage

$250,000
CODE ERA
DESTIN
Set in beautifully landscaped gardens, a modern property with a covered patio
£137,500

🛏 3 | 🌸 with a garden and marina | 🏬 close to amenities and attractions

🛑 not located on a main road | 🚗 room for parking

$250,000
CODE PAR
PONCE DE LEON
A spacious home in a secluded area, with a pool, hot tub and games room
£137,500

🛏 3 | 🌸 with 14.5 acres | 🏬 in a secluded location | 🛑 not located on a main road

🚗 room for parking, with a two-car garage

$287,900
CODE ERA
MARY ESTHER
Spacious and modern, an ideal family property with a swimming pool and large garden
£158,345

🛏 4 | 🌸 with a spacious garden | 🏬 near to the shops | 🛑 not located on a main road

🚗 room for parking

PRICE GUIDE

THE PANHANDLE

$300,000—$520,000
(£165,000–£286,000)

Stunning, surprisingly cheap waterfront properties, both newly built and resale

$339,900   CODE ERA
FORT WALTON BEACH
A brand new property set in woodlands, with a hot tub and separate workshop
£186,945

4 | with spacious grounds | within easy reach of amenities | not located on a main road | room for parking, with a garage

$357,700   CODE ERA
CRESTVIEW
Situated in a verdant setting, a modern, spacious property close to the town centre
£196,735

5 | with a large garden | close to the town centre and schools | not located on a main road | room for parking, with a two–car garage

$357,700   CODE ERA
CRESTVIEW
A comfortable home in a wonderful, serene setting overlooking its own private lake
£196,735

4 | in 7.2 acres | within driving distance of amenities | not on a main road | room for parking

$489,800   CODE ERA
FORT WALTON BEACH
Set in a gated community, with a pool, this newly built home comes with all mod cons
£269,390

4 | with a large garden | situated close to the beach and amenities | not located on a main road | room for parking

$519,000   CODE ERA
DESTIN
A Gulf-front condo with stunning views, on the beachfront, with a pool and a gym
£285,450

2 | with a balcony and communal gardens | situated close to amenities | not located on a main road | room for parking

PRICE GUIDE

THE PANHANDLE

$520,000 — $775,000
(£286,000 – £426,250)

The most competitively priced luxury beachfront homes in the state of Florida

PRICE GUIDE

$535,900　　　　　　　　　　　　　　　　　　　　　　　　　CODE ERA
FORT WALTON BEACH
Currently under construction, a stunning new property with a fully fitted kitchen
£294,745

🛏 5　　🌸 with a large garden　　🏢 close to the town centre　　🚸 not on a main road

🚗 room for parking, with a two-car garage

$590,000　　　　　　　　　　　　　　　　　　　　　　　　　CODE ERA
FORT WALTON BEACH
A modern home situated on the seafront with access to Fort Walton's sandy beaches
£324,500

🛏 2　　🌸 with a small garden　　🏢 situated close to amenities　　🚸 not on a main road

🚗 room for parking

$595,000　　　　　　　　　　　　　　　　　　　　　　　　　CODE ERA
FORT WALTON BEACH
With waterfront views and a private dock, this home is ideal as a relaxing retreat
£327,250

🛏 3　　🌸 with a large garden　　🏢 situated close to amenities　　🚸 not on a main road

🚗 with three private parking spaces

$719,000　　　　　　　　　　　　　　　　　　　　　　　　　CODE ERA
DESTIN
Built in a contemporary design, a property in large grounds perfect for a family
£395,450

🛏 3　　🌸 with a large garden　　🏢 situated close to amenities　　🚸 not located on a main road　　🚗 with three parking spaces

$775,000　　　　　　　　　　　　　　　　　　　　　　　　　CODE ERA
DESTIN
A large cottage, extremely cosy and with a pool, ideal as a holiday home
£426,250

🛏 4　　🌸 with a large garden　　🏢 within easy reach of amenities and shops　　🚸 not located on a main road　　🚗 room for parking

90

THE PANHANDLE

$775,000 – $1,000,000
(£426,250 – £550,000)

Waterfront townhouses and magnificent resale homes that represent great value

$776,000
CODE ERA
FORT WALTON BEACH
A waterfront home on a quiet road with a boat dock, enjoying fabulous views
£426,250

- 3
- with a large garden
- close to the town centre
- not on a main road
- room for parking

$795,000
CODE ERA
DESTIN
With spectacular views and private beach access, an excellent prospect for rentals
£437,250

- 4
- with a garden
- situated close to amenities
- not located on a main road
- room for parking

$1,250,000
CODE ERA
PERDIDO KEY
A stunning property, with a private boat dock, patio and gazebo, on the waterfront
£687,500

- 5
- with a large garden
- situated close to town
- not located on a main road
- room for parking

$2,750,000
CODE ERA
DESTIN
With views over the Gulf of Mexico, a comfortable residence ideal as a holiday home
£1,512,500

- 4
- with a garden
- situated close to shops and attractions
- not located on a main road
- room for parking

$2,950,000
CODE ERA
DESTIN
A stunning beach property built to the highest quality overlooking the Gulf of Mexico
£1,622,500

- 6
- with a porch
- situated close to the town centre
- not on a main road
- room for parking

PRICE GUIDE

0161 351 2160

escapes2.com
florida property

Our Best Seller

WINSLOW ESTATES ORLANDO

3, 4 and 5 bed detached homes with private pool. Gated entrance with walled perimeter. 10 minutes to Disney.

From £166,000
Including a FREE Furniture Pack

Fantastic Investment Opportunity

FLORIDAY'S ORLANDO RESORT

Mediterranean style 2 and 3 bedroom condominiums with five star hotel facilities. Excellent rental potential.

120 sq metres + balcony

From £128,000

holiday homes · residential homes · thousands of resales · view over 80 new development projects
rental management · investment properties · 1-2-1 inspection trips · mortgages and remortgages arranged
UK head office: escapes house 228 bury new road whitefield manchester M45 8QN

Experience the difference of buying in Florida

New & re-sale homes in the Disney area from £90,000
New home deposits from as little as 10%

Would you like a home like this? I am not only a homeowner, I am legally licensed to sell property in Florida. You can benefit from my years of experience and excellent continuing after-sales care when it is needed most.

- Having me as your realtor costs you nothing yet could save you thousands
- Friendly staff both in the UK and the US
- Impartial advice on location, financing, management, rental potential etc.
- Inspection visits with NO pressure for new or re-sale homes: the choice is always yours
- Up to $2,000 cashback and accommodation costs for buyers
- Contact with other homeowners and referrals from previous buyers if required
- Great investment opportunity/pension plan that you & your family get to enjoy!

For a brochure & information, please contact Karen Evans
Tel/Fax UK 01502 514122
E-mail evans@westridge-florida.freeserve.co.uk
www.executivevillas4florida.com

Ideal Florida Homes

We are delighted to offer luxury resort and marina homes at **Key Largo**, **Bahia Beach** and **St Augustine**

We have homes to fulfil everyone's dream of Florida living, whether waterfront, boating, golf, or just relaxing, a comfortable, rewarding lifestyle is ensured.

Please visit our website or call Andy Lowe on **01923 85 67 66** or mobile **07973 675 477** for a brochure or email:
andy@idealfloridahomes.com

Golfers who dream about a property that overlooks one of three signature golf courses, ought to consider the potential of our **Fort Myers** or **Orlando** Resorts.

www.idealfloridahomes.com

The North East

The oldest US city, motor racing Mecca and beaches galore

- **Population** 1.3 million
- **Population increase** Between 1992–2002 the population grew by 22%
- **Migration** 46,500 people migrated to the North East between 2000–2002 of which 16% were international migrants
- **Median age** 36.2, the state average is 38.7
- **Median home price** $117,800. This is 17% lower than the state average (141,100) and 26% lower than the national average
- There has been a 10% increase in prices over the last year
- There is huge interest from 'snowbirds' from America's northern states and Canada and the North East is a healthy retirement market

Profile 94
Hotspots 96

Price Guide

$100,000–$150,000	100
$150,000–$200,000	101
$200,000–$270,000	102
$270,000–$425,000	103
$425,000–$570,000	104
$570,000 +	105

THE NORTH EAST

GETTING THERE

AIR There are no direct flights into Daytona Beach Airport from the UK, so it would require a transfer. **British Airways** (0870 850 9850; www.britishairways.com) recommend travelling to Atlanta or New York and then securing a transfer to Daytona Beach via **Delta** (www.delta.com; +1 800 221 1212) or **Continental Airlines** (www.continental.com; 0129 377 6464/ 0845 607 6760). To reach Jacksonville Airport it would require flying from Heathrow to Miami and then securing a transfer with **American Airlines** (www.aa.com; 0845 7789 789). **Virgin Atlantic** (www.virgin-atlantic.com; 0870 380 2007) fly into Orlando International from Manchester and Gatwick, and Miami Airport from Heathrow. From Orlando, it's a straightforward drive up Route 4 to the north east coast.

ROAD It is essential to hire a car in order to navigate the north east coastline. From Jacksonville in the north Route 1 and the I-95 run down the eastern coast, through St Augustine, Daytona Beach and New Smyrna. From Orlando Airport, Route 1 and 4 take you up to the east coast. The A1A also runs along the coastline linking a number of the coastal resorts from St Augustine to Ormond Beach and beyond.

RAIL The **Amtrak** rail services (www.amtrak.com; +1 800 872 7245) run from Orlando to Jacksonville, and also run to Deland and from here you can get a connection to Daytona Beach. There is a direct Amtrak service to Palatka and from here you can take Highway 207 all the way to St Augustine.

COACH Greyhound buses (+1 800 229 9424; www.greyhound.com) offer a comprehensive network of services to Daytona Beach, Gainesville, Jacksonville, Lake City, Ocala and St Augustine.

Area profile

THE NORTH EAST OF FLORIDA OFFERS VISITORS AND RESIDENTS A RARE blend of state-of-the-art technology, old world charm and natural beauty. The area is the last frontier of the Sunshine State, stretching from Cape Canaveral to Georgia, taking in many sights and sounds along the way.

The primary draw for tourists is Kennedy Space Center – listed among Florida's top five attractions. NASA shares its 'Space Coast' with unlikely bedfellows the National Wildlife Refuge and the Canaveral National Seashore Park, meaning that neighbours include bald eagles, alligators and even the shy manatee. Continuing north up US Highway 1 we reach New Smyrna Beach, a popular spot with young families due to its proximity to the theme parks. With its self-styled 'World's Safest Bathing Beach', it's home to 13 miles of pristine white sand and excellent year-round fishing, while the city itself – the second oldest in Florida – boasts street after street of beautifully restored turn-of-the-century houses.

Daytona Beach – a little further up the coast again – is famed for its stretch of hard-packed sand which became a Mecca for automotive racing enthusiasts between 1903 and 1935; in fact, no fewer than 13 records were set here. The tradition continues with world-famous annual events such as the Daytona 500. The beach is full of bustle, and has many activities on offer such as boat trips, canoeing and excellent surfing.

By the time you get to St Augustine, the coast becomes a lot less developed and it's characterised by nature reserves and quaint seaside towns. The city itself was founded in 1565 by Spanish settlers, making it America's oldest European-settled city; it contains over 144 blocks of historic buildings and sites. Many of the structures – from forts to bandstands – are made from coquina, Florida's oldest building material. Formed over millions of years, coquina is a soft, porous, but durable stone.

The North East is home to many fine historic towns, some of which date back to the 16th century

THE NORTH EAST

The economy and housing market

North East Florida has a very strong economy that is supplemented by the impressive tourist figures achieved by the Space Coast and Daytona Beach. Jacksonville is known as America's hottest city. An industrial hub the geographical size of New York, Jacksonville plays host to numerous successful companies dealing in avionics and biomedicine. Excellent infrastructure and low administrative costs are very appealing to other big businesses and it is estimated that almost 50 per cent of Florida's high-tech companies are located here.

In spite of the area's economic blessings and beautiful topography, house prices in the North East remain well below those found in the rest of Florida. Just outside St Augustine, family-sized homes can be purchased for $100,000, while the median cost of a three-bedroom home in Jacksonville is around $119,000.

Daytona Beach is a booming market in terms of real estate with a price growth of 30 per cent reported in just two years. Nonetheless, it remains affordable with oceanfront condos priced from around $200,000. Taking advantage of these good value beachfront condos makes sense at the moment as prices are continuing to rise, which makes for an excellent long-term investment. During sporting events and the summer months, rental prospects at Daytona are excellent. Be prepared to move quickly if you're planning to buy here because demand is outstripping supply.

Another indication of a growing property market is the increase in construction of more upmarket properties. Both Ponce Inlet and Ormond have seen their first $2 million property sales recently and this will attract the attention of the bigger spenders.

The idea of buying an old house might be appealing to some, given the plethora of historic property along the North East coast. Be warned though that prices will be higher than those associated with the new-build market, and preservation regulations and building restrictions could turn your slice of the past into a modern day nightmare. It's important to always seek proper legal advice in these matters.

Social groups

The largest group of US buyers in North East Florida are retirees from New York, New Jersey and the east coast who move to take advantage of the excellent infrastructure and facilities.

The North East is still a new area in terms of the overseas market though realtors predict a boom in the near future owing to the wealth of cheap properties and fabulous weather. There is a small but growing British expat community and other northern Europeans are beginning to catch on, too. Families tend to gravitate towards New Smyrna Beach due to its proximity to Orlando, the sandy beaches and other excellent amenities. ●

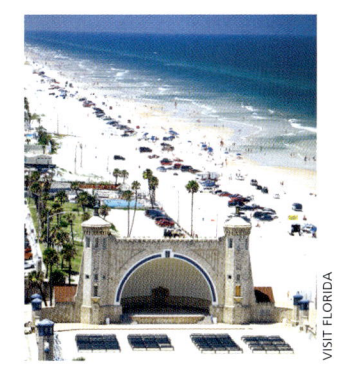

Daytona Beach's wide, hard-packed sands have attracted motor racers for 100 years

Realtors predict a boom owing to the cheap property and fantastic weather

Average monthly temperature °C (Celsius)

THE NORTH EAST		LONDON	
23	Dec	7	
22	Nov	10	
25	Oct	14	
27	Sept	19	
28	Aug	21	
28	July	22	
27	June	20	
25	May	17	
25	April	13	
20	March	10	
18	Feb	7	
18	Jan	6	

Average monthly rainfall mm (millimetres)

THE NORTH EAST		LONDON	
69	Dec	81	
110	Nov	78	
130	Oct	70	
194	Sept	65	
158	Aug	62	
144	July	59	
170	June	58	
119	May	57	
72	April	56	
84	March	64	
64	Feb	72	
79	Jan	77	

Florida Climate Center (www.coaps.fsu.edu/climate_center)

AVERAGE HOUSE SALE PRICES

Hotspot	2-bed	3-bed	4-bed	5-bed
Daytona Beach	$148K (£80K)	$305K (£166K)	$447K (£244K)	$740K (£405K)
New Smyrna Beach	$218K (£119K)	$508K (£277K)	$639K (£348K)	$917K (£500K)
St Augustine	$342K (£186K)	$550K (£300K)	$1.13M (£613K)	$1.5M (£838K)
Ormond Beach	$133K (£73K)	$296K (£162K)	$467K (£254K)	$613K (£335K)
Ponte Vedra Beach	$247K (£135K)	$388K (£212K)	$903K (£494K)	$2.9M (£1.6M)

■ THE NORTH EAST

Property hotspots

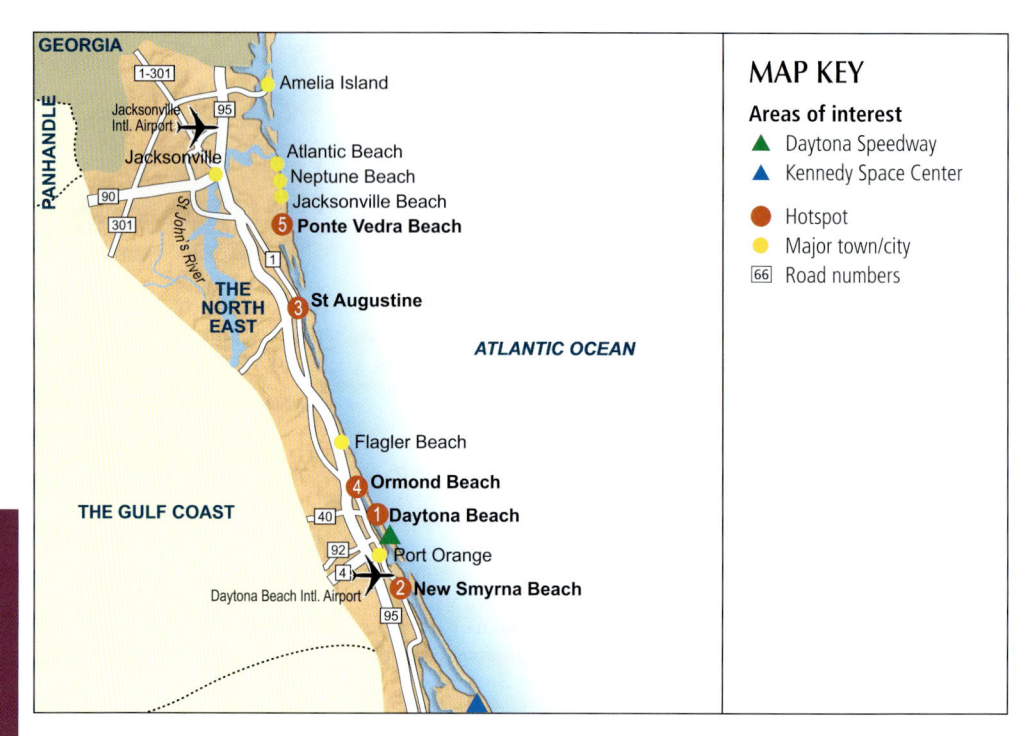

MAP KEY

Areas of interest
▲ Daytona Speedway
▲ Kennedy Space Center
● Hotspot
○ Major town/city
66 Road numbers

1. Daytona Beach

ESSENTIALS ■ **Pop** 64,000 ■ **Airport** Daytona Beach International Airport, 700 Catalina Drive, Suite 300, Daytona Beach, 32114, Tel: +1 386 248-8030 ■ **Tax** Property tax per $1,000: $15

KEY FACTS

■ **Schools** A Child's Place Inc, 142 Fairview Av, Daytona Beach, FL 32114-2104, Tel: +1 386 258-7611 ■ Daytona Beach Community College, Adult High School, 940 10th St, New Smyrna Beach, FL 32168-7563, Tel: +1 386 423-0703
■ **Medical** Halifax Community Health System, 303 N Clyde Morris Blvd, Daytona Beach, FL 32114-2709, Tel: +1 386 238-6078 ■ Health Line, 303 N Clyde Morris Blvd, Tel: +1 386 258-4848
■ **Rentals** Popular rentals area, especially during rally time and Spring Break, when prices can double ■ Average weekly rentals for a one-bed condo range from $420 per week during winter to $425 in autumn, $528 in spring and $654 in summer ■ Few restrictions; some restricted to one per month
■ **Pros** Downtown Daytona has been recently restored, offering continual activity ■ Thriving market, now increasingly becoming a retirement hotspot ■ You can still buy a beachside property for between $200,000 and $250,000, one of Florida's cheapest property markets ■ The average cost of a one-bedroom home is $75,900
■ **Cons** Not for those seeking a leisurely lifestyle ■ Saturated with American second home buyers, with a limited amount of international interest, although it is increasing ■ Prices have shot up

In the late 19th century, Matthias Day purchased a parcel of land on the banks of the Halifax River and founded a small community. The 1890s saw the arrival of the railroad and Daytona Beach became a tourist haven. However, it wasn't until people started to race cars on its hard-packed sands that it really made a name for itself; it's now the home of NASCAR, which attracts thousands of fans every year. The best part of Daytona is still the eponymous beach, which stretches for more than 20 miles. The town itself houses a wealth of attractions, shops and restaurants. For may years it was a popular 'Spring Break' destination, the time when thousands of American college kids descend on Florida towns to 'indulge' themselves before their examinations. Although the students have since moved on, Daytona Beach is still home to a number of fairly raucous events which generally involve vehicles, be it bikes or cars.

After being a rather under-valued coastal town for many years, the housing market has seen a large growth in activity and properties are being snapped up very quickly. Oceanfront homes in Ponce Inlet and Ormond have recently sold for over $2 million. Apartments with a view of the ocean can be snapped up for around $350,000, although inland they can still be bought for under $100,000. ●

THE NORTH EAST

2. New Smyrna Beach

ESSENTIALS ■ **Pop** 20,048 ■ **Airports** Daytona Beach International Airport, 700 Catalina Drive, Suite 300, Daytona Beach, FL 32114, Tel: +1 386 248-8030 ■ **Tax** Property tax per $1,000: $18

New Smyrna Beach was originally settled as a colony by a Scottish physician named Andrew Turnbull in 1769. It was Turnbull's intention for it to be a new Mediterranean community; he brought over hundreds of people from Greece, Corsica and Minorca to the new world. Unfortunately, disease and shortages saw most settlers flee to St Augustine and it wasn't until the early 1900s that the city really began to expand.

Less commercial than Daytona Beach, it's home to a flourishing artistic community. With more than 13 miles of white sand beaches, it's one of the best naturally protected areas in the region. The Canaveral National Seashore Park sits to the south and offshore rock ledges protect the bathing areas from undercurrents. It's popular with people who want to visit the beach but are staying in the Orlando region.

In comparison with many of Florida's cities, New Smyrna Beach is laid back to the point of being sleepy; the median age of residents is over 50. New oceanfront condo projects are underway and it's a popular area for golfers. Small detached houses within walking distance of the beach can still be picked up for around $250,000 but you can pay up to $2 million for beachfront condos. ●

KEY FACTS

■ **Schools** Riviera Pre School, 103 Desoto Drive, New Smyrna Beach, FL 32169 ■ Daytona Beach Community College, Adult High School, 940 10th St, New Smyrna Beach, FL 32168-7563, Tel: +1 386 423-0703
■ **Medical** South Seminole Hospital, 555 West State Road 434, New Smyrna Beach, FL 32168, +1 904-221-4223
■ **Rentals** A popular beach resort with an abundance of accommodation makes this area an excellent and cheap investment ■ For a condo that sleeps up to six, average weekly rentals range from $478 and $483 in winter and autumn and goes up to $558 for spring and summer
■ **Pros** An excellent area for surfing and swimming, with a protected cove ■ With an unspoilt 13 mile long beach, the area is fairly isolated and it remains unpretentious ■ With a tropical climate, year-round swimming and watersports can be enjoyed ■ This area is undergoing major development and is an excellent investment prospect ■ Ideal for a retirement home
■ **Cons** Wealthy incomers from Orlando are driving prices up ■ The property tax rate is high compared with the state average of $16.43

3. St Augustine

ESSENTIALS ■ **Pop** 16,000 ■ **Airport** Daytona Beach International Airport, 700 Catalina Drive, Suite 300, Daytona Beach, FL 32114, Tel: +1 386 248-8030 ■ **Tax** Property Tax per $1,000: $18

St Augustine lays claim to being the oldest city in the whole of the United States. Founded in 1565 by Spanish settlers, it's an engaging place with a distinctly European feel. Its turbulent history has seen it passed between the Spanish and the British a number of times before it was finally ceded to America in 1821. Nowadays, St Augustine bustles with tourists who come from all over the world; the famous National Historic Landmark District covers almost 150 blocks and features renovated buildings and cobbled streets lined with shops, galleries and restaurants. Horse-drawn carriages trot along the streets and many workers sport period costumes giving the town an almost theme park-like feel. With its palm-lined sandy beaches, sidewalk bistros and bars and wealth of other attractions, it's one of the finest small cities in the US.

Tourism provides a major chunk of the region's economy and with visitors, the population is generally larger than the recognised 14,000 (approx). The property market is extremely active, especially in the Historic District and on the waterfront. Houses on the Intracoastal Waterway with views of the sea often sell for over $1 million, while condos can go up to $500,000. With limited building land, properties sell quickly and often close to the asking price. ●

KEY FACTS

■ **Schools** Secondary Schools, Bartram Trail High School, 2050 Roberts Rd, St Augustine, FL 32084, Tel: +1 904 819-83 ■ Nease Allen D High School, 1455 N Whitney St, Saint Augustine, FL 32084-2475, Tel: +1 904 824-5281
■ **Medical** Flagler Hospital, Saint Augustine, FL 32084, Tel: +1 904 797-2663 ■ Healthsouth St Augustine Surgery Center, 180 Southpark Blvd, Saint Augustine, FL 32086-4120, Tel: +1 904 823-1447
■ **Rentals** Average weekly rentals for a condo range from $630 in winter, to $615 in autumn, and rising to $698 in spring and $745 in summer
■ **Pros** Charming European-style town with bags of charm ■ Abundance of amenities and distractions ■ Average property price is $117,180 compared with the national average of $146,102 ■ Prices vary from $71,544 for a mobile home to $650,000 for a new home on the Intracoastal Waterway, offering something for everyone ■ Market is still strong
■ **Cons** This is a resort rather than a relocation area and few people buy here ■ The area is dominated by locals and not the international market ■ There has been a 9.5 per cent appreciation over the last year ■ Pickings are very slim for buyers in the $150K-$250K range which represents an 'average' three-bed, two-bath home

Have **you** ever dreamed of owning a home in **Orlando, Florida**?

Free independent advice on all aspects of purchasing, financing, renting and managing your home.

Also available, affordable buy-to-let.

DREAM HOMES ORLANDO

Telephone Carol on +44 (0)1392 278230 for a brochure
Email: dhorlando@lycos.co.uk or visit our website
www.dreamhomesorlando.us

Sunshine State Properties Ltd
Florida Property Consultants

BEAUTIFUL PROPERTIES FOR SALE CLOSE TO DISNEY

★ Full Property Management Service Available
★ Comprehensive Rental Programme
★ Mortgage Services and Inspection Tours

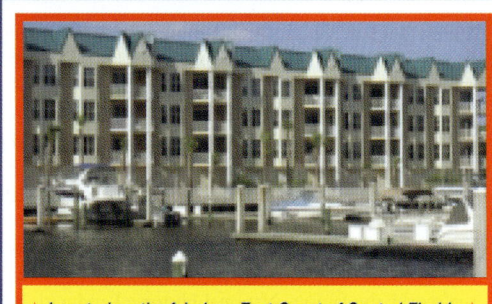

★ Located on the fabulous East Coast of Central Florida ★

— *"a little bit of paradise"* —

NEW SMYRNA BEACH

For more information call us on

(01344) 752358 or Fax (01344) 771272

Email: sales@sunshinestateproperties.co.uk   www.sunshinestateproperties.co.uk

THE NORTH EAST

4. Ormond Beach

ESSENTIALS ■ **Pop** 36,301 ■ **Airport** Daytona Beach International Airport, 700 Catalina Drive, Suite 300, Daytona Beach, FL 32114, Tel: +1 386 248-8030 ■ **Tax** Property Tax per $1,000: $21

Ormond Beach is a quiet, refined seaside town which came to prominence as a winter resort after railroad and oil baron Henry Flagler extended his east coast railway further south from St Augustine in the late 19th century. The 75 room Ormond Hotel boasted a star-studded, wealthy clientele including Henry Ford and John D Rockefeller, and its wide beaches attracted so many car racers that it was named the 'Birthplace of Speed'. These days, it's a family-orientated resort, genteel when compared with its commercial neighbour Daytona Beach.

The population of around 40,000 consists mainly of middle class Americans (with a few retirees from abroad) and the median age of residents is almost 50. However, the population is supplemented by a further 15,000 people who live just outside the centre in areas that are not officially incorporated in the city.

Ormond Beach's economy relies less on tourism than many other resorts in the North East and the local property market is very strong. The oceanfront sees very limited development; property is scarce and demand and prices are high. Those with a huge budget can spend more than $3 million, while ocean-view apartments sell for between $200,000 and $300,000. ●

KEY FACTS

■ **Schools** Center Academy, 308 N Nova Rd, Ormond Beach, FL 32174-5126, Tel: +1 386 677-7944 ■ The Children's House, 2010 W Granada Blvd, FL 32174-2531, Tel: + 1 386 672-1620
■ **Medical** Halifax Medical Center-Ormond Beach, 1688 W Granada Blvd, Ormond Beach, FL 32174-1851, Tel: +1 386 254-4000
■ **Rentals** Prices range from $408 a week during autumn to $1,368 in summer ■ A good influx of renters from the US, although it's less popular with international renters
■ **Pros** Popular retirement destination because of its golf courses, boating, and beaches ■ Top rated schools and hospitals ■ There is huge demand and development within Ormond Beach so it's an excellent investment opportunity ■ There is favourable development within the light industry centres and economic prospects are good. The average property costs just $102,130 compared with the state average of $141,100 ■ Well-located with a good infrastructure, it's easily accessible for Orlando and Jacksonville
■ **Cons** New-build market sees builders scrambling to keep up with demand and prices are rising rapidly ■ Few properties currently available and if this continues prices will be forced up

5. Ponte Vedra Beach

ESSENTIALS ■ **Pop** 28,057 ■ **Airport** Jacksonville Airport Authority, P.O. Box 18018, Jacksonville, FL 32229, Tel: +1 904 741-2000 ■ **Tax** Property Tax rate per $1,000: $17.1

The city of Ponte Vedra Beach is an exclusive resort of beautiful beaches, fine golf courses (including Sawgrass, home of the PGA), elegant restaurants and smart shops. It wasn't always this way: in 1914, engineers discovered that the beaches harboured a wealth of minerals suitable for the production of titanium and after the National Lead Company settled here it became a mining community dubbed Mineral City. When mineral demand dropped, the company launched the area as a fashionable resort and named it Ponte Vedra Beach. Rapid development in the last 20 years of the 20th century saw the population quadruple to almost 30,000 and it's now the most desirable, picturesque resort in the North East.

Property prices are almost prohibitively high and the average household income of $120,000 per annum illustrates just how wealthy the inhabitants of this town are. A one-bed apartment in the least exclusive areas costs almost $150,000 and you can pay anything up to $10 million for large waterfront plots. The median price for a property is almost $300,000. With new construction continuing, the area's population and economy is expected to grow rapidly, particularly as it's within easy commuting distance of Florida's largest city Jacksonville. ●

KEY FACTS

■ **Schools** Bolles School Ponte Vedra, 202 Atp Tour Blvd, Ponte Vedra Beach, FL 32082-3211, Tel: +1 904 285-4658 ■ Nease Allan D High School, 230 Landrum Ln, Ponte Vedra, FL 32082-3825, Tel: +1 904 824-5
■ **Medical** Baptist Primary Care, 520 A1a N, Ponte Vedra Beach, FL 32082-5212, Tel: +1 904 273-69 ■ Northeast Florida Neurology Clinics & First Coast Medical Center, 520 A1a N, Ponte Vedra Beach, FL 32082-5212, Tel: +1 904 273-4694
■ **Rentals** A three-bed house costs between $1,483 in autumn through to $1,825 in summer for a week's rental ■ This area is more expensive for lettings than Daytona Beach and St Augustine and this is due to the luxurious developments and the area ■ Healthy rental market because it's the most refined resort in the North East
■ **Pros** Well known for its sporting facilities and there are many golfing developments ■ Hugely sought-after due to its proximity to the ocean and the Intracoastal Waterway ■ Easy to get to St Augustine and Jacksonville ■ Low interest rates allow buyers in this area to get more for their money
■ **Cons** Very prestigious so prices are very high ■ Limited development land available means that waterfront properties sell for a premium.

■ THE NORTH EAST

$100,000 — $150,000
(£55,000–£82,500)

A wealth of beachfront properties to choose from, all with great potential

$119,900 — CODE WCO
DAYTONA BEACH
Full of potential, this modern property comes fully furnished, an excellent investment
£65,945

2 | with a large garden | situated close to the town centre | not located on a main road | room for parking, with a garage

$119,900 — CODE WCO
DAYTONA BEACH
Located on the Intracoastal Waterway, a fantastic condo, furnished with all mod cons
£65,945

2 | with a fenced yard | close to shops and amenities | located on a main road | room for parking, with a garage

---

$124,900 — CODE WCO
DAYTONA BEACH
Located on the Intracoastal Waterway, a modified condo, with a balcony and river view
£68,695

1 | with a balcony | situated close to the town centre | not located on a main road | room for parking

---

$139,900 — CODE SUR
ST AUGUSTINE
A single family property, with a modern interior, located close to all attractions
£76,945

4 | with a garden | situated close to amenities | not located on a main road | room for parking

---

$149,900 — CODE WAT
PONTE VEDRA BEACH
A townhouse located in a comfortable development, with all mod cons and a pool
£82,445

2 | with a small garden | situated close to the town centre | not located on a main road | room for parking

PRICE GUIDE

100

THE NORTH EAST

$150,000 – $200,000
(£82,500–£110,000)

For those seeking a modern, oceanfront property, there is plenty of choice

$154,000 — CODE LIN
FLAGLER BEACH
Located near the beach and golf courses, this beachside townhouse is fully furnished
£84,700

2 | with a garden | situated close to amenities and the beach | not located on a main road | room for parking

---

$165,000 — CODE WCO
DAYTONA BEACH
With a porch and splendid view of the river, a condo home offering all mod cons
£90,750

2 | with a deck and porch | situated in the city centre | located on a main road | room for parking

---

$185,000 — CODE CEN
FLAGLER BEACH
A townhouse property overlooking an excellent golf course, with all mod cons
£101,750

2 | with a large garden and pool | situated close to the town centre | not located on a main road | room for parking

---

$185,000 — CODE WCO
JACKSONVILLE
This stunning home has a jacuzzi in the master bedroom and offers a large porch
£101,750

3 | with a garden | within easy reach of shops and attractions | not located on a main road | room for parking, with a two-car garage

---

$199,900 — CODE CEN
ST AUGUSTINE
A single family home, fully air conditioned, with all mod cons and furnishings
£109,945

3 | with a garden | situated close to the town centre | not located on a main road | room for parking, with a two–car garage

PRICE GUIDE

101

■ **THE NORTH EAST**

$200,000 – $270,000
(£110,000–£148,500)

More upmarket properties, ideal for families and tremendous value for money

PRICE GUIDE

$220,000   CODE REX
PONTE VEDRA BEACH
A recently built home, fully air conditioned, with a hot tub and shared swimming pool
£121,000

🛏 2   🌼 with a large garden   🏬 situated close to amenities   🅰 not located on a main road   🚗 room for parking, with a garage

---

$227,900   CODE WCO
DAYTONA BEACH
With ocean views, this modern home has a balcony, deck and a patio
£125,345

🛏 2   🌼 with a large garden   🏬 situated close to amenities   🅰 not located on a main road   🚗 room for parking, with a garage

---

$242,500   CODE WCO
AMELIA ISLAND
Recently renovated, this home is extremely spacious and is ideal as a family holiday home
£133,375

🛏 3   🌼 with a large garden   🏬 situated close to amenities   🅰 not located on a main road   🚗 room for parking, with a garage for three cars

$250,000   CODE LIN
FLAGLER BEACH
A resale ranch, with a swimming pool, only a short walk from the beach and attractions
£137,500

🛏 3   🌼 with a sun deck and large garden   🏬 only a short distance from amenities   🅰 not located on a main road   🚗 room for parking, with a garage

---

$265,000   CODE PAS
ORMOND BEACH
Only a short walk to the beach, fully air conditioned and with all mod cons
£145,750

🛏 3   🌼 with a garden   🏬 situated close to the town centre   🅰 not located on a main road   🚗 room for parking, with a garage

THE NORTH EAST

$270,000—$425,000
(£148,500–£233,750)

The North East offers buyers some truly magnificent modern condos and villas

$279,500 — CODE TED
AMELIA ISLAND
With a swimming pool and all mod cons, this home has excellent rental potential
£153,725

🛏 4 | 🌼 with a large garden | 🏙 situated within easy reach of amenities | 🚧 not located on a main road | 🚗 room for parking

---

$289,500 — CODE TED
AMELIA ISLAND
A single family property, located in the centre of the island, with an open fireplace
£159,225

🛏 3 | 🌼 with a large garden | 🏙 situated close to all amenities | 🚧 not located on a main road | 🚗 room for parking

---

$339,000 — CODE CEN
FLAGLER BEACH
A modern condo, fully air conditioned and offering all mod cons
£186,450

🛏 2 | 🌼 with a balcony | 🏙 situated close to the town centre | 🚧 located on a main road | 🚗 room for parking, with a one–car garage

$424,000 — CODE BAL
FLAGLER BEACH
Ideal for development, this home comes with a parcel of land and is close to the beach
£233,200

🛏 3 | 🌼 with a garden | 🏙 situated close to the beach and amenities | 🚧 not located on a main road | 🚗 room for parking

---

$425,000 — CODE CAR
PONTE VEDRA BEACH
Located in a development, with a spa and hot tub and a communal swimming pool
£235,950

🛏 3 | 🌼 with a large garden | 🏙 situated close to shops and attractions | 🚧 not located on a main road | 🚗 room for parking

PRICE GUIDE

THE NORTH EAST

$425,000 — $570,000
(£233,750–£313,500)

Some luxurious homes, fully air conditioned, with all mod cons and furnishings

$429,000   CODE CAR
ST AUGUSTINE
This townhouse enjoys onsite amenities, with a shared swimming pool and clubhouse
£235,950

3 | with a garden | situated close to the town centre | not located on a main road | room for parking

---

$469,000
PALM COAST
Fully air-conditioned and with all mod cons, a three–storey family home
£257,950

3 | with a large garden | situated close to shops and amenities | not located on a main road | room for parking, with a garage

$495,000   CODE TED
AMELIA ISLAND
Located in the historic district, a home with stained glass windows, and full of charm
£272,250

4 | with a garden | close to all amenities | not located on a main road | room for parking

---

$499,900   CODE JJM
PALM COAST
Arranged over two storeys, a fully air-conditioned home, with a swimming pool
£274,945

4 | a large, well maintained garden | situated close to shops and amenities | not located on a main road | room for parking

---

$565,000   CODE WCO
DAYTONA BEACH
Situated on the waterfront, a newly built condo, fully furnished with all mod cons
£310,750

2 | with a balcony | situated in the town centre | not located on a main road | room for parking

PRICE GUIDE

THE NORTH EAST

$570,000+
(£313,500+)

For those with deep pockets there is a vast array of homes on the market

$629,000 — CODE TED
AMELIA ISLAND
With a communal swimming pool, this air-conditioned home has all mod cons
£345,950

- 4 | with a garden | situated close to amenities | not located on a main road
- room for parking

$649,000 — CODE WCO
DAYTONA BEACH
With a jacuzzi, this condo property is located on Daytona Beach and offers great views
£356,950

- 3 | with a balcony | close to the town centre | not located on a main road
- room for parking

$749,000 — CODE TAV
FLAGLER BEACH
A single family property, arranged over three storeys, with glorious ocean views
£411,950

- 4 | with a garden | situated close to amenities | not located on a main road
- room for parking, with a two–car garage

$829,000 — CODE BER
PONTE VEDRA BEACH
Ideal for nature lovers this home is located along the Intracoastal Waterway
£455,950

- 5 | with a garden | within easy reach of amenities | not located on a main road
- room for parking

$900,000 — CODE LIN
FLAGLER BEACH
Overlooking the Intracoastal Waterway, this property enjoys a spa and has a balcony
£495,000

- 3 | with a garden | situated close to amenities | not located on a main road
- room for parking, with a four-car garage

PRICE GUIDE

ORLANDO | KISSIMMEE | DAVENPORT | DISNEY AREA | GULF COAST

Vacation Homes

Investment Properties

Businesses & Commercial

Looking for low-pressure, no-nonsense, down-to-earth, independent, unbiased, truthful advice, with second-to-none after sales service?

Then look no further than **DOLBY PROPERTIES INC**.

As Licensed Realtors, we can show you ALL properties for sale in the Orlando/Disney area – OUR HOMETOWN!

Our professional services to you, as a Buyer, are at no cost and we will negotiate the best deal for YOU, whether your choice is resale or new.

- We give the best advice on how to maximise rental income.
- US or UK mortgages easily arranged from 20% to 30% down.
- Inspection trips and tours arranged.

Dolby Properties' team of Licensed Realtors is headed by Broker Lesley Dolby, CCIM (Certified Commercial Investment Member), member of the board of directors of Orlando Regional Realtor Association and Florida Association of Realtors, assisted by Sales Associate Steve Schaffer, CIPS (Certified International Property Specialist) and ABR (Accredited Buyer Representative). With our team of RESIDENT BRITISH REALTORS, we are dedicated to raising the standards of professionalism and consumer protection in the real estate industry.

In working with you as our partner to find you the best investment, our goal is to create a positive and successful real estate experience!

Website **www.dolbyproperties.com**
Email **lesley.dolby@dolbyproperties.com**
Telephone **001 407 352 3664**

WHO IS LOOKING OUT FOR YOU?

dolbyproperties inc.

Licensed Real Estate Broker
Orlando, Florida

FLEXIBLE MORTGAGES
IN THE USA

RATES AS LOW AS
1.0%

DOWN PAYMENT AS LOW AS
20%

NO NEED TO DOCUMENT INCOME NOR LIQUID ASSETS!!!

Rates are subject to change according to market conditions

INTERNATIONAL FINANCING CONSULTANTS

ORLANDO
6220 S. Orange Blossom Trail, Suite 165, Orlando FL 32809
Tel: 001-407-856-6677 Fax: 001-407-856-8131

MIAMI
2100 Coral Way, Suite 502, Miami FL 33145
Tel: 001-305-859-8366 Fax: 001-305-859-8926

Alfonso Muelle
www.financeandsales.com

The Gulf Coast

The City of Culture, a stunning coastline and the 'best beach'

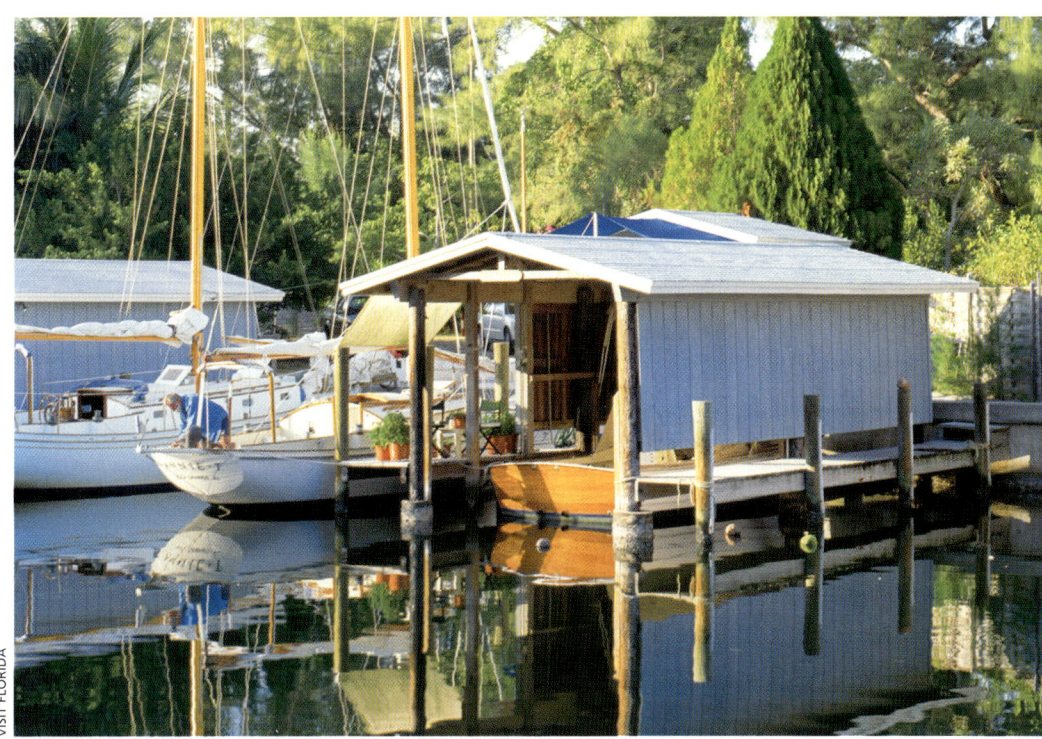

- **Population** 5.1 million
- **Population increase** Between 1992–2002 the population grew by 19% on Tampa Bay, 21.1% in North Central Florida, and 39% in the South West generally
- **Migration** 219,800 people migrated to the Gulf Coast between 2000–2002, of whom 51,896 were international migrants
- **Median age** 41.7 in Tampa Bay, 33.8 in North Central Florida and 46.4 in the South West; the state average is 38.7
- **Median home price** $153,200 in Tampa Bay, $130,000 in North Central Florida and $133,600 in the South West, compared with the average of $141,100
- **Cost of living** The ACCRA cost of living index rates Tampa Bay as 96.4/100, 93.4/100 in North Central Florida, and the South West as 95.3/100

Profile **108**

Hotspots **110**

Price Guide

$100,000–$250,000 **117**

$250,000–$300,000 **118**

$300,000–$400,000 **119**

$400,000–$1,000,000 **120**

$1,000,000 + **122**

THE GULF COAST

GETTING THERE

AIR The main airport on the Gulf Coast is Tampa International. **American Airlines** (0845 778 9789; www.aa.com) flies from Heathrow to Tampa via New York (JFK), Chicago or Miami and from Gatwick via Dallas Fort Worth. **British Airways** (0870 850 9850; www.ba.com) flies directly to Tampa from Gatwick on Mondays, Wednesdays and Saturdays. **Continental Airlines** (0845 607 6760; www.continental.com) does not offer any direct flights to Florida but flies via Newark to Tampa. **Virgin Atlantic** (0870 574 7747; www.virgin-atlantic.com) fly directly to Miami and Orlando from Heathrow and from there connections are available. **Continental Airlines** offers connections from Tampa to Sarasota, Bradenton from Newark and Tampa to Fort Myers. Flights are also available to St Petersburg-Clearwater airport from many major American cities including New York, Chicago, Los Angeles and Newark with **American Trans Air** (www.ata.com; 001 800 435 9282).

RAIL Amtrak (+ 1 800 872 7245; www.amtrak.com) offers mainline services to Tampa, and Thruway connecting bus services to St Petersburg, Clearwater, Bradenton, Sarasota, Port Charlotte and Fort Myers.

ROAD As public transport along the Gulf Coast is fairly limited it is essential to have a car. The I-75 runs from north to south to the east of Tampa, Bradenton, Sarasota, Port Charlotte and Fort Myers and the I-275 runs through Tampa and down to St Petersburg. US Route 60 runs east to west between Clearwater and Tampa and US route 41 runs along the coast from Tampa to south of Fort Myers. There are also many smaller roads, providing a comprehensive network.

COACH Greyhound buses (+1 800 231 2222; www.greyhound.com) serves Spring Hill, Clearwater, St Petersburg, Tampa, Bradenton, Sarasota, Venice, Port Charlotte, Punta Gorda, Fort Myers and Bonita Springs.

Area profile

THE STUNNING GULF COAST STRETCHES FOR HUNDREDS OF MILES DOWN Florida's west side, offering endless beautiful white sand beaches and temperate azure waters all year round. For all the competition, it is Fort De Soto Park that claims the prestigious title of best beach in continental USA. Spread over five islands and boasting 900 unspoiled acres of major waters' edge, the park is a prime attraction for bird watchers.

Tampa is the largest city on the Gulf Coast and has styled itself as the business and commercial centre. The metropolis is also home to the region's top attractions: Busch Gardens, Florida Aquarium and the Museum of Science and Industry.

Clearwater and St Petersburg sit on the edge of Tampa Bay, surrounded by thriving resorts and suburbs. Popular with holidaymakers, these coastal cities are more sedate than Tampa and offer plenty of parks (130 in St Petersburg alone) and every watersport imaginable. Dubbed the 'Sunshine Capital', this area is famed for an average of 361 sunny days a year.

Further south is the gem of the Gulf Coast, Sarasota. Oozing culture and refinement, the city is home to a professional symphony orchestra, ballet and opera, as well as 10 theatres and 30 art galleries. It also exudes natural beauty and has 35 miles of beaches. Continuing downwards and the Gulf Coast begins to take on a slightly different atmosphere. This stretch exudes Old South ambience and a quiet, unpretentious feel. Fort Myers is known as the City of Palms; to see why simply take a stroll down McGregor Boulevard where no fewer then 1,800 trees line the street. The town's beach is seven miles long and though lively and attractive, it is a lot less exclusive – and consequently less expensive – than others nearby.

Naples is the ultimate lifestyle statement boasting more beach (11 miles worth), golf courses per person (more than 35) and quality shopping than anywhere else in Florida. Its boatyards have been turned into fashionable boutiques and galleries, and there's an abundance of chic sidewalk bistros and bars. The city's architecture has a strong Mediterranean influence, giving it a very cosmopolitan feel.

The Gulf Coast is home to cultured cities such as Naples and Sarasota which boasts ballet and its own symphony orchestra

VISIT FLORIDA

THE GULF COAST

The economy and housing market

Boasting low business costs, good infrastructure and a highly skilled, entrepreneurial workforce, the Gulf Coast has laid its claim as one of the business centres of Florida. The Charlotte, Lee and Collier counties alone house over 600 hi-tech companies while the Florida Gulf Coast University and the emerging Florida Gulf Coast Technology and Research Park draw new businesses to the area. Further north, Tampa forms the commercial centre of the west coast complete with a busy international port.

The Gulf Coast is the second most popular real estate area in Florida after Orlando, though prices are higher with realtors advising a budget of $300,000 for a well-located, good-sized property. As a general rule, the same house in Orlando and on the Gulf Coast will cost around $50,000 more in the latter due to the desirable beach proximity. Another factor in the price discrepancy is construction cost – these are higher on the west coast than inland due to hurricane safety precautions. Your insurance will feature a weighty premium for the same reason.

From its swampy origins in the 1860s, Naples has proved itself to be one of the biggest real estate success stories in the States. Today it is reckoned to be the most expensive market in mainland Florida with a $389,000 median sales price in 2004, and an annual median price growth of a staggering 42 per cent. Nearby Fort Myers has seen similar price increases, though property remains cheaper with a median price of $135,300.

More affordable than Naples is Sarasota, but a large four-bed, three-bath home could still set you back by over $1,000,000. You might want to be hasty though; some reports state that Florida's cultural epicentre witnessed the second highest property appreciation last year at 26 per cent.

At the north end of the coast Tampa, St Petersburg and Clearwater offer comparative bargains with some of the lowest property prices on the Gulf Coast stretch, though prices have risen considerably in the last five years.

Along the length of the Gulf Coast rental restrictions mean that investors might not do particularly well from buy-to-let property, but in terms of capital appreciation the stretch offers prime real estate.

Social groups

The Gulf Coast is known as a magnet for retirees and snowbirds, though singles and families are moving here to benefit from the job opportunities and lifestyle. Brits have always had a special relationship with the west coast and many have made a permanent home for themselves here. ●

Fort De Soto Park boasts some of the finest beaches in the United States

Average monthly temperature °C (Celsius)

GULF COAST		LONDON
17	Dec	7
21	Nov	10
24	Oct	14
28	Sept	19
28	Aug	21
28	July	22
28	June	20
25	May	17
22	April	13
20	March	10
17	Feb	7
16	Jan	6

Average monthly rainfall mm (millimetres)

GULF COAST		LONDON
58	Dec	81
41	Nov	78
58	Oct	70
166	Sept	65
193	Aug	62
165	July	59
140	June	58
72	May	57
46	April	56
72	March	64
68	Feb	72
58	Jan	77

Florida Climate Center (www.coaps.fsu.edu/climate_center)

AVERAGE HOUSE SALE PRICES

Hotspot	2-bed	3-bed	4-bed	5-bed
Clearwater	$230K (£125K)	$364K (£198K)	$530K (£289K)	$902K (£501K)
St Petersburg	$225K (£122K)	$421K (£229K)	$568K (£309K)	$1.22M (£665M)
Sarasota	$400K (£220K)	$801K (£436K)	$1.79M (£975K)	$3.30M (£1.7M)
Englewood	$545K (£297K)	$707K (£385K)	$1.21K (£657K)	$2.22M (£1.2M)
Venice	$294K (£160K)	$361K (£197K)	$780K (£425K)	$1.88M (£1M)
Naples	$389K (£214K)	$863K (£470K)	$2.65M (£1.44M)	$3.70M (£2M)
Fort Myers	$430K (£234K)	$590K (£321K)	$457K (£250K)	$2.03M (£1.1M)
Bradenton	$280K (£153K)	$645K (£351K)	$867K (£472K)	$1.5M (£806K)
Punta Gorda	$242K (£132K)	$500K (£272K)	$619K (£337K)	$946K (£515K)
Cape Coral	$156K (£85K)	$608K (£331K)	$816K (£446K)	$1.75M (£953K)

■ THE GULF COAST

Property hotspots

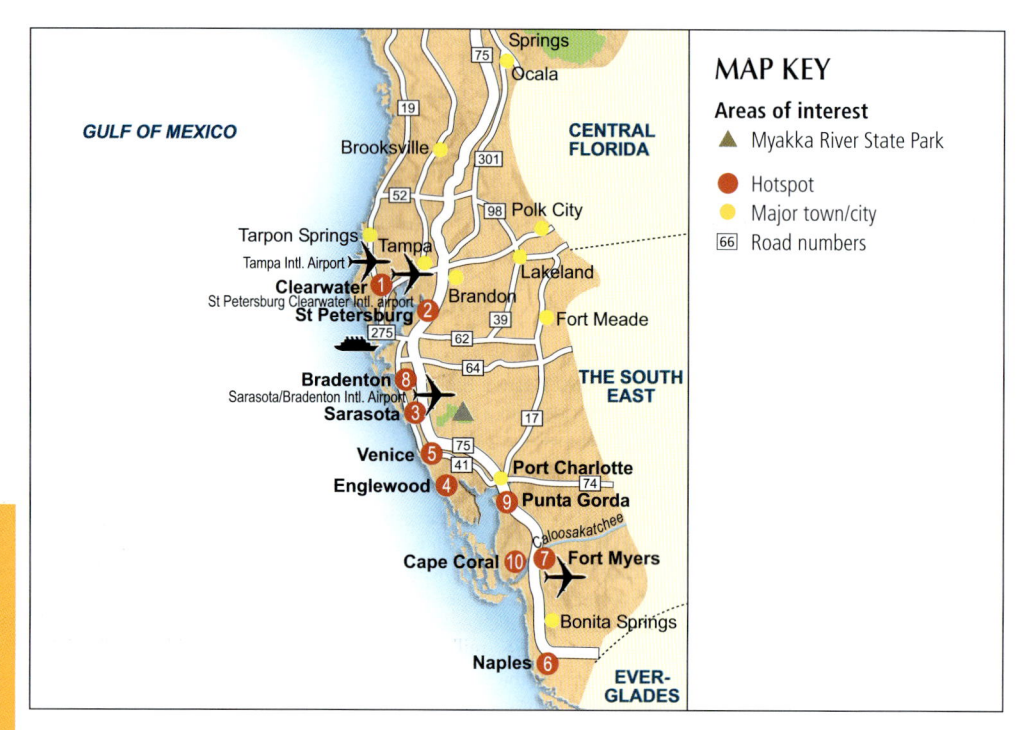

MAP KEY
Areas of interest
- ▲ Myakka River State Park
- ● Hotspot
- ● Major town/city
- 66 Road numbers

1. Clearwater

ESSENTIALS ■ **Pop** 108,787 ■ **Airport** St. Petersburg-Clearwater International Airport, 14700 Terminal Boulevard, Suite 221, Clearwater, FL 33762 USA, Tel: +1 727-453-7800 ■ **Tax** Property tax per $1,000: $14

KEY FACTS

■ **Schools** Clearwater Central Catholic High School, 2750 Haines Bayshore Rd, Clearwater, FL 33760-1435, Tel: +1 727 536-6983 ■ Oak Grove Elementary School, 6315 North Armenia Avenue, Tampa, FL 33604-5709, Tel: +1 813 356-15
■ **Medical** Mease Countryside Hospital, 3231 N McMullen Booth Rd, Clearwater, FL 33761-2045, Tel: +1 727 725-6111 ■ Mease Dunedin Hospital, 601 Main St, Clearwater, FL 33755, Tel: +1 727 733-1111
■ **Rentals** There are rental restrictions; most areas offer monthly rentals only from $1,600 with peak time luxury two-bedroom condos costing $3,800
■ **Pros** Good transportation network ■ Close to the amenities and job markets of St Petersburg and Tampa ■ Condos are currently selling at a faster rate than private homes ■ Cheaper than the central and east coast of Florida ■ Buyers can expect substantial appreciation in the price of their property
■ **Cons** Clearwater Beach is overdeveloped ■ It's a seller's market; prices increased 10 per cent last year ■ Over the last three years prices for one property have increased by 75 per cent and $116,000: from $154,000 to $270,000 for a three-bed property ■ Appreciation has slowed over the last 12 months to 4.6 per cent; the market is nearing its peak

Clearwater is a popular, lively resort city that attracts more than a million visitors each year, including many Europeans. Before the settlers arrived, it was a place known to Native American tribes for its clear springs that bubbled and gurgled on the banks of the bay. The natural springs had long disappeared by the time the railroad arrived in 1888, swiftly followed by a real estate boom that included the building of several large grand hotels. A two-mile causeway links the city to the miles of crisp white sand at Clearwater Beach, now a blossoming resort in its own right. Hotels and condos line the oceanfront and the Intracoastal Waterway, and the best value properties are to be found in the more commercial city of Clearwater. In fact, Clearwater offers excellent value for money, especially in comparison with neighbouring St Petersburg. Condos in the more exclusive Clearwater Beach can sell for anywhere between $400,000 and $2 million. Better value can be found in the city suburbs, where you can buy a three-bedroom, single storey house with a pool for around $200,000. However, demand is growing and prices are rising. Interestingly, in the last census, Clearwater ranked number one in the percentage of the population aged 65 or older (21.5 per cent) in all major American cities. ●

THE GULF COAST

2. St Petersburg

ESSENTIALS ■ **Pop** 248,232 ■ **Airport** St. Petersburg-Clearwater International Airport, 14700 Terminal Boulevard, Suite 221, Clearwater, FL 33762 USA, Tel: +1 727-453-7800 ■ **Tax** Property tax per $1,000: $14

St Petersburg is without doubt one of Florida's finest cities. Tucked inside the south eastern tip of the Pinellas Peninsula, its structured avenues and boulevards house a vast array of shops, restaurants, galleries and museums, and the 250,000 inhabitants enjoy, on average, more than 360 days of fabulous sunshine every year. Indeed, in the late 1960s, St Petersburg racked up almost 800 consecutive days of sunshine.

The city's focal point is its pier, which rises up at the end in the shape of an inverted pyramid and boasts an aquarium and an observation deck. Once the preserve of pensioners – and it remains a popular destination for retired folk – St Petersburg is now a much more lively proposition. The median age of residents has dropped below 40, and the area's combination of great weather and low unemployment ensures that demand for property is high. Prices rose eight per cent across the board last year, but historic neighbourhoods such as Kenwood, Old Northeast and Crescent Lake have seen houses triple in value in a three year period. You can still pick up houses in these areas for under $180,000, but equally, you can pay upwards of $3 million for a luxury waterfront condo. Realtors report that prices rose around eight per cent in 2003. ●

KEY FACTS

■ **Schools** Shorecrest Preparatory School, 5101 First Street NE, # 20, Saint Petersburg, FL 33703, Tel: +1 727-522-2111, www.shorecrest.org ■ Wellington School, 5175 45th Street N, Saint Petersburg, FL 33707, Tel: +1 727-397-4565, www.wellingtonschool.com
■ **Medical** Bayfront Medical Center, 701 6th St S, St Petersburg, FL 33701, Tel: +1 727 895-3 Edward White Hospital, 2323 9th Ave N, St Petersburg, FL 33713, Tel: +1 727 323-1111
■ **Rentals** Snowbirds spend between two and six months of the winter here ■ Primarily a long-term market between November and April ■ Rentals vary in cost from $1,400 to $2,500 per month for a two-bedroom condo ■ Weekly rentals for a two-bedroom condo range from $600 to $1,500
■ **Pros** Property is appreciating at 8% annually ■ Great weather, low unemployment ■ Demand has resulted in some homes increasing in value by 80% over recent years ■ St Petersburg has been listed in the top 23 most desirable areas to live in the US
■ **Cons** Many of the locals have been priced out of their own market ■ After the boom, it's become a seller's market ■ This area is renowned for its ageing population and is a prime retirement location, not for those seeking a vibrant lifestyle

3. Sarasota

ESSENTIALS ■ **Pop** 52,715 ■ **Airport** Sarasota – Bradenton International Airport, 6000 Airport Circle, Sarasota, FL 34243, Tel: +1 941-359-2770 ■ **Tax** Property tax per $1,000: $12

Sarasota is a small, affluent city that lies adjacent to the barrier islands of Longboat Key, Lido Key and Siesta Key. At the turn of the 20th century, it became a popular resort for wealthy entrepreneurs and industrialists and one of its wealthiest winter residents, John Ringling, left a cultural legacy that resounds today. He was a circus manager who travelled Europe extensively collecting art and his estate is now a fabulous museum and one of the city's finest attractions.

As well as 35 miles of sandy beaches, Sarasota's well-heeled inhabitants enjoy great cafes, restaurants, bookshops and galleries. In fact, arts, tourism and catering provide a healthy 15 per cent of the region's employment. Not only was Sarasota recently named 'Best Small City in the US' by CNN, its real estate value grew 26 per cent last year, the second highest growth in the country. Huge demand means prices are high: a two-bed condo in Longboat Key can cost upwards of $500,000, although it is possible to buy cheaper houses in suburban areas such as Woodland. Large waterfront properties, however, often rise above $6 million. Buyers are constantly demonstrating that they are more than willing to pay high prices for Sarasota's combination of small town chic and metropolitan-quality arts and restaurants. ●

KEY FACTS

■ **Schools** Cardinal Mooney High School Development Ofc, 4171 Fruitville Rd, Sarasota, FL 34232-1618, Tel: +1 941 379-2647 ■ Marjorie G. Kinnan Elementary School, 3415 Tallevast Road, Sarasota, FL 34243-3969, Tel: +1 941 358-2888.
■ **Medical** Sarasota Memorial Hospital and Health Care System, 1700 S Tamiami Trl, Sarasota, FL 34239, Tel: +1 941 957-3302
■ **Rentals** Only one rental allowed every 30 days in Sarasota County, limiting rental income ■ Demand from snowbirds for long-term winter rentals is very strong ■ Some condos allow weekly rentals but generally these are monthly and range from $900 to $3,000 for a two-bedroom condo
■ **Pros** Sarasota is modern with varied architecture, art galleries, and museums ■ The 'Cultural Capital of Florida' ■ Second most popular destination for US retirees and snowbirds ■ The National Association of Realtors has classed Sarasota as having 'Second Fastest Medium Home Appreciation in 2003' with excellent future growth ■ 2003 saw 23% appreciation making Sarasota an excellent location for investment
■ **Cons** Very few beachside properties sell for less then $1 million ■ The popularity of the market means there is very little property available

■ THE GULF COAST

4. Englewood

ESSENTIALS ■ **Pop** 16,196 ■ **Airport** Tampa International Airport, 5503 W. Spruce Street, Tampa, FL 33607-1475, Tel: +1 813 870-8770 ■ **Tax** Property tax per $1,000: $15

KEY FACTS

■ **Schools** Lemon Bay High, 2201 Placida Rd, Englewood, FL 34223, Tel: +1 941 474-7702
■ **Medical** Englewood Community Hospital, 700 Medical Blvd, Englewood, FL 34223-3964, Tel: +1 941 475-6571
■ **Rentals** Primarily a long-term, monthly rentals market ■ Prices vary from $1,500 a month for a mobile home to $2,750 for a two-bedroom house overlooking the Gulf of Mexico ■ This is an expensive rentals market and the limitations on the frequency of rentals reduce the amount of income to be gleaned from your property.
■ **Pros** A relatively undiscovered area, there are a number of luxurious new waterfront developments and now is an excellent time to invest with prices destined to continue rising ■ Excellent watersport and fishing facilities and stunning tropical beaches ■ There are new constructions planned in North Englewood and the Rotunda West area ■ Easily accessible and well located for the Gulf Coast area ■ The most popular price bracket is $100,000 to $124,999, below the state average
■ **Cons** The popular waterfront properties are selling quickly. Demand in the area is high and prices are consequently being driven up ■ An average three-bed property costs $707,000

In 1884, Herbert Nicholas and his two brothers arrived in Florida with the express intention of building a business growing lemons, for which there was a huge demand as a guard against scurvy. They named the town Englewood after their hometown in Illinois. After a couple of mammoth freezes put paid to the lemon-growing business, Englewood rebranded itself as a quiet, family-orientated town to lure investors. However, although Englewood wasn't hit with the same kind of freezes ever again, people have long since neglected its citrus growing potential.

Today it's a relaxed beach community of around 16,000 inhabitants, with an exceptionally high median age of 63. Englewood is proud of its cultural lifestyle – it even has a movie cafe where you can watch films while eating seated at a table. The tropical environment gives it a great year-round temperature, generally from the mid 60s in winter to the mid 90s in summer. Unspoiled by high rises, the lovely sandy beaches and laid back atmosphere ensure that property is in demand and prices are rising. You can pay more than $1 million for a new build, ocean-front, three-bedroom condo in sought-after Manasota Key. At the other end of the market, for just over $200,000 you can pick up a three-bed home with a pool in the Rotunda West suburb. ●

5. Venice

ESSENTIALS ■ **Pop** 17,764 ■ **Airport** Sarasota – Bradenton International Airport, 6000 Airport Circle, Sarasota, FL 34243, Tel: +1 941-359-2770 ■ **Tax** Property tax per $1,000: $14

KEY FACTS

■ **Schools** Manatee Community College, North Port, FL 34287, Tel:+1 941 426-0611 ■ North Port Elementary School, 7050 Glenallen Blvd, North Port, FL 34287, Tel: +1 941 426-9517
■ **Medical** Bon Secours Venice Hospital, 540 The Rialto, Venice, FL 34285-2900, Tel: +1 941 485-7711 ■ Walk-In Care, 540 The Rialto, Venice, FL 34285, Tel: +1 941 483-7034
■ **Rentals** Dominated by long term-rentals from snowbirds ■ Some condos allow only three months rental at the minimum ■ Prices range from $1,500 a month to $3,000
■ **Pros** Healthy property market, with an average of one home being sold every five days ■ With fewer high–priced properties being sold, prices are dropping as demand is centred around mid-priced homes market ■ There is a strong retirement market with many people investing in holiday homes to which they intend to retire ■ There is a lot of investment underway, with new house, golf courses, and a new Venetian walkway on Venice Beach
■ **Cons** The market is still favouring the seller and prices are set to rise ■ Waterfront properties cost a premium due to their location ■ High–end homes are not selling; demand is centred on the lower end of the market where there's a limited inventory

Venice is a small, picturesque city that lies on a quiet stretch of the Gulf Coast 18 miles south of Sarasota. One of the few cities on the west coast that isn't separated from the Gulf by a barrier island, its beaches are renowned for being the best place in the United States to collect sharks teeth that wash up on its beaches. Venice not only calls itself the 'Shark Tooth Capital of the World', it has an annual Shark's Tooth and Seafood Festival which attracts many thousands of visitors to the region.

With a wealth of inland waterways, miles of white sandy beaches, and carefully restored Italianate buildings (now on the Historical Register), it's a popular area for retirees; in fact, the population of around 20,000 has a median age of 68. Central Venice is relatively sleepy and uncommercial, but further out there are lots of exciting real estate projects underway. High rise condos are being built (and snapped up quickly) on the Intracoastal Waterway, and on the Island of Venice, homes are selling for $100,000 more than the Florida median price. The average price for a home on the island is now more than $450,000. At the lower end of the scale, you can acquire a two-bed, single storey house on the Waterford estate for just over $250,000. They sell quickly and usually for the asking price. ●

112

Homesearch-Overseas.com

A HOME ON FLORIDA'S GULF COAST TO BUY OR TO RENT

Buying a property overseas is easy; being several thousand miles away can make it more difficult. At Homesearch Overseas we understand this and we work with our clients from the early stages through construction, finance, completion and beyond, via our continuing service offering management, maintenance and rentals.

We offer:

- A top local builder
- 19 different floor plans and also custom builds
- regular updates on the progress of your build
- Homeowners Club to maximise rental potential
- US loans available
- Full management, maintenance and rental programme

Email: info@homesearch-overseas.com Tel: +44 (0) 1635 550 363 Web: www.homesearch-overseas.com

Buying a property in Florida?
you need to speak to the currency experts...

SGM-FX offers a friendly and commission-free service to ensure you secure the best possible exchange rate when converting your funds into US Dollars. There are no hidden fees and no nasty surprises; in short **there is nothing to lose and everything to gain.**

For more information contact SGM-FX

Contact us:

- UK tel: +44 (0) 20 7778 0123
- UK fax: +44 (0) 20 7778 0234
- Email: info@sgm-fx.com
- Web: www.sgm-fx.com

sgm-fx™

SGM-FX Ltd, Prince Rupert House, 64 Queen Street, London EC4R 1AD

THE GULF COAST

6. Naples

ESSENTIALS ■ **Pop** 20,976 ■ **Airports** Southwest Florida International Airport, 16000 Chamberlin Parkway, Fort Myers, FL 33913, Tel: +1 239-768-4381 ■ **Tax** Property tax per $1,000: $14

KEY FACTS

■ **Schools** Collier County Public Schools, 7878 Shark Way, Naples, FL 34119-6751, Tel: +1 239 593-2600 ■ Cedar Montessori School, 10904 Winterview Dr, Naples, FL 34109, Tel: 1 239 597-7190
■ **Medical** Brzezinski Diane DO PA, 848 1st Ave N Ste 340, Naples, FL 34102-6063, Tel: +1 239 261-9990 ■ The Willough at Naples, 9001 Tamiami Trl E, Naples, FL 34113, Tel: +1 239 775-4500
■ **Rentals** There are rental restrictions to be aware of when buying a property for investment purposes ■ Some properties are only available for rent for three months ■ A two-bed condo costs between $1,500 and $4,000 a month on average ■ Peak season is generally between January and March when the snowbirds arrive from the north
■ **Pros** The market remains very strong with both resale and new properties selling well ■ Lots of development planned for the coming years and property is continuing to appreciate ■ Plenty of attractions and amenities, long sandy beaches and a number of waterfront properties for sale
■ **Cons** Limited number of resale properties available ■ There are few properties remaining on golfing developments ■ This is an affluent area with a high cost of living ■ Prone to hurricanes

When the early settlers arrived in the 1860s, the area's fine climate and bountiful fishing waters led them to describe it as 'surpassing the bay in Naples, Italy'. With the city named and suitably promoted, outside investors were attracted. A huge pier was constructed and it stretched 600 feet out into the Gulf of Mexico, its innovative 'T' shape allowing large ships to dock. A number of vast hotels were built and Naples quickly developed into a popular winter resort. The Naples Hotel was patronised by Hollywood stars including Gary Cooper and Greta Garbo, as well as wealthy industrialists such as Harvey Firestone and Thomas Edison.

Now it's a sophisticated, prosperous, and rather exclusive city with a wealth of restaurants, boutiques and galleries. The financial and real estate sector provides around 16 per cent of the employment, a much higher percentage than in other Florida cities. The median age, income, and house values are all well above average; the 2004 median price is $389,000 – the fastest rising median price in the state. You can buy a two-bed, two-bath home in the Emerald Woods area for under $200,000, but as the median price attests, this is not typical of the market. For those with deep pockets, a condo in the Marco Island complex costs about $3 million. ●

7. Fort Myers

ESSENTIALS ■ **Pop** 47,103 ■ **Airport** South Florida International Airport, 6000 Chamberlin Parkway, Suite 8671, Fort Myers, FL 33913, Tel: +1 239 768 1000 ■ **Tax** Property tax per $1,000: $12

KEY FACTS

■ **Schools** Denicole Private High School, 12995 S Cleveland Avenue, Fort Myers, FL 33907 – 3890, Tel: +1 239 415 0368
■ **Medical** Gulf Coast Hospital, 13681 Doctors Way, Fort Myers, FL 33912, Tel: +1 239 768 8575
■ **Rentals** The rentals market has been described as one of the strongest in the US ■ The influx of people to the town is continuing and rental prices are increasing ■ Fort Myers achieves a consistent number of visitors meaning that an annual rental season is likely
■ Rentals in the town can earn up to $30,000 per year ■ On average, a two–bedroom property will rent for about $2,250 per month.
■ **Pros** A new shopping mall is opening at Coconut Point ■ The Fort Myers river front is in the midst of an urban renewal again encouraging investors into the area ■ Delightful mix of old Floridian architecture and modern designs ■ Amenities include golf courses, restaurants and clubs ■ The average property price is $135,300, way below the state average
■ **Cons** High-end properties are not selling as well as others ■ The market favours the seller rather than the buyer because there are more buyers than available properties.

Fort Myers was a rowdy cattle town when it was first established on the Caloosahatchee River in the 1860s. After the Seminole Indian Wars ended, the fort was disassembled and settlers began to cultivate the land. Thomas Edison visited the settlement in 1885 and he liked it so much he built a home and laboratory, Seminole Lodge, on the banks of the river. He also landscaped tropical gardens and planted palm trees along McGregor Boulevard, which has led to Fort Myers being nicknamed the 'City of Palms'. Henry Ford visited Edison in 1914 and ended up buying the house next door. Their majestic homes are now the city's biggest attractions, along with Fort Myers Yacht Basin and Centennial Park.

With a low median age of 32, Fort Myers' lively downtown area has been extensively renovated and caters for the younger crowd. New apartments, shops, restaurants, galleries and nightclubs have sprung up, and the centre is minutes from miles of beautiful sandy beaches. Property prices are rising but it still offers better value than illustrious neighbours Sarasota and Naples. A single storey, three-bed home in the suburb of Lehigh Acres can be picked up for under $140,000 (and often cheaper), but a four-bed beach home in exclusive Sanibel costs around $3 million. ●

THE GULF COAST

8. Bradenton

ESSENTIALS ■ **Pop** 48,318 ■ **Airport** Sarasota-Bradenton International Airport, 6000 Airport Circle, Sarasota, FL 34243, Tel: +1 941 359 2770 ■ **Tax** Property tax per $1,000: $16

Bradenton's first brush with fame was back in 1539 when Spanish adventurer Hernando De Soto landed at Shaw's Point to begin his search for El Dorado, the fabled lost city of gold. However, the famous fruit juice producer Tropicana is the city's greatest claim to fame these days; Florida's south west is the ideal climate for nurturing many thousands of acres of orange and grapefruit trees. Downtown Bradenton has miles of office blocks which lie on the banks of the Manatee River, and the area in general is far more industrial than its illustrious neighbour Sarasota, which lies just over 10 miles to the south.

That said, the Manatee Village Historical Park houses restored buildings, and the chain of barrier islands and the Bradenton beaches are major selling points for a region now regarded as one of the hottest real estate spots in the state. The median property price rose 24 per cent to $235,700 last year, and the county's population has grown by 70,000 in the last 13 years. A four-bed home in the suburb of Windsor Park sells for under $200,000, but you can spend more than $5 million for a home in Longboat Key. There is currently a lot of real estate developement in the Bradenton area, the majority of it in the $250,000 to $380,000 bracket. ●

KEY FACTS

■ **Schools** Contact the School Board of Manatee County, 215 Manatee Avenue West, Bradenton, FL 34205-8840, Tel: +1 941 708 8770
■ **Medical** Manatee Glens Hospital, 2020 26th Avenue East, Bradenton, FL 34208, Tel: +1 941 741 3805
■ **Rentals** The demand for houses in Bradenton is higher than ever and the area has a strong rentals market ■ On average, a two-bed property will rent for around $1,400 per month ■ This market is primarily long term
■ **Pros** Prices have risen 24 per cent from last year and the number of sales has gone up by 70 per cent ■ Breath-taking sunsets, sandy white beaches ■ The restaurants, schools and golf courses provide a good quality of life in the town ■ Affordable area, cheaper than others in South West Florida
■ **Cons** Prices here are rising steeply ■ There are perhaps too many rental properties ■ The median price tag of $235,700 was up 24 per cent from last year ■ It is recommended that buyers seek to invest soon before interest rates begin to slow the market

9. Punta Gorda

ESSENTIALS ■ **Pop** 12,686 ■ **Airport** Southwest Florida International Airport, 16000 Chamberlin Parkway, Suite 8671, Fort Myers, FL 33913, Tel: +1 239 768 1000 ■ **Tax** Property tax per $1,000: $14

Punta Gorda is a waterfront community opposite Port Charlotte on the south bank of the narrow, winding Peace River. Its small downtown area has been meticulously restored and the cobbled streets and gaslight lamps give the town an air of charming tranquillity. Excellent shops and restaurants are complemented with a number of small statues and murals. The pleasant riverfront area houses a Fisherman's Village, which comprises a marina and a selection of quirky shops. Punta Gorda is home to the Florida Adventure Museum and the Ponce de Leon Historical Park. With a resident's median age of almost 64, the town emphasis is clearly on retirees. House prices are fairly high; the median price is well over $200,000. Burnt Store Marina on the Southshore offers three-bed condos for around $325,000. In upmarket Sunlake Villas, $450,000 will buy you a four-bed home with a pool on a two acre plot. The market is expected to strengthen in the next few years.

Punta Gorda actually came fourth in America's Best Places To Live in 2003. More than 330 metropolitan areas were rated by the influential Sperling's Best Places study group in a number of categories including cost of living, crime rate, education, home prices and weather, and only Punta Gorda's lack of recreation options were criticised. ●

KEY FACTS

■ **Schools** Contact the Charlotte County School Board, 1016 Education Avenue, Punta Gorda, FL 33950, Tel: +1 941 255 7519
■ **Medical** Charlotte Regional Medical Center, 809 E Marion Avenue, Punta Gorda, FL 33950-3819, Tel: +1 941 639 3131
■ **Rentals** On average, a two–bedroom property will rent for around $2,400 per month.
■ **Pros** The property market is very healthy ■ Prices are rising, but it's still possible to buy a waterfront home for under $250,000 ■ Punta Gorda has a good infrastructure ■ The atmosphere is laid back, with a rich mix of cultures ■ Architecture reflects a Southern style, with most houses fronting onto the sea
■ **Cons** The beaches are not as attractive as many on the Gulf Coast ■ There is a large community of retired workers here and not many younger families ■ This is predominantly a seller's market, with more potential buyers than there are houses available

HOTSPOTS

115

■ GULF COAST

10. Cape Coral

ESSENTIALS ■ **Pop** 101,894 ■ **Airport** South Florida International Airport, 16000 Chamberlin Parkway, Suite 8671, Fort Myers, FL 33913, Tel: +1 239 768 1000 ■ **Tax** Property tax per $1,000: $11

KEY FACTS

■ **Schools** School District of Lee County, Mariner High/Middle Schools, 701 Chiquita Blvd. N, Cape Coral, FL 33993-7222, Tel: +1 239 772 3324
■ **Medical** Cape Coral Hospital, 636 Del Prado Blvd. S., Cape Coral, FL 33990-2668, Tel: +1 239 574 2323
■ **Rentals** This is a strong rentals market with good rental potential ■ On average, a two-bedroom property will cost around $2,000 per month ■ There are rental restrictions on letting property in this area
■ **Pros** Thousands of waterfront homes located along 400 miles of canals ■ Developers are now choosing to locate near schools, excellent for family relocation ■ Cape Coral is one of the fastest growing cities in Florida, ranked first for new constructions ■ High-end homes and small gated communities are springing up in north west Cape Coral ■ Riverfront and saltwater access properties are climbing in value, and in the last year, prices increased by 22 per cent ■ Properties are low priced in comparison to other areas
■ **Cons** There is potential for overdevelopment in this area which could lead to overpopulation ■ Although prices are low now, they are predicted to rise quickly in future

Although it was only developed just over 40 years ago, Cape Coral is geographically, at 114 square miles, the second largest city in Florida and the 12th largest in population. In 1957, two brothers named Leonard and Jack Rosen purchased a huge tract of land (around 60,000 acres) and dug more than 400 miles of canals, which flow into the Caloosahatchee River and the Gulf of Mexico. This enabled them to develop a huge number of waterfront plots at affordable prices – they sold almost 350,000 plots, mostly to people from other states. One of the reasons why they were able to sell so many plots was due to the fact that people were able to pay for them in instalments, so even blue collar workers could invest in the region.

Cape Coral remains one of the fastest growing cities in Florida and continues to attract people relocating from northern states. Properties fronting the canals are most sought after, and you can pay anything from $100,000 to over $1 million. Developments are springing up and although prices are on the increase, it remains a relatively affordable city in comparison to its more historic neighbours.

Despite the rapid development, Cape Coral residents still find time to decorate their boats with lights at Christmas and parade along the many miles of canals. ●

Although it has many hundreds of miles of coastline, Florida also has an abundance of inland lakes

VISIT FLORIDA

THE GULF COAST

$100,000–$250,000
(£55,000–£137,000)

For those on a tight budget there is still a variety of great homes to choose from

$200,693   CODE HOM
ROTONDA
A modern, fully furnished property with a heated swimming pool and a pool deck
£110,382

3 | with a garden | situated close to the town centre | not located on a main road | room for parking, with a two-car garage

---

$221,383   CODE HOM
ROTONDA
With 2,241 square feet, a fully fitted property with wooden floors throughout
£121,760

3 | with pool and large garden | situated close to amenities | not located on a main road | room for parking, with a garage

---

$232,400   CODE SUS
PORT CHARLOTTE
A series of off-plan properties, with 1,730 square feet living area and a pool
£127,820

3 | with a small garden | situated close to the town centre | not located on a main road | room for parking, with a garage

---

$238,785   CODE HOM
ROTONDA
With a heated swimming pool, this open plan modern property is a great investment
£131,332

3 | with a large garden and pool deck | close to shops and amenities | not located on a main road | room for parking, with a two-car garage

---

$241,353   CODE HOM
ROTONDA
Set in a popular development, a delightful home complete with furnishings and pool
£132,744

3 | with a garden and pool deck | situated close to the town centre | not located on a main road | room for parking, with a two-car garage

PRICE GUIDE

■ THE GULF COAST

$250,000—$300,000
(£137,500–£165,000)

There are many fully furnished community homes available for a bargain price

$255,983
CODE HOM

ROTONDA
A large, fully fitted property, offering spacious rooms and a heated swimming pool
£140,790

4 | with a large garden | situated close to amenities | not located on a main road | room for parking, with a two-car garage

$259,123
CODE HOM

ROTONDA
Ideal as a family home, a fully furnished property with air conditioning and a pool
£142,518

3 | with a landscaped garden | situated close to amenities | not located on a main road | room for parking, with a three-car garage

$268,160
CODE HOM

ROTONDA
Luxuriously designed and furnished, a spacious home with a study and a heated pool
£147,488

3 | with a large garden | situated close to amenities | not located on a main road | room for parking, with a three-car garage

$269,000
CODE SUS

PUNTA GORDA
A custom-built home, located in a golfing development, overlooking woodlands
£147,950

4 | with a large garden | situated close to amenities and the beach | not located on a main road | room for parking, with a garage

$277,660
CODE HOM

ROTONDA
With a total living area of 3,342 square feet, a fully furnished home with a pool
£178,475

4 | with a large garden | situated close to amenities | not located on a main road | room for parking, with a two-car garage

PRICE GUIDE

THE GULF COAST ■

$300,000—$400,000
(£165,000–£220,000)

Those seeking a holiday home for family and friends will find a wealth of choice

$364,000   CODE MIS
SOUTH SARASOTA
Overlooking a golf course, a home with a hot tub, offering stunning country views
£200,200

| 2 | with a large garden | situated close to amenities | not located on a main road | room for parking, with a garage |

$369,900   CODE MIS
SOUTH SARASOTA
Newly built, this modern 1,864 square foot residence offers stunning bay views
£203,445

| 2 | with a balcony | situated close to the town centre | not located on a main road | room for parking, with a three-car garage |

$370,170   CODE HOM
ROTONDA
Spacious and fully furnished, well located with a large swimming pool and pool deck
£203,594

| 5 | with landscaped gardens | situated close to the town centre | not located on a main road | room for parking, with a two-car garage |

$372,658   CODE HOM
ROTONDA
Ideal for a family, this newly built home offers all mod cons, a heated pool and a deck
£204,962

| 4 | with a large garden | situated close to amenities | not located on a main road | room for parking, with a garage |

$372,900   CODE MIS
VENICE
A spectacular home, located in a private country club community, with a pool and spa
£205,095

| 3 | with a large garden and panoramic views | situated close to all amenities | not located on a main road | room for parking |

PRICE GUIDE

119

■ **THE GULF COAST**

$400,000 — $1,000,000
(£220,000–£550,000)

From community dwellings to sprawling waterfront homes, something for everyone

$420,000   CODE FLC

NAPLES
Only seven minutes from the beach, a modern property with a swimming pool
£231,000

🛏 4   🌼 6,600 square feet   🏬 situated three minutes from the shops   🚗 not located on a main road   🏠 room for parking, with a garage

---

$420,000   CODE FLC

VENICE
With a swimming pool and a spa, a comfortable modern house ideal for the family
£231,000

🛏 5   🌼 with a 8,400 foot garden   🏬 situated close to the town centre   🚗 not located on a main road   🏠 room for parking, with a garage

---

$449,000   CODE MIS

SARASOTA
With dazzling views across the bay, this community offers a gym, pool and concierge
£246,950

🛏 2   🌼 with a communal pool and garden   🏬 situated close to the town centre   🚗 not located on a main road   🏠 room for parking

---

$479,000   CODE WOF

NEW PORT RICHEY
Situated 60 miles north of Tampa, backing onto the Intracoastal Waterway, with a dock
£263,450

🛏 5   🌼 with a garden   🏬 situated close to the shops   🚗 not located on a main road   🏠 room for parking

---

$485,000   CODE FLC

ENGLEWOOD
A modern property only eight minutes from the beach, with a pool and ocean views
£266,750

🛏 6   🌼 14,000 square feet   🏬 situated 10 minutes from the shops   🚗 not located on a main road   🏠 room for parking, with a garage

PRICE GUIDE

THE GULF COAST

$574,900   CODE WOF

NAPLES
Located in a popular development, a spacious holiday home, with a swimming pool
£316,195

3 | with a garden | situated close to the town centre | not located on a main road | room for parking

---

$769,000   CODE MIS

VENICE
A home built to the highest standards, with a deluxe master bedroom suite
£422,950

4 | in five acres of grounds | situated close to amenities | not located on a main road | room for parking, with a garage

$799,000   CODE MIS

BRADENTON
Located within a golf and country club, a Mediterranean style home on the canal front
£439,450

5 | with a large, mature garden | situated close to the town centre | not located on a main road | room for parking

---

$895,000   CODE MIS

SOUTH SARASOTA
An elegant, traditional property, with spacious rooms and wooden floors. With a pool
£492,250

5 | with a large, private garden | situated close to amenities | not located on a main road | room for parking

---

$930,000   CODE MIS

SOUTH SARASOTA
Surrounded by oak trees, a custom-built residence with french doors and a pool
£511,500

5 | with a large garden | situated close to amenities | not located on a main road | room for parking

---

$970,000   CODE MIS

SOUTH SARASOTA
Beautifully landscaped and surrounded by fruit trees, a spacious family home
£533,500

3 | with a large landscaped garden | situated close to amenities | not located on a main road | room for parking

PRICE GUIDE

■ **THE GULF COAST**

$1,000,000
(£550,000+)

Luxurious waterfront mansions, exquisitely designed for the discerning buyer

PRICE GUIDE

$1,150,000   CODE MIS
SOUTH SARASOTA
With a traditional open porch and a view overlooking a lake, a luxurious country home
£632,500

- 5 | with a large garden | situated close to the shops | not located on a main road | room for parking

$3,750,000   CODE MIS
DOWNTOWN SARASOTA
A spectacular penthouse apartment, in the heart of Sarasota's popular cultural district
£2,062,500

- 3 | with a balcony | situated in the town centre | located on a main road | room for parking

$4,350,000   CODE MIS
LONGBOAT KEY
Set on the southernmost point, overlooking the beachfront, truly luxurious
£2,392,500

- 4 | with a large garden and pool | situated close to amenities | not located on a main road | room for parking

$4,500,000   CODE MIS
CASEY KEY
An elegantly designed beachfront home, stretching over an acre of grounds
£2,475,000

- 4 | with one acre of grounds | situated close to Sarasota's amenities | not located on a main road | room for parking

$8,900,000   CODE MIS
LIDO KEY
A splendid estate set right on the waterfront, splendidly designed, in spacious grounds
£4,895,000

- 6 | with extensive grounds | situated close to the centre | not located on a main road | room for parking

Florida Keys • Gulf of Mexico • Disney World • Florida Keys • Gulf of Mexico • Disney World

freedom homes usa

www.freedomhomesusa.co.uk

real estate

immigration

property management

rentals

'To discuss your Florida property requirements, call us today on 02920 383 453.'

'We look forward to your call.'

'live the dream'

Florida Keys • Gulf of Mexico • Disney World • Florida Keys • Gulf of Mexico • Disney World

Forget the heartache.....Discover the right property the easy way........

FLORIDA SPECIALISTS

We can offer you the most comprehensive choice of properties currently available in Orlando, Florida, as we have local contacts in all key areas, providing up to the minute details on all the best deals available. You will speak to local people with local knowledge and we will handle all the fine details for you with a personal & efficient service.

FLORIDAYS HOTEL CONDOS

from $235,000

Fully serviced luxurious hotel condos on International Drive. Full Turnkey Package. Designer furniture, superb central location.
2 Bed 2 Bath or
3 Bed 2 Bath available.

GREAT INVESTMENT OPPORTUNITY

DETACHED HOMES

from $294,900

Nestled minutes from Disney. Wonderfully appointed. State of the art clubhouse. Resort Pool & Spa Children's & Sports facilities.

Solana

GOOD AVAILABILITY
from $269,000

Detached Pool Homes.
4 Bedrooms / 3 Bathrooms.
Full Turnkey Package.
Some Conservation lots.
EXCELLENT RENTAL POTENTIAL.

This is just a small selection from our extensive listings of New & ReSale homes in Orlando, Florida. All are unique and set in the best locations for all the main attractions.

NAEA — NATIONAL ASSOCIATION OF ESTATE AGENTS

"USE US AS YOUR LOCAL UK CONTACT"

www.parsonfloridahomes.com

PARSON International
Victoria Road, Diss, Norfolk.

kevin @ parson.ltd.uk
PHONE +44 (0)1379 650680

Central Florida

Theme parks, lakes and the beautiful Ocala National Forest

- **Population** 2 million
- **Population increase** Between 1992–2002 the population grew by 505,600
- **Migration** 101,884 people migrated to Central Florida between 2000–2002 of which 20% were international migrants
- **Median age** 38.6 years; the state average is 38.7
- **Median home price** $136,600
- **Cost of living** The ACCRA cost of living index rates Central Florida as 102.8/100

Profile 126
Hotspots 128

Price Guide

$20,000–$75,000	130
$75,000–$200,000	132
$200,000–$240,000	133
$240,000–$300,000	134
$300,000–$385,000	136
$385,000–$450,000	139
$450,000–$920,000 +	140

CENTRAL FLORIDA

GETTING THERE

AIR Orlando International Airport (001 407/825-2001, www.orlando-mco.com); Orlando Sanford International (001 407/585-4000, www.orlandosanford airport.com) receives a lot of UK charter flights. **American Airlines** (0845 778 9789, www.aa.com) operates flights from Gatwick, Heathrow and Manchester to Orlando. **British Airways** (0870 850 9850, www.ba.com) flies direct from Gatwick to Orlando International Airport, while **Continental Airlines** (0845 607 6760, www.continental.com) flies to Orlando via Washington Airport. **Virgin Atlantic** (0870 574 7277, www.virgin-atlantic.com) flies directly to Orlando International Airport from Gatwick and Manchester Airport.

RAIL Amtrak-Orlando, 800-USA-RAIL, 1400 Sligh Blvd, Downtown, Orlando, (+1 407/843-7611). There are stations in Winter Park (+1 407/645-5055) and Kissimmee (+1 407/933-1170).

BUS Lynx bus services offer the most coverage of the Orlando area (+1 407/841-2279, www.golynx.com). It services all the three counties around Orlando and regularly stops at the airport, Disney World, SeaWorld and Universal Studios. There are also bus and shuttle services. **Gray Line of Orlando** (+1 407 422-0744).

ROAD There are a number of car rental firms operating around Orlando International Airport, but they are generally very busy and need to be booked in advance. There are many private shuttle and coach services operating in Orlando and they're also busy and need to be booked in advance. **Mears Transportation Group** (+1 407/423-5566). There are many taxis in Orlando but these are expensive, although in order to get around at night there is little option for the non-driver. For those who are driving, the roads are generally clear and fast-moving, with Route 4 being the main road that stretches from Daytona Beach, through Orlando and past Davenport heading towards Tampa. Travelling to Florida from within the US is cheapest on the **Greyhound** buses (+1 800/231-2222, www.greyhound.com).

Area profile

FIFTY YEARS AGO CENTRAL FLORIDA WAS A SLEEPY BACKWATER OF farming communities, a fact that is hard to imagine when you consider that today it is the epicentre of tourist and house buying activity in the Sunshine State.

The 'tourist triangle' stretches from Walt Disney World (approximately 35 kilometres south west from downtown Orlando) on Interstate 4, to Kissimmee (approximately 19 kilometres east of Walt Disney World) on Highway 192 and back up north to Orlando (approximately 29 kilometres) via combined Highways 17/92 and 441. Incorporated in this area are attractions such as SeaWorld, Universal Studios and Wet 'n Wild.

As visitor figures soared, so did development. Today Orlando has all but absorbed its neighbours Kissimmee and upmarket Windermere, with shopping malls, resorts, hotels, crazy golf and restaurants lining US Highway 192 and catering for every possible tourist whim. The population has soared by almost 80 per cent thanks to the real estate boom in the area.

While pastel coloured holiday villas and raucous family entertainment are all very well, it is worth exploring a little further afield during a visit. Continuing south from Kissimmee along combined Highway 17/92 the countryside changes back to dust dotted with cattle and orange groves. Lake Kissimmee State Park is in the heart of cattle country and offers nature trails, campsites, fishing and even canoeing. At weekends, visitors can step back in time and relive the days of cattle drives and cow camps.

Winter Haven is an hour's drive from Disney World and offers a striking contrast to the area's more commercially popular tourist attractions. This community of around 25,000 people is surrounded by 23 beautiful freshwater lakes, 14 of which are joined by navigable canals. Davenport also offers the best of both worlds, being just 30 minutes away from Walt

Walt Disney World attracts millions of visitors to Central Florida

CENTRAL FLORIDA

Disney World and an hour from the Gulf Coast, yet it sits peacefully surrounded by a wealth of top class golf courses and rolling hills once used for citrus growth.

Economy and housing market

Central Florida is rich in tourist gold thanks to the millions of visitors that flock there each year. The opening of Walt Disney World in 1971 really put Orlando on the international map and the appeal has been enduring, with other crowd-pulling attractions springing up in close proximity.

The entertainment, leisure and tourist industry remains the economic driving force of the area. Unsurprisingly, the Disney empire is the largest private employer with over 53,000 people on its books, and Universal Studios is another huge employer with around 14,500 staff.

Orlando itself is one of the fastest growing cities in the United States with an estimated 5,000 new residents arriving monthly. For this reason the housing market is very buoyant, although most sales are for second or holiday homes. Property prices have increased by around 11 or 12 per cent over the past year, yet they remain well below the state and national averages and generally offer excellent value for money. A three or four bedroom house can be purchased for around $250,000, though the closer to Disney World your property is, the more it is likely to cost.

Buying in the Orlando or Davenport area makes for an excellent investment, too. Rental returns are high and there is never a shortage of customers, though you should double check that your property is in the correct rental zone to ensure you are not subject to limiting restrictions. Thanks to the 'snowbird' phenomenon, the rental season here is virtually year-round. When residents of colder areas in the northern US and Canada head south for the winter to avoid the snow and freezing cold, they create an extremely high rental demand from November to April.

While Orlando and further south to Kissimmee could be described as over developed, the north provides a refreshing contrast. Here property becomes a little more exclusive and, of course, rather more expensive as it tends to focus around the proliferation of golf courses in the area.

Social groups

As you might expect, most of central Florida is populated by young families who take advantage of the child-oriented entertainments of the area and the reasonable property prices. The area is also very popular with American retirees from metropolises such as New York and New Jersey who want a change of pace and a break from the big city life.

Some realtors estimate that as many as two thirds of the homes around Orlando are used primarily as rentals which does mean a very low ratio of owner occupiers. Many of these rentals will be for months at a time, however, so there is a community feel and a relatively constant population.

Central Florida is popular with UK buyers and it remains an attractive proposition. The strength of sterling against the dollar means that Orlando represents great value for money, and many couples in their fifties are releasing equity from their UK property to take advantage of this. •

Orlando is popular with retired second home buyers, mostly 'snowbirds'

The strength of sterling against the dollar means that Orlando represents great value for money at present

Average monthly temperature °C (Celsius)

ORLANDO		LONDON
17	Dec	7
20	Nov	10
24	Oct	14
27	Sept	19
28	Aug	21
28	July	22
27	June	20
25	May	17
22	April	13
20	March	10
17	Feb	7
16	Jan	6

Average monthly rainfall mm (millimetres)

ORLANDO		LONDON
59	Dec	81
59	Nov	78
69	Oct	70
69	Sept	65
159	Aug	62
182	July	59
187	June	58
95	May	57
62	April	56
90	March	64
60	Feb	72
62	Jan	77

Florida Climate Center (www.coaps.fsu.edu/climate_center)

AVERAGE HOUSE SALE PRICES

Hotspot	2-bed	3-bed	4-bed	5-bed
Orlando	$287K (£156K)	$303K (£165K)	$660K (£360K)	$912K (£497K)
Kissimmee	$147K (£80K)	$237K (£129K)	$401K (£219K)	$551K (£300K)
Davenport	$166K (£90K)	$265K (£144K)	$132K (£72K)	$178K (£97K)

CENTRAL FLORIDA

Area hotspots

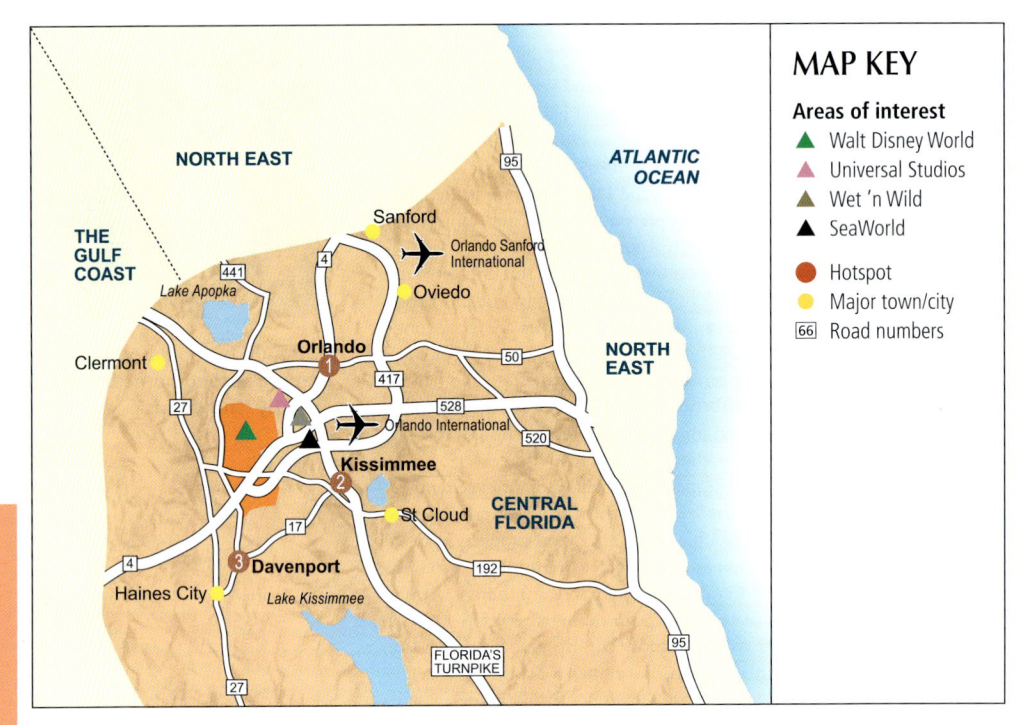

MAP KEY

Areas of interest
▲ Walt Disney World
▲ Universal Studios
▲ Wet 'n Wild
▲ SeaWorld

● Hotspot
● Major town/city
66 Road numbers

Map shows Central Florida region including North East, The Gulf Coast, Atlantic Ocean, with locations: Sanford, Orlando Sanford International, Lake Apopka, Oviedo, Clermont, Orlando (1), Orlando International, Kissimmee (2), St Cloud, Haines City, Davenport (3), Lake Kissimmee, Florida's Turnpike.

1. Orlando

ESSENTIALS ■ **Pop** 200,000 ■ **Airports** Orlando International Airport, Tel: 001 407/825-2001, www.orlando-mco.com, Orlando ■ Sanford International, 001 407/585-4000, www.orlandosanfordairport.com ■ **Taxes** Property tax per $1,000: $18

KEY FACTS

■ **Schools** Northstar High School, 8291 Curry Ford Rd, Orlando, FL 32822-7890, Tel: +1 407/273-1188 ■ Pathways Private School Inc, 514 E Central Blvd, Orlando, Fl 32801-1935, Tel: +1 407/843-9988 ■ Windows Preschool, 1014 Park Lake St, Orlando, FL 32803-4028, Tel: +1 407/898-1267
■ **Medical** Arnold Palmer Hospital, 22 West Underwood Street, Orlando, FL 32806, Tel: +1 407-648-7899 ■ Florida Hospital Centra Care 12139 South Apopka Vineland Road, Orlando, FL 32836, Tel: +1 407-238-2000 ■ Orlando Regional Healthcare, 9400 Turkey Lake Road, Orlando, FL 32819, Tel: +1 407-351-8500
■ **Rentals** Zoned for short-term rentals, making it easy to secure regular year-round lets ■ Peak season focuses around Christmas, Easter and New Year ■ Off peak varies from $300 to $695 for a one to four-bedroom property ■ Peak time varies from $400 to $895 for a one to four-bed property
■ **Pros** Far and away the best bet for investment buyers ■ Lots of golfing developments ■ Central Orlando is a busy commercial district of skyscrapers, restaurants and hotels
■ **Cons** Orlando is a 90 minute drive from the coast in both directions ■ This is a highly developed area ■ Neighbours will be constantly changing

Orlando has expanded massively since the establishment of Disney World in 1971. It's now a huge resort encompassing a number of theme parks spread over a huge site of 43 square miles. After New York and Los Angeles, Orlando attracts the highest number of overseas visitors in the US, on average 33 million a year. The resort is actually 23 miles south of downtown Orlando and so the city itself is relatively free of people sporting rodent ephemera. However, many tourists visit the downtown area's shops and restaurants after the parks have closed. Orlando's most refined neighbourhoods of Winter Park and Loch Haven Park are located north of the city centre. In the late 19th century, wealthy northerners built their winter homes in these districts, and these days prices in Winter Park can rise as high as $10 million. However, there is good value to be had in other districts, and although Orlando is inland, the wealth of lakes in the region means that waterfront properties are available.

Those with a slightly smaller budget of around $120,000 will discover a huge range of properties at their disposal. Orlando has more of a multiracial population than other Florida cities and perhaps not surprisingly, more than 20 per cent of the employment in the city is linked to tourism, entertainment and catering. ●

CENTRAL FLORIDA

2. Kissimmee

ESSENTIALS ■ **Pop** 48,000 ■ **Airport** Orlando International Airport, Tel: 001 407/825-2001, www.orlando-mco.com ■ Orlando Sanford International, 001 407/585-4000, www.orlandosanfordairport.com ■ **Taxes** Property tax per $1,000: $10

Kissimmee lies to the south of Orlando not far from the Disney World Resort. For those tourists that don't wish to stay in the resort's bespoke accommodation, Kissimmee offers a wealth of motels and malls that are cheaper than their Disney equivalents. Once a cattle boom town, its major attraction these days is the recreated old town which features more than 75 shops, and Gatorland, a huge working alligator farm with a variety of related attractions including gator wrestling. Kissimmee is also surrounded by some of Florida's finest freshwater lakes. The population of almost 50,000 is over 40 per cent Hispanic, particularly high for this region of Florida, and the median age of residents is very low at just over 30. Tourism and entertainment provide almost 40 per cent of the city's employment. Although there has been an upsurge in real estate prices in general, your money still stretches further in Kissimmee than in a lot of other Florida cities.

A new four-bed home in the Pleasant Hill suburb on a good-sized plot sells for well under $250,000. Slightly further out is the Disney-created, utopian town of Celebration which was built in 1996. Property is expensive but it's an idyllic setting, with architect-designed houses set over 5,000 acres. ●

KEY FACTS

■ **Schools** Northstar High School, 8291 Curry Ford Rd, Orlando, FL 32822-7890, Tel: +1 407/273-1188 ■ Page Private Schools Inc, 10250 University Blvd, Orlando, FL 32817, Tel: +1 407/678-0333
■ **Medical** Florida Hospital Centra Care, 4320 West Vine Street, Kissimmee, FL 34746, www.centracare.org, Tel: +1 407-660-8118 ■ Celebration Health – Osceola, 400 Celebration Place, Kissimmee, FL 34747, Tel: +1 407-764-4000
■ **Rentals** Kissimmee is a hugely popular area for rentals due to its proximity to the theme parks ■ An excellent area for investment, average weekly prices range from $483 for a two-bedroom property off season (from January to May), and $660 during the peak season of Christmas, Easter and New Year ■ For a three-bedroom property, prices range from $399 out of season and $1,120 during peak season
■ **Pros** Kissimmee developments are focused along Highway 192 where there are a number of amenities, hotels and restaurants ■ Ideal spot for a family home and those seeking rental income ■ This is a residential area zoned for short-term rentals, ideal for those seeking an active family life
■ **Cons** This is an area slightly more expensive than the rest of Orlando ■ Highway 192 suffers from having too many bland concrete motels and malls

3. Davenport

ESSENTIALS ■ **Pop** 2,000 ■ **Airports** Orlando International Airport, Tel: 001 407/825-2001, www.orlando-mco.com, Orlando Sanford International, 001 407/585-4000, www.orlandosanfordairport.com ■ **Taxes** Property tax rate per $1,000: $14.63

Although the population of Davenport is only around 2,000, its location near Disney World means it's becoming an increasingly popular area for real estate construction. Exclusive resort communities and gated developments are springing up, and many thousands of acres will be developed in the coming years, along with world class golf courses and other leisure facilities. Although there isn't a huge number of facilities in the downtown area of Davenport, they are improving rapidly as more and more people move into the vicinity. The rentals market has expanded simply because the theme parks attract millions of visitors to the region. However, those not looking to buy-to-let can purchase property in residential-only areas at around half the price of real estate that falls within short-term rental zones. The Reunion Resort and Club attempts to recreate the ambience of small-town America but with added luxury – it houses three championship-quality golf courses and there are shops and restaurants. Existing custom-built homes sell for between $300,000 and $750,000, while condominiums cost anything between $280,000 to over $400,000. There is good value to be had on the Fairways Lake Estate where you can buy a four-bed home with a screened pool for $250,000. Prices have risen by over a third in the past couple of years. ●

KEY FACTS

■ **Schools** Four Corners Charter Elementary School, 9100 Teacher Lane, Davenport, FL 33897, Tel: +1 407-787-4300 ■ Ridgeview Global Studies Academy, 1000 Dunson Road, Davenport, FL 33896, Tel: +1 863-419-3171
■ **Medical** Heart of Florida Regional Medical Center, 40100 Highway 27, Davenport, Tel: +1 863-419-2272
■ **Rentals** The average rental cost for a three-bed home varies from $300 to $715 in autumn and winter, through to $500 to $790 for spring months ■ Prices for summer vary from $650 to $850, while the peak season of Christmas, Easter and New Year average at $895
■ **Pros** Many people are investing in property in Davenport prior to these properties being built, and then selling them on completion and making a 40 per cent profit ■ Ideal location for a family home
■ **Cons** The majority of properties are zoned for short-term rentals and neighbours are constantly changing ■ It's a holiday home environment year-round, not ideal for the older couple seeking a quiet retreat ■ Residential properties in Davenport are 50 per cent cheaper if they do not fall within the short-term rentals zone ■ The area is prone to water shortages due to the huge number of developments

■ CENTRAL FLORIDA

$20,000—$75,000
(£11,000–£41,250)

Orlando is one the most affordable areas in Florida and offers some bargain homes

$29,891   CODE MED
DAVENPORT
This townhouse is located in a development and comes fully fitted and furnished
£16,440

🛏 1   🌼 no garden   🏬 situated close to shops and amenities   🚫 not located on a main road   🅿 room for parking

$54,990   CODE MED
ORLANDO
An expansive cottage style property, this home is fully furnished and has great views
£30,245

🛏 3   🌼 with a large garden   🏬 close to amenities and shops   🚫 not located on a main road   🅿 room for parking

$63,815   CODE MED
ORLANDO
With a communal pool and tennis courts onsite, a comfortable development home
£35,100

🛏 2   🌼 with a small garden   🏬 situated close to the town centre   ✅ located on a main road   🅿 room for parking, with a garage

$69,897   CODE MED
ORLANDO
This beautiful property is zoned for short-term rentals and is ideal as an investment
£38,443

🛏 3   🌼 with a garden   🏬 all amenities on site   🚫 not located on a main road   🅿 room for parking

$74,480   CODE MED
ORLANDO
This development home comes fully fitted and with all amenities onsite
£40,964

🛏 3   🌼 with a small garden   🏬 situated close to the town centre   ✅ located on a main road   🅿 room for parking

PRICE GUIDE

Beautiful vacation homes in
ORLANDO
Florida

At The Florida Store, we believe in a friendly, supportive and honest approach.

A British owned and managed company, we have been in Orlando for over ten years. In that time we have grown to become one of the most successful companies of its kind, highly respected by builders and major tour operators alike.

With us you will find no sales gimmicks, no rental lock-outs and no over-optimistic predictions. What you *will* find is real knowledge, experience and advice plus full assistance at every stage of your home purchase.

You will also find an unrivalled partner for the future maintenance and rental management of your home. With two offices right on the spot in Orlando, as well as in the UK, you can enjoy real peace of mind. Book an inspection trip and meet our friendly Orlando office staff. See how it all works and ask any questions you like.

So you really *do* know who you're dealing with.

THE FLORIDA STORE

To find out more, call us free on
Tel: 0800 169 6247
Or visit our website at
www.floridastore.uk.com

The Florida Store, Florida House, 35 High Street, Spennymoor, Co.Durham DL16 6AA

■ **CENTRAL FLORIDA**

$75,000 – $200,000
(£41,250–£110,000)

Spacious family homes are available for the price of a one-bedroom flat in the UK

$78,086 — CODE MED

ORLANDO
Expansive and enjoying all the benefits of community living, a modern, furnished house
£42,947

🛏 3 | 🌼 with a garden | 🏢 all amenities onsite | ⚠ not located on a main road
🚗 room for parking, with a garage

$84,651 — CODE MED

ORLANDO
Newly built, this home is close to all the development amenities and is fully furnished
£46,560

🛏 4 | 🌼 with a large garden | 🏢 situated close to amenities | ⚠ not located on a main road | 🚗 room for parking

---

$110,000+ — CODE COL

ORLANDO
Great value, quality homes with many leisure facilities including a superb golf course
£60,500

🛏 1/2 | 🌼 with a garden | 🏢 all amenities on site | ⚠ not located on a main road
🚗 room for parking

$155,000 — CODE BHG

KISSIMMEE
Located in a popular short-term rentals neighbourhood, this home is close to Disney
£85,250

🛏 3 | 🌼 with a garden | 🏢 situated close to attractions and amenities | ⚠ not located on a main road | 🚗 room for parking

---

$183,000+ — CODE COL

ORLANDO
Beautiful homes with pools and gardens close to all the main attractions in Orlando
£100,650

🛏 3/5 | 🌼 with a private garden | 🏢 all amenities on site | ⚠ not located on a main road | 🚗 room for parking

PRICE GUIDE

CENTRAL FLORIDA ■

$200,000–$240,000
(£110,000–£132,000)

Attractive homes with swimming pools, close to amenities, at attractive prices

$206,990+
CODE COL
ORLANDO
Attractive homes, designed for outdoor living with a beautiful pool and decking
£113,795

3/5   with a private garden   close to amenities and attractions   not located on a main road   room for parking

$214,900
CODE PAR
ORLANDO
A fully furnished, detached home featuring a large swimming pool and spa
£118,195

4   with a large garden   close to amenities   not located on a main road   room for parking

$219,000+
CODE COL
ORLANDO
Suite apartments in a first-class resort with pools, games room and kids activity centre
£120,450

2/3   with a communal garden   all amenities on site   located on International Drive   room for parking

$227,270
CODE FRE
DAVENPORT
Located five miles from Disney, this superb family home has a heated pool
£125,000

3   with a garden   situated close to all amenities   not located on a main road   room for parking

$231,900
CODE ABG
ORLANDO
Located on International Drive, a condo development with fully-furnished apartments
£127,545

2/3   with a balcony   close to the centre of Orlando   located on a main road   room for parking

PRICE GUIDE

133

■ CENTRAL FLORIDA

$240,000 – $275,000
(£132,000–£151,250)

Ideal, spacious family homes, just a stone's throw away from Disney World

$250,000   CODE ABG
ORLANDO
Set amidst a golf course, a community property, fully fitted, and close to Disney World
£137,500

- 3
- with a spacious garden
- within minutes of the shops and theme parks
- not located on a main road
- room for parking, with a garage

$252,490   CODE JUF
DAVENPORT
With a children's play area, tennis courts and pool, an attractive and spacious home
£138,870

- 4
- with a garden
- situated one mile from the shops
- not located on a main road
- room for parking, with a two-car garage

$267,900   CODE TFS
ORLANDO
With a den and swimming pool this home is ideal as a family holiday home
£147,345

- 3
- with a garden
- close to shops and amenities
- not located on a main road
- room for parking, with a garage

$274,900   CODE WOF
DAVENPORT
Situated in a small development, a modern property, fully furnished, with a pool
£151,195

- 4
- with a garden
- situated close to shops and Disney
- not located on a main road
- room for parking, with a garage

$274,900   CODE ABG
ORLANDO
A resale property recently upgraded, sold fully furnished, with a swimming pool
£151,195

- 5
- with a garden
- situated close to amenities
- not located on a main road
- room for parking, with a garage

PRICE GUIDE

CENTRAL FLORIDA ■

$275,000–$300,000
(£151,250–£165,000)

Secure, gated, private properties in well-located areas, close to local attractions

$271,500   CODE ULV
DAVENPORT
A fully furnished, custom-built family home, zoned for short-term rentals
£149,325

4+ | with a large garden | situated close to amenities | not located on a main road | room for parking, with a garage

---

$275,000   CODE WOF
DAVENPORT
Located in a secure, gated community, with a pool and tennis court, ideal for a family
£154,820

5 | with a garden | close to shops and Disney World | not located on a main road | room for parking, with a two-car garage

$285,000   CODE ULV
ANDAVENPORT
Located in a gated community, this house is well located and is an ideal investment home
£156,750

4 | with a garden | situated close to shops and attractions | not located on a main road | room for parking

---

$293,000   CODE FLC
KISSIMMEE
Located in a resort with a putting green, cyber cafe and spa, a newly built property
£161,150

4 | with a garden | one minute from the shops, 17 minutes from Disney World | not located on a main road | room for parking, with a garage

---

$298,000   CODE FLC
KISSIMMEE
Located in a private community, a modern home with all amenities on site
£163,900

4 | with a garden | situated only 15 minutes from Disney World | not located on a main road | room for parking, with a garage

PRICE GUIDE

135

■ **CENTRAL FLORIDA**

$300,000 – $360,000
(£165,000–£198,000)

Ideally situated garden homes offering all mod cons

$311,990   CODE ESC
ORLANDO
Located close to the local schools and restaurants, in affordable gated community
£171,945

4 | with a small garden | all amenities on site | not located on a main road | room for parking, with a garage

$337,900   CODE ESC
DAVENPORT
A stunning two-storey house set in a community only 10 minutes from Disney World
£185,845

5 | with a large garden | all amenities on site | not located on a main road | room for parking, with a garage

$342,300   CODE WOF
ORLANDO
Located in a development on Highway 27, this home features a pool and all mod cons
£188,265

4 | with a garden | situated close to Kissimmee and Orlando | not located on a main road | room for parking, with a garage

$360,000   CODE DRV
DAVENPORT
A detached villa, with a private pool and a spacious living area, close to Disney World
£198,000

5 | with a large garden | situated close to amenities | not located on a main road | room for parking

$360,000   CODE FLC
KISSIMMEE
Set on a lake and enjoying a swimming pool and spa, only 10 minutes from Disney
£198,000

4 | with a garden | situated 3 minutes from shops | not located on a main road | room for parking, with a garage

PRICE GUIDE

Orlando, Florida
Buying made easy...

- **Comprehensive range of quality new apartments, town homes and villas, all close to Disney**
- **English owned and operated UK and Florida offices**
- **Low cost, no obligation, one to one viewing tours**
- **Advice and assistance with financing your purchase**
- **Assistance with rental and management**
- **In house legal services**
- **Foreign currency exchange assistance**

...from the initial viewing tour through to the enforcement of after sales service beyond completion, we're on hand to offer all the advice and assistance you need!

GATEWAY
OVERSEAS HOMES

t: 01347 825650 w: gatewaygroup.co.uk
e: overseashomes@gatewaygroup.co.uk

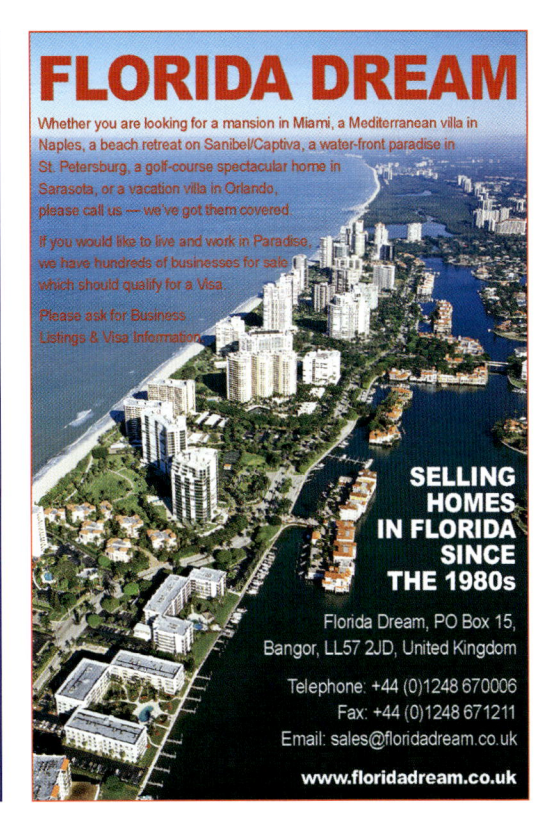

FLORIDA DREAM

Whether you are looking for a mansion in Miami, a Mediterranean villa in Naples, a beach retreat on Sanibel/Captiva, a water-front paradise in St. Petersburg, a golf-course spectacular home in Sarasota, or a vacation villa in Orlando, please call us — we've got them covered.

If you would like to live and work in Paradise, we have hundreds of businesses for sale which should qualify for a Visa.

Please ask for Business Listings & Visa Information

SELLING HOMES IN FLORIDA SINCE THE 1980s

Florida Dream, PO Box 15, Bangor, LL57 2JD, United Kingdom

Telephone: +44 (0)1248 670006
Fax: +44 (0)1248 671211
Email: sales@floridadream.co.uk

www.floridadream.co.uk

Kissimee Example:
4 bedroom, 3 bathroom $330,000
(£183,000 @ $1.80 to £1)

- Luxurious detached homes from $250,000 (£139,000 @ $1.80 to £1)
- Locations include Orlando/Kissimmee and the Gulf Coast
- Set in quiet, landscaped communities close to shops, restaurants and the major attractions
- Excellent rental income opportunities
- Full property management services
- Personalised inspection visits arranged
- We have 16 years' experience in the sale of Florida property
- Rental Homes prices: 3 bedroom with pool from £480 per week
  4 bedroom with pool from £500 per week

THE FLORIDA CONNECTION LTD

"We are an independent UK company who specialise in the sale and letting of Quality Florida Property"

Kissimmee example:
3 bedroom, 2 bathroom $294,000
(£163,000 @ $1.80 to £1)

For Brochure: Tel 01293 615034   Fax 01293 553884   E-mail floridaconnection@talk21.com

■ CENTRAL FLORIDA

$360,000 – $385,000
(£198,000–£211,750)

Beautiful, large family homes in newly built and luxurious resorts

$370,000 — CODE FLC

KISSIMMEE
Located in a newly built development, a modern property with a swimming pool
£203,500

🛏 6 | 🌼 with a garden | 🛍 situated two minutes from the shops | 🚫 not located on a main road | 🏠 room for parking, with a garage

---

$378,290 — CODE ESC

REUNION
Set amidst a stunning golfing community, with all amenities onsite, close to Disney
£208,060

🛏 3 | 🌼 with a communal garden | 🛍 all amenities onsite | 🚫 not located on a main road | 🏠 room for parking

---

$379,900 — CODE WOF

KISSIMMEE
A detached property located close to Disney World, with a swimming pool
£208,945

🛏 6 | 🌼 with a garden | 🛍 situated close to amenities | 🚫 not located on a main road | 🏠 room for parking, with a garage

---

$380,000 — CODE ULV

ORLANDO
A single family home, including a swimming pool, situated in a gated golfing community
£209,000

🛏 3 | 🌼 with a small garden | 🛍 situated in the town centre | 🚫 located on a main road | 🏠 room for parking, with a garage

---

$382,900 — CODE TFS

ORLANDO
This property comes with a fully fitted kitchen and has a swimming pool and sun deck
£210,595

🛏 5 | 🌼 with a large garden and a sun deck | 🛍 situated close to town | 🚫 not located on a main road | 🏠 room for parking

PRICE GUIDE

138

CENTRAL FLORIDA

$385,000—$450,000
(£211,750–£247,500)

Fantastic lifestyles for sale, with executive and custom-built homes

$385,000+ CODE COL
OSCEOLA COUNTY
Lovely houses situated in a luxurious, new resort, featuring 3 golf courses and a spa.
£211,750

various | with a private garden | all amenities onsite | not located on a main road | room for parking

$396,990 CODE ESC
REUNION
Homes on golfing development, close to Disney World, offering an active lifestyle
£218,345

4 | with a garden | situated close to amenities | located on a main road | room for parking

$398,700 CODE JUF
DAVENPORT
Executive homes located in a gated development, with a swimming pool and jacuzzi
£219,285

5 | with a garden | situated only 10 minutes from Disney World | not located on a main road | room for parking, with a two-car garage

$449,000 CODE BHG
HYDE PARK
A beautifully renovated bungalow, with a luxurious interior and garden with sun deck
£246,950

3 | with a large, fenced garden | close to shops and amenities | not located on a main road | room for parking

$469,000 CODE BHG
CELEBRATION
A custom-built home, well located, with a separate study and family room with fireplace
£257,950

3 | with a large garden | situated close to the town centre | not located on a main road | room for parking, with a two-car carport

PRICE GUIDE

139

■ CENTRAL FLORIDA

$450,000–$920,000
(£247,500–£506,000)

Glamorous homes in spectacular settings, with all amenities on your doorstep

$580,000+   CODE COL
OSCEOLA COUNTY
Stunning, luxury homes in a 2,300 acre resort with conservation areas and several lakes
£319,000

4/5 | with a large garden | all amenities on site | not located on a main road | room for parking

---

$629,900   CODE BHG
CELEBRATION
Recently decorated, this home offers all amenities, including a swimming pool and a spa
£329,945

4 | with a large garden | situated close to town | not located on a main road | room for parking, with a garage

$699,000   CODE BHG
CELEBRATION
A luxurious property, customised and built in a colonial style, close to the town centre
£385,000

3 | with a large garden | situated close to the town centre | not located on a main road | room for parking

---

$799,000   CODE BAL
ORLANDO
A modern home, set within minutes of attractions, offering all mod cons and furnishings
£439,450

3 | with a large garden | situated within minutes of shops and attractions | not located on a main road | room for parking

---

$921,000+   CODE COL
ORLANDO
Large detached houses in a spectacular seaside resort with amazing leisure facilities
£506,550

4+ | with a large garden | all amenities on site | not located on a main road | room for parking

PRICE GUIDE

140

CENTRAL FLORIDA ■

$920,000+
(£506,000)

Magnificent, well appointed, detached properties offering all conceivable amenities

---

$921,000+ — CODE COL
ORLANDO
Spacious homes in an exclusive ocean-side community with a large marina and beach
£506,550

4+ | with a garden | all amenities onsite | not located on a main road | room for parking

---

$999,000 — CODE MED
CELEBRATION
With a waterfront view, this pristine mansion has a swimming pool and gazebo
£549,450

4 | with a large garden | situated close to amenities | not located on a main road | room for parking, with a three-car garage

---

$1,250,000 — CODE MED
CELEBRATION
Located on a prestigious estate, a stunning mansion with waterfront views and a pool
£687,500

6 | with a large garden | situated close to amenities | not located on a main road | room for parking, with a three-car garage

---

$2,750,000 — CODE BHG
CELEBRATION
Offering all conceivable amenities, a stunning mansion, with a cinema and swimming pool
£1,512,500

7 and guest quarters | with a balcony, and a garden with a fountain | situated close to the town centre | not located on a main road | ample room for parking

---

TURN TO PAGE 232 TO FIND THE CONTACT DETAILS FOR THE AGENT OF YOUR CHOICE

PRICE GUIDE

141

Reach for the stars, with Ultra Villas...

Florida – 'A sunshine state of mind'

All year round sunshine, pristine golf courses, miles of rolling beaches and the cosmopolitan cities of Miami, Tampa & Orlando are just a phone call away.

Properties are very affordable with excellent capital growth and rental opportunities. We understand that your needs are as individual as the properties we represent and as independent agents we will provide completely unbiased advice on your choice of home-from-home. A personal service is guaranteed. So why not join us on a 'try before you buy' viewing-visit and get into a sunshine state of mind.

A typical Floridian Villa
Prices start from around £125,000 for
3 bedroom villa with 2 bathrooms and pool

An Award Winning Company

BEST INTERNATIONAL USE OF TECHNOLOGY
GOLD WINNER

BEST SPANISH APARTMENT
GOLD WINNER

BEST INTERNATIONAL LUXURY DEVELOPMENT
SILVER WINNER

Ultra Villas
FLORIDA
International Estate Agents & Constructors

A founder member of FOPDAC
The Federation of Overseas Property Developers, Agents & Consultants.

Ultra Villas Limited, Clarendon House, 42 Clarence Street, Cheltenham, GL50 3PI
Tel: +44(0)1242 221700 Fax: +44(0)1242 226388 Email: post@ultravillas.co.uk

**To purchase your own property in Florida or Spain,
call today on 0845 1305464** (quoting FBGAUG) **or visit www.ultravillas.com**

The South East

Opulent Palm Beach, fine boutiques and miles of canals

- **Population** 3.2 million
- **Population increase** Between 1992–2002 the population grew by 23.8%
- **Migration** 153,299 people migrated to the South East between 2000–2002 of which 76,701 were international migrants
- **Median age** 38.3; the state average is 38.7
- **Median home price** $197,000 in the South East, 28.4% higher than the state average of $141,100
- This is a hugely affluent market offering very luxurious properties
- Property costs 22% more than the average cost of property in Florida

Profile 144

Hotspots 146

Price Guide

$100,000–$230,000 150

$230,000–$500,000 151

$500,000–$1,000,000 152

$1,000,000–$3,000,000 153

$3,000,000–$10,000,000 154

$10,000,000 + 156

THE SOUTH EAST

GETTING THERE

Air There are a limited number of airlines that fly directly from the UK into the South East and the main airport is Miami. **American Airlines** (0845 778 9789; www.aa.com) flies directly into Miami from Heathrow and from there offers connections to Fort Lauderdale and West Palm Beach. **British Airways** (0870 850 9850; www.ba.com) flies directly into Miami from Heathrow and again can organise connections to Fort Lauderdale and West Palm Beach with **American Airlines** (see above). **Continental Airlines** (0845 607 6760; www.continental.com) does not offer any direct flights to Florida but flies via Newark to Miami, Fort Lauderdale and West Palm Beach. **Virgin Atlantic** (0870 574 7747; www.virgin-atlantic.com) flies directly to Miami from Heathrow and from there connections are available to Fort Lauderdale and West Palm Beach.

Rail Amtrak (+ 1-800 872 7245; www.amtrak.com) offers mainline services all along the eastern coastline.

Road Both US 1 and I-95 run along the eastern coastline from both the north and south and the A1A runs directly to the coastline off of these. This links Fort Lauderdale in the south right up to Palm Beach and beyond.

Coach Greyhound buses (+1 800 231 2222; www.greyhound.com) serves Fort Lauderdale, Delray Beach, Hollywood, Fort Myers, Sebastian and West Palm Beach.

Area profile

THE GOLD AND TREASURE COASTS RUN MIDWAY DOWN THE PENINSULA'S east coast and their names are thought to derive from a Spanish shipwreck in 1715 that spilled its cargo of gold, treasure and jewels into the ocean.

Hollywood is the most southerly destination of note primarily as it houses Port Everglade – the second largest cruise port in the world after near neighbour Miami – and an international airport. That is not to say the city should be dismissed; Hollywood boasts seven miles of fabulous white sandy beaches, Florida's only oceanfront broadwalk and serves as the headquarters for the Seminole Indian tribe.

Further up the Gold Coast is the wealthy residential resort of Fort Lauderdale. Scored by hundreds of miles of waterways and canals, the city claims to be the largest yacht basin in America. The Intracoastal Waterway makes travel between Fort Lauderdale's opulent homes and chic recreational areas a pleasure, though as a means of getting around, water taxi is rivalled by a drive down the spectacular A1A coast road.

Continuing north up this road brings the driver to Palm Beach County, so-called because 20,000 coconuts were planted by early settlers. As well as a proliferation of palm trees, the area is home to in excess of 160 golf courses and a fascinating cultural scene encompassing everything from modern dance to watercolour painting. The first city within its borders is Boca Raton which has numerous pretty parks and plenty of water sport activities. Unusually, Boca manages to retain a small town feel despite its prosperity and popularity. It's home to many blue chip technology companies as well as some of the world's best-known tennis players.

Of course, the jewel of the Gold Coast is Palm Beach itself; rich, beautiful and vibrant. There is simply nothing you can't do here, from sports to beauty treatments. The shopping is out of this world. Worth Avenue has its own valet service and price tags are rarely displayed but, as the old adage goes, if you have to ask… After hours, over 2,000 restaurants entice diners while cafes, bars, theatres, galleries and discos continue the entertainment long into the night.

West Palm Beach's historic downtown streets and waterfront have been recently renovated and property prices are rising rapidly

THE SOUTH EAST

North of Palm Beach, the Treasure Coast offers a more laidback approach to life and is dotted with small towns inhabited by 'real folk'. Port St Lucie is situated in the heart of the area and offers a taste of old Florida. Horse rides along deserted beaches, paddling down tranquil rivers and hiking through nature reserves are all on the itinerary for visitors. Down-to-earth Sebastian is noted for its excellent fishing, surfing and watersports.

The economy and housing market

As you might expect from two coastlines littered with upmarket resorts, both the Gold and Treasure Coasts are very wealthy areas. Dubbed the 'Internet Coast', the area is at the cutting edge of advances in voice, video and data technology; the first IBM PC was developed in Boca Raton in the early 1980s. Other communication advantages, including the proximity of several international airports and deep-sea water ports, appeal to many businesses that make a base for themselves here. The local infrastructure is also excellent with roads continually undergoing improvement.

Accordingly, the cost of living on the South East coast of Florida is higher than average and this extends to property. Palm Beach was recently ranked as one of the richest cities in the US by Worth Magazine, which might go some way to explaining the median sales price for a family home: a staggering $2 million and an annual price increase of 27 per cent. Boca Raton boasts similar price tags. Fort Lauderdale contains costly property, too, with price tags sitting considerably above the state average. Demand is high and supply is dwindling which has led to property values in the city shooting up an estimated 70 per cent in six years. Of course, some outlying areas are cheaper; a hot tip at the moment is fast–growing Palm Beach Gardens where homes can be found from $200,000.

Though less developed, the Treasure Coast is hot on the heels of its Gold Coast neighbour with homebuilding growing 92 per cent in 2003 – the fastest in the country on a percentage basis. Prices are comparatively low at the moment – the median sales price in St Lucie is $141,600, just below the state average – but as properties become more expensive and hard to come by on the Gold Coast, boom time could be just around the corner. Realtors working over both stretches of coastline report that places along the Intracoastal Waterway and homes in gated golf communities are the properties that have seen the most capital appreciation.

Social groups

Residents of the Gold and Treasure Coasts can essentially be defined as 'wealthy'. Buyers are people who are often involved in business in the area. They desire luxurious accommodation, hence the predominance of gated communities here. Though primarily the preserve of rich Americans, UK buyers are opening their eyes to the charms of Florida's South East coast and other international families too are choosing to relocate here. ●

Fort Lauderdale's canals, which were dredged in the 1920s, can be traversed using the water buses and taxis

Palm Beach ranks as one of the richest cities in the whole of the United States

THE SOUTH EAST		LONDON		THE SOUTH EAST		LONDON	
Dec	23	Dec	7	Dec	69	Dec	81
Nov	22	Nov	10	Nov	110	Nov	78
Oct	25	Oct	14	Oct	130	Oct	70
Sept	27	Sept	19	Sept	194	Sept	65
Aug	28	Aug	21	Aug	158	Aug	62
July	28	July	22	July	144	July	59
June	27	June	20	June	170	June	58
May	25	May	17	May	119	May	57
April	25	April	13	April	72	April	56
March	20	March	10	March	84	March	64
Feb	18	Feb	7	Feb	64	Feb	72
Jan	18	Jan	6	Jan	79	Jan	77

Average monthly temperature °C (Celsius)

Average monthly rainfall mm (millimetres)

Florida Climate Center (www.coaps.fsu.edu/climate_center)

AVERAGE HOUSE SALE PRICES

Hotspot	2-bed	3-bed	4-bed	5-bed
Palm Beach	$651K (£355K)	$822K (£448K)	$3M (£1.66M)	$5.3M (£2.9M)
Fort Lauderdale	$365K (£199K)	$424K (£231K)	$- (£-)	$- (£-)
Port St Lucie	$142K (£78K)	$234K (£128K)	$295K (£161K)	$- (£-)
Hollywood	$150K (£83K)	$407K (£224K)	$586K (£319K)	$1.2M (£651K)
Boca Raton	$376K (£205K)	$1.22M (£663K)	$1.44M (£786K)	$2.87M (£1.5M)

■ THE SOUTH EAST

Property hotspots

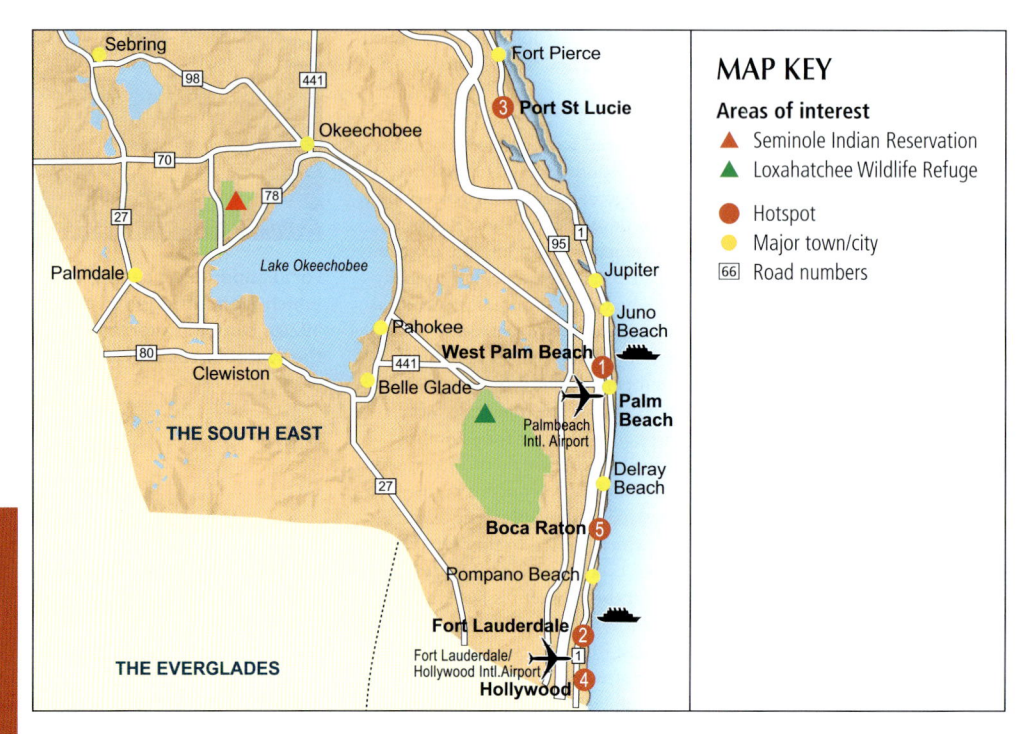

MAP KEY
Areas of interest
▲ Seminole Indian Reservation
▲ Loxahatchee Wildlife Refuge
● Hotspot
● Major town/city
66 Road numbers

1. West Palm Beach

ESSENTIALS ■ **Pop** 82,103 ■ **Airports** Palm Beach International, FL 33401, Tel: +1 561 471-7481 ■ Fort Lauderdale Hollywood International, 320 Terminal Drive, FLL, FL 33315, Tel: +1 954 359-1200 ■ **Tax** Property tax per $1,000; $17

KEY FACTS

■ **Schools** Educational Services Center, 3300 Forest Hill Boulevard, West Palm Beach, FL 33406, Tel: +1 561 434-8000 ■ Royal Palm Beach Community High School, 3505 Shiloh Dr, West Palm Beach, FL 33407-6870, Tel: +1 561 753-4007 ■ Coastal Middle & Senior High School, 730 5th St, West Palm Beach, FL 33401-4145, Tel: +1 561 842-6349
■ **Medical** Good Samaritan Medical Center, 1309 S Flagler Dr, West Palm Beach, FL 33401-6736, Tel: +1 561 655-5111 ■ Columbia Hospital, 2201 45th St, West Palm Beach, FL ZipCode, Tel: +1 561 845-0021
■ **Rentals** A popular area for rentals, excellent for investment ■ The average rental for a two-bed apartment is $500-$600 per week
■ **Pros** With the home of the PGA at Palm Beach Gardens, Palm Beach has 15 golf courses ■ Home of the Grapefruit League, fans from all over come every year to watch baseball ■ Spectacular snorkelling and award winning scuba diving ■ Palm Beach County enjoys mild tropical temperatures all year-round with an excellent quality of life
■ **Cons** Liable to hurricanes between June and November ■ The seasonal population swells from 10,000 to 30,000 during the summer months ■ The median price of housing has risen by 27% in the past ■ Construction and growth is very evident

When the small, exclusive island town of Palm Beach was undergoing construction in the 1920s West Palm Beach, on the other side of Lake Worth, housed the building workers. Naturally, it was always the more rowdy of the two locations but in recent years the city has been refurbished; its historic downtown streets and waterfront areas have been restored and revitalised, and new condos, restaurants and shops are being built. West Palm Beach is also home to the Norton Museum of Art, regarded by many as the finest in the state. Paintings by Cézanne, Matisse, Picasso and Jackson Pollock are the highlights, although there is a great deal of 20th century American art and ancient artefacts from China.

The area is extremely expensive compared with the average cost of housing throughout the state. However two-bedroom, single storey homes in a gated community are available for under $200,000, and large, four-bed, new-build homes are on the market for under $500,000. New executive homes on Cote Azur Drive in an executive country club setting are selling for over $1 million. As the area becomes more desirable, demand is growing and prices are rising. With Palm Beach, one of the most desirable real estate markets in the US on the other side of Lake Worth, West Palm Beach can cling to its shirt-tails. ●

146

THE SOUTH EAST

2. Fort Lauderdale

ESSENTIALS ■ **Pop** 152,397 ■ **Airport** Fort Lauderdale Hollywood International, 320 Terminal Drive, FLL, Fort Lauderdale, FL 33315, Tel: +1 954 359-1200, Fax: +1 954 359-0027 ■ **Tax** Property tax per $1,000; $16

In the 1920s, Charles Green Rhodes purchased a large parcel of swampland, dredged it into canals and used the fill to develop peninsulas, providing prime real estate and creating the 'Venice of America' in the process. Indeed, the process used was not dissimilar to that used in Italy. In the 1930s, Fort Lauderdale became a popular venue for Collegiate Aquatic Forums and swimmers came from campuses all over the country to compete. Over the years, students from across the US continued to visit the city every spring and in the 1980s, it was attracting over 300,000. The Spring Break crowd has since diminished to more manageable levels.

Today Fort Lauderdale is a culturally rich and cosmopolitan city of just over 150,000 inhabitants, and the waterways remain the dominant feature. It's also a popular stop-off point for cruise ships.

Development land in the region is now at a premium, so the trend is for old homes to be destroyed and replaced. Prices for detached homes rose around 20 per cent last year. The most desirable areas to live are the peninsulas, known as The Isles, where houses can cost well in excess of $10 million, but the suburbs offer a range of properties under $200,000. Demand is also high in the $200–$400,000 bracket and locals agents point out that it shows no sign of slowing. ●

KEY FACTS

■ **Schools** Broward Community College, 225 E Las Olas Blvd, Fort Lauderdale, FL 33301-2208, Tel: +1 954 201-7465 ■ Larkdale Elementary School, 3250 NW 12th Pl, Fort Lauderdale, FL 33311-4942, Tel: +1 954 797-4690 ■ Cypress Bay High, 3600 Nw 5th Ct, Fort Lauderdale, FL 33311-7546, Tel: +1 954 358-6768
■ **Medical** Atlantic Shores Hospital, 4545 N Federal Highway, Fort Lauderdale, FL 33308, Tel: +1 954 771-2711 ■ Fort Lauderdale Hospital, 1601 East Las Olas Blvd, Fort Lauderdale, FL 33301-2357, Tel: +1 954 463-4321
■ **Rentals** You can expect to pay around $600 per week for a two-bedroom property out of season
■ **Pros** Great for snorkellers and divers, offering tropical sea life, sunken ships, and coral reef ■ Historical region ■ Year-round festivals and recreational events ■ Previously a tourism-based economy, Fort Lauderdale now supports a diverse range of industries ■ Good location for investors with a healthy property market and good appreciation
■ **Cons** Demand has resulted in a limited amount of available property ■ Prices in this area are continuing to rise, making it a seller's market

3. Port St Lucie

ESSENTIALS ■ **Pop** 88,769 ■ **Airport** Fort Lauderdale Hollywood International, 320 Terminal Drive, FLL, Fort Lauderdale, FL 33315; Tel: +1 954 359-1200, Fax: +1 954 359-0027 ■ **Tax** Property tax per $1,000: $18

Port St Lucie wasn't incorporated as a city until 1961 but now it's one of the fastest growing cities in the whole of the United States. Primarily a residential area, its population grew by an amazing 60 per cent in the 1990s. Essentially, it's a new city – more than 25 per cent of its housing has been developed since 1995. While it lacks the historical charm of many of its neighbours, it's a good proposition for young families and it provides some of the most affordable housing in the state. More than 4,000 single family units are springing up rapidly every year and there are extensive gated developments; St Lucie West, a gated golf development, covers 4,700 acres. Only half of the city's land has been developed thus far and if development continues at the current pace, in the long term its population could reach 250,000.

The building boom means there are many types of property available. A large three-bed home with a pool and a view of the golf course in the exclusive PGA Village (owned and run by the PGA itself) costs around $550,000, but similar sized homes in less exclusive suburbs sell for less than half this price. Natural attractions include the 6,000 acre preserve 'the Savannas' and the Indian River Lagoon Estuary, and there are beaches six miles away. ●

KEY FACTS

■ **Schools** St. Lucie County, 4204 Okeechobee Rd, Fort Pierce, FL 34947-7299, Tel: +1 772-429-3600
■ **Medical** St Lucie Medical Center, 1800 SE Tiffany Avenue, Port St. Lucie, FL 34952, Tel: +1 772 335-4000, Fax: +1 772 398-360
■ **Rentals** The average weekly rate is $400 for a two-bedroom property
■ **Pros** Port St Lucie is one of the fastest growing counties in the state of Florida ■ With building lots still affordable, it's experiencing a building boom ■ Contains the last undeveloped beaches in the area ■ Excellent area for investment with record levels of appreciation ■ The average property price is only $142,000; the state average is $141,100
■ **Cons** Port St Lucie itself could be considered overdeveloped ■ The market is destined to slow and begin tailing off ■ This is essentially a seller's market and not favourable to buyers

THE SOUTH EAST

4. Hollywood

ESSENTIALS ■ **Pop** 139,357 ■ **Airport** Fort Lauderdale Hollywood International, 320 Terminal Drive, FLL, Fort Lauderdale, FL 33315, Tel: +1 954 359-1200 ■ **Tax** Property tax rate per $1,000: $16

KEY FACTS

■ **Schools** McArthur High School, 6501 Hollywood Blvd, Hollywood, FL 33024-7647, Tel: +1 954 985-3150 ■ Hollywood Central Elementary school, 1700 Monroe St, Hollywood, FL 33020-5539, Tel: +1 954 926-0930 ■ Driftwood Middle School, 2751 NW 70th Ter, FL 33024-2853, Tel: +1 954 985-3100
■ **Medical** Hollywood Pavilion Hospital, 1201 N 37th Ave, Hollywood, FL 33021-5414, Tel: +1 954 962-1355 ■ Memorial Hospital, 3501 Johnson St, Hollywood, FL 33021-5421, Tel: +1 954 987-2000
■ **Rentals** Strong rentals market ■ Low interest rates are attracting buyers with a range of budgets ■ A four-bed property costs an average of $550 a week for low season, and $710 peak season
■ **Pros** Racial diversity, cultural variety, and a blend of old and young ■ Miami Airport and the Port of Miami less than 25 miles away ■ Downtown area has been renovated ■ Located on the beachfront and with the vibrancy of a thriving city, Hollywood offers everything with sumptuous shopping and party life to a quiet retirement lifestyle ■ Low interest rates are fuelling the local property market
■ **Cons** Properties are available but those priced correctly sell very quickly ■ Prices are up on resale condos, homes and townhomes ■ Inventory is slow due to limited development

Hollywood was designed in 1921 and grew rapidly into a beautifully planned city with a fabulous beach casino and high class hotel. The casino, built at a cost of $250,000, comprised an Olympic-sized swimming pool, 80 showers and over 800 dressing rooms. Five years later it was in ruins after a vicious hurricane ripped through the centre. It slowly recovered and after rapid growth in the 1950s and 1960s, it's now a multicultural city with an extremely stable population; it has only risen by 15,000 in the past 30 years, which is pretty amazing when compared with the general trend of massive expansion in Florida. Recently, the historic park Young's Circle and the broadwalk along Hollywood Beach have been renovated.

Nicknamed 'Diamond of the Gold Coast', Hollywood is home to fine beaches and 1,500 acres of mangrove preserves, and it's a popular resort for many French Canadians who spend winter in Florida. Hollywood is seeing significantly less new real estate development than some areas of the Gold Coast, notably neighbouring Port St Lucie. Prices are high in Hollywood Lakes on the Intracoastal Waterway (up to $3 million for a large plot), but further inland the suburbs offer cheaper options. The median price in the district is around $150,000 plus, and most of the properties are over 20 years old. ●

5. Boca Raton

ESSENTIALS ■ **Pop** 77,411 ■ **Airports** Palm Beach, West Palm Beach, FL 33401, Tel: + 1 561 471-7481 ■ Fort Lauderdale-Hollywood, 320 Terminal Drive, FLL, Fort Lauderdale, FL 33315, Tel: +1 954 359-1200 ■ **Tax** Property tax per $1,000; $17

KEY FACTS

■ **Schools** Spanish River High School, 5100 Jog Rd, Boca Raton, FL 33428-2215, Tel: +1 561 241-2200 ■ Eagles Landing Middle School, 19500 Coral Ridge Dr, Boca Raton, FL 33428-6521, Tel: +1 561 470-7000 ■ Waters Edge Elementary School, Boca Raton, FL 33428, Tel: +1 561 883-8070
■ **Medical** Boca Raton community hospital inc, 800 Meadows Road, Boca Raton, FL 33486-2304, Tel: +1 561 955-4123 ■ West Boca Medical Center, 77070 W Palmetto Park Rd, Boca Raton, FL 33433-3411, Tel: +1 561 620-8707
■ **Rentals** A two-bedroom property costs between $600 and $1,500 per week, with higher rates during the winter ■ A world-renowned resort with a healthy rentals market
■ **Pros** With its many country clubs, high fashion stores and malls it's one of the most sought after areas of Florida ■ Lush scenery and aquatic activities ■ Primarily a retirement location ■ Healthy economic market, ideal for those with business interests
■ **Cons** Decrease in new construction due to less vacant land for new home developments ■ High-profile residents push living costs and housing prices up ■ Low inventory means the market remains favourable to the seller

Boca Raton was originally planned as a world class resort in 1925. The town council commissioned architect Addison Mizner, noted for his work in Palm Beach, to design a resort hotel and town hall. Despite a real estate crash in 1926, his Spanish-influenced architecture remains intact; his hotel is now the exclusive Boca Raton Resort and Club.

Although the city was little more than a hamlet for many years, a boom in the 1960s encouraged new investment and now Boca Raton is one of the most affluent cities in the state with a population of over 75,000. Its parks are outstanding, and the array of restaurants, shops and cultural facilities (including 145 golf courses in the area) ensure Boca Raton is one of the Gold Coast's most sought-after cities.

The median price for a property is well over $250,000 and median age for inhabitants just over 42 years. Lakefront, gated communities with courses – of which there are many – demand premium prices, and large waterfront properties stretch into many millions. A smaller plot comprising of a four-bed home with a pool in the Palm Beach Farms suburb costs around $400,000. The further west you travel in this sprawling city, the cheaper the real estate, but with less vacant land for new developments, prices are rising for older homes. ●

YOUR FLORIDA COASTAL CONNECTION
From North Florida to the Florida Keys and The Gulf Coast

KATIE STACK
Licensed Realtor and Mortgage Broker
BOCA RATON, FLORIDA

RE/MAX Services

Offering beachfront, single family, high rise and golf communities — from £55,000 to £22million

ARRANGING FOR IMPORTANT REAL ESTATE SERVICES:
- INVESTMENT PROPERTIES • PROPERTY SALES • INSPECTIONS
- HOMES TO LET • MORTGAGES • LEGAL SERVICES • INSURANCE
- TITLE SERVICES

Telephone: 001 561 271 8281 Fax: 001 561 391 6205
Email: katiestack@adelphia.net

'On parle français'

35 YEARS IN FLORIDA

AMERICAN FIRST REALTY
AND INVESTMENT CORPORATION

CENTRAL FLORIDA INVESTMENT PROPERTIES

★ Independent Realty Co. for personal service
★ We negotiate the best deal for you at no cost to you
★ Full package of support services and guaranteed rental schemes
★ Resale properties from $220k

NEW DEVELOPMENTS
Zoned for short-term rental & within 10 minutes of Disney

Caribe Cove 2 & 3 bedroom condiminium resort
Tuscany 3, 4 & 5 bedroom homes within gated community
Calabria 3, 4 & 5 bedroom Estate Homes with Italian theme

For further information, prices and waiting list, contact Charlotte on 020 7624 8700 or email floridasun@btconnect.com

www.a-f-realty.com

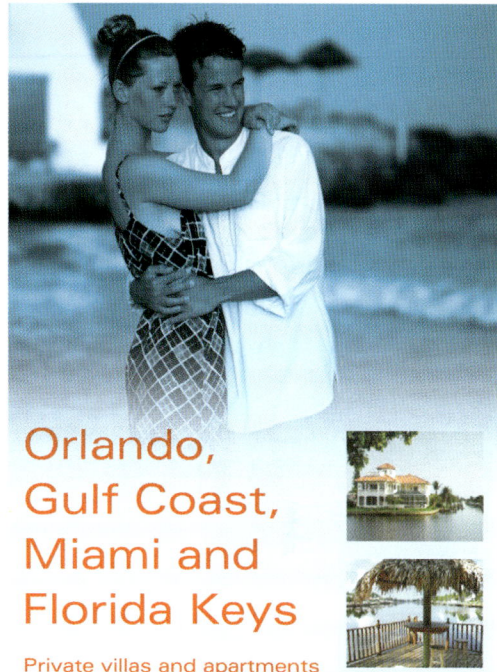

Orlando, Gulf Coast, Miami and Florida Keys

Private villas and apartments from 2-7 bedrooms for sale

- Second homes and rental investment properties
- Full on site management programme
- International rental programme
- Easy financing up to 80% of purchase price
- 15 years experience in the Florida property market
- Our comprehensive service is entirely FREE to buyers

Holiday in Private Villas, Apartments, Boutique Hotels & Resorts

- Stay at 1, 2 or more locations with flexible arrival days
- On airport car rental with no one-way drop off fees

Call for brochure or details of our regional exhibitions

Living the dream....

Select Destinations
01782 394546
(Ireland) 028 9048 9660
www.selectdestinations.com

■ **THE SOUTH EAST**

$100,000—$230,000
(£55,000–£126,500)

As well as luxurious mansions, the South East can offer some real bargains

PRICE GUIDE

$126,500　　　　　　　　　　　　　　　　　　　　　　　　CODE MFJ
DELRAY BEACH
A condo, set in a development and enjoying a clubhouse, theatre and swimming pool
£69,575

- 2　with a balcony　situated close to town　not located on a main road
- with private parking

$152,000　　　　　　　　　　　　　　　　　　　　　　　　CODE MFJ
LANTANA
Located in a small community, this townhouse is ideal as a family holiday home
£83,600

- 2　with a large garden　all amenities on site　not located on a main road
- room for parking

$188,000　　　　　　　　　　　　　　　　　　　　　　　　CODE MFJ
BOCA RATON
A townhouse set in a popular development, with views over the Intracoastal Waterway
£103,400

- 2　with a small garden　situated close to the town centre　not located on a main road　room for parking

---

$188,000　　　　　　　　　　　　　　　　　　　　　　　　CODE MFJ
PALM BEACH
With beach access, this condo is located in a development with a pool and a gym
£103,400

- 4　with a garden　situated close all amenities　located on a main road
- room for parking

$229,900　　　　　　　　　　　　　　　　　　　　　　　　CODE BAL
LAKE WORTH
An excellent investment opportunity, a triplex apartment, located close to the beach
£126,400

- 3　with a small garden　situated close to the town centre　located on a main road　room for parking

THE SOUTH EAST

$230,000–$500,000
(£126,500–£275,000)

Away from the glitz of the waterfront, some real bargains can be found

$275,000
CODE MFJ
BOCA RATON
Ideal as a family home, this property has views over a lake and a swimming pool
£151,250

3 | with a garden | within easy reach of amenities | not located on a main road | room for parking

$299,999
CODE BAL
COCONUT CREEK
Located in a modern community, a newly-built home, overlooking a nature preserve
£165,000

4 | with a garden | situated close to the town centre | not located on a main road | room for parking, with a two-car garage

$389,900+
CODE BAL
BOCA RATON
An outstanding townhouse, with a stunning lake view and secluded patio
£214,445

3 | with a large garden | situated close to town | not located on a main road | room for parking, with a garage

$459,000
CODE BAL
LIGHTHOUSE POINT
Recently upgraded, this house is extremely spacious and enjoys a landscaped garden
£252,450

3 | with a large garden | close to shops and amenities | not located on a main road | room for parking, with a two-car garage

$499,000+
CODE BAL
FORT LAUDERDALE
Offering penthouses, condos and villas, a luxury oceanfront development
£274,450

1+ | with a balcony and a communal garden | situated close to the town centre | located on a main road | room for parking

PRICE GUIDE

151

■ THE SOUTH EAST

$500,000 — $1,000,000
(£275,000–£550,000)

Waterfront townhouses and magnificent resale homes can be purchased for a bargain

PRICE GUIDE

$599,900   CODE BAL
BOYNTON
A beautifully renovated property with a large balcony and a pool, ideal for a family
£329,945

4 | with a large garden | situated close to amenities | not located on a main road
room for parking, with a two-car garage

$600,000+   CODE BAL
SOUTH PALM BEACH
Set on the Intracoastal Waterway, a prestigious community, with County Club facilities
£330,000

2+ | with spacious communal gardens | situated a mile from amenities and shops | not located on a main road | room for parking

$649,000   CODE BAL
POMPANO
Built in a Mediterranean style, a development of luxury townhouses, near the beach
£356,950

3 | with a sun deck | situated near the town centre | located on a main road
room for parking, with a two-car garage

$799,000   CODE BAL
HILLSBORO BEACH
A lovingly reconditioned property, with private access to the beach and a pool
£439,450

3 | with a large garden | situated close to amenities | not located on a main road
room for parking

$799,900   CODE BAL
HILLSBORO BEACH
Located on the Intracoastal Waterway, a luxurious townhouse with fabulous views
£439,945

3 | with a garden | situated close to the beach and amenities | not located on a main road | room for parking, with a two-car garage

THE SOUTH EAST

$1,000,000–$3,000,000
(£550,000–£1,650,000)

Those with deep pockets can choose from a host of sumptuous mansions

$1,950,000 — CODE SOT
WEST PALM BEACH
A recently renovated property, with a separate guest house and a swimming pool
£1,072,500

3 | with a large garden | close to shops and amenities | not located on a main road | room for parking, with a garage and car port

$1,975,000 — CODE SOT
PALM BEACH
Fully furnished, a modern townhouse residence, Mediterranean in style, with a pool
£1,086,250

4 | with a large, landscaped garden | situated a short drive from amenities | not located on a main road | room for parking, with a two-car garage

---

$2,270,000 — CODE JAT
NORTH PALM BEACH
A luxurious property, with marble floors throughout, and private docking space
£1,248,500

4 | with a large garden | situated on the waterfront close to amenities | not located on a main road | room for parking

---

$2,650,000 — CODE SOT
PALM BEACH
Set on the beachfront, with yacht dockage, an exclusive, fully furnished townhouse
£1,457,500

3 | with a large garden | situated close to all amenities | not located on a main road | room for parking, with a two-car garage

---

$2,995,000 — CODE JAT
MANALAPAN
Located on the waterfront, a stunning, custom-built house, complete with furnishings
£1,647,250

5 | with a large garden | situated close to amenities | not located on a main road | room for parking

PRICE GUIDE

153

■ THE SOUTH EAST

$3,000,000 — $10,000,000
(£1,650,000–£5,500,000)

Luxury is the byword for the discerning buyer with a large budget

PRICE GUIDE

$3,750,000   CODE SOT

WEST PALM BEACH
Overlooking the beach and Intracoastal Waterway, a luxurious condo development
£2,062,500

- 3 | with a large terrace | situated on the waterfront close to amenities
- located on a main road | room for parking

$5,300,000   CODE SOT

PALM BEACH
Built in a Mediterranean style, an elegant property with a patio and swimming pool
£2,915,000

- 4 | with a large garden | situated close to amenities | not located on a main road
- room for parking, with a garage

$5,500,000   CODE SOT

PALM BEACH
An island residence, fronting onto Lake Worth Lagoon, with a guest house
£3,025,000

- 5 | with a large garden | within walking distance of shops and amenities
- not located on a main road | room for parking, with a two-car garage

$6,900,000   CODE SOT

PALM BEACH
A stylish estate residence, located on the waterfront, fully furnished with a pool
£3,795,000

- 4 | with a large garden | situated a short drive from amenities | not located on a main road | room for parking, with a garage

---

$7,950,000   CODE SOT

PALM BEACH
A newly built family property, designed in an Italian style, with a separate guest house
£4,372,500

- 7 | with a large landscaped garden | situated close to amenities | not located on a main road | room for parking

ORLANDO FLORIDA

Vacation Homes, Villas and Condos

Coldwell Banker Team Realty is part of the largest real estate company in the U.S.A. with over 3,500 offices and should always be your first call when buying a holiday or investment home.

from **THE** *Florida Real Estate Specialists!*

Here is just a small sample of new homes available through **Coldwell Banker Team Realty**

Southern Dunes

Southern Dunes *From the* $110's
A new condominium community within Southern Dunes, one of the finest resort developments in the Orlando area with a world famous Golf Course and the condominiums overlook beautiful Lake Joe.

Sandy Ridge *From the* $250's
A super new development just fifteen minutes from Disney World and the other main attractions

Floridays Resort

Floridays Resort *From the* $230's
Enjoy the amenities of a world class resort as the owner of a Suite Apartment at Floridays Orlando Resort and receive outstanding rental income on your investment.

Sandy Ridge

Solana

Coldwell Banker Team Realty is pleased to introduce a new community just minutes from Walt Disney World™.

The Solana Resort will feature over two hundred vacation homes, along with state-of-the-art clubhouse facility in a gated community.

THE SOLANA CLUB CENTRE INCLUDES PLANS FOR:
- 4,000 sq.ft. clubhouse with sundry shop, cyber café, gathering area and snack bar
- Interactive children's water play area
- Large resort pool and spa
- Sand Volleyball court
- Putting green
- Recreation field

4 Bed with pool *From the* **$280's**

ALL PRICES CORRECT AT TIME OF GOING TO PRESS

COLDWELL BANKER
TEAM REALTY

THE Florida Real Estate Specialists!

Coldwell Banker Team Realty

116 Polo Park East Blvd.
Davenport FL 33897
Phone: +1 (863) 420-9404
Fax: +1 (863) 420-3104

EACH OFFICE IS INDEPENDENTLY OWNED AND OPERATED

Coldwell Banker Team Realty   Phone: **0871 780 1180**

www.ColdwellBankerTeamRealty.com

THE SOUTH EAST

$10,000,000+
(£5,500,000+)

Situated on Florida's most exclusive waterfront, most can only dream…

$12,500,000   CODE SOT

PALM BEACH
With stunning views and resting in landscaped grounds a truly luxurious property
£6,875,000

- 7   with a large garden   situated on the ocean front, close to all amenities
- not located on a main road   room for parking, with a garage

---

$13,200,000   CODE SOT

PALM BEACH
Directly situated on the ocean front, set in a private street, an elegant residence
£7,260,000

- 7   with a large garden   situated on the waterfront close to amenities
- not located on a main road   room for parking, with a garage

---

$27,900,000   CODE SOT

PALM BEACH
With a spectacular oceanfront view, located on a newly built estate, a luxurious home
£15,345,000

- 9   with a large landscaped garden   situated only minutes from the shops
- not located on a main road   room for parking, with a garage

---

$35,000,000   CODE SOT

PALM BEACH
Part of a desirable community, a newly built mansion, with a lake and ocean views
£19,250,000

- 9   with a large, landscaped garden   situated a short drive from amenities
- not located on a main road   room for parking, with a garage

---

$48,000,000   CODE SOT

PALM BEACH
Set on 475 feet of stunning coastline, a unique estate, with a pool and tennis courts
£26,400,000

- 7   with 6 acres   situated minutes from amenities   not located on a main road
- room for parking, with a garage

PRICE GUIDE

Thinking about property in Florida?

For FREE, immediate, in depth consumer information, facts and case studies on the pitfalls to avoid when buying property and living in Florida, contact us today.

www.FloridaPropertyFacts.com
Andrew@floridapropertyfacts.com

0871 222 1745 UK • 941 966 3426 USA

COLDWELL BANKER

The only British group specializing in The Gulf Coast of Florida with Coldwell Banker — the largest Real Estate Company in America — specializing in Sarasota, Siesta Key, Longboat Key, Venice, Rotonda, Naples, Marco, Fort Myers, Fort Lauderdale, Miami and St. Petes from a uniquely British perspective.

Mortgages are available for your Florida Home

Obtain complete, up to date information on available mortgage programmes from a uniquely British perspective.

www.Lynxbanc.com • sparnell@Lynxbanc.com
0207 681 2653 UK • 561 392 8044 USA

ANGLO AMERICAN

The only British owned, Florida based mortgage company specializing in British nationals since 1992.

BUYING IN FLORIDA?

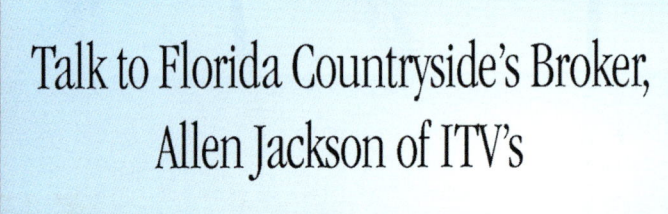

Talk to Florida Countryside's Broker, Allen Jackson of ITV's

'I Want That House'

Telephone 08456 444 747

www.floridacountryside.com

FLORIDA COUNTRYSIDE

THE EVERGLADES

The Everglades

An ecological wonder, exotic wildlife and outdoor pursuits

- **Population** 2.35 million
- **Population increase** Between 1992-2002 the population grew by 29.1%, a total of 53,000 people
- **Migration** 4,274 people migrated to the Everglades area in 2003
- **Median age** 40.3, the state average is 38.7
- **Median house price** $121,200

Profile **160**

Hotspots **162**

Price Guide

$100,000–$145,000	**164**
$145,000–$225,000	**165**
$225,000–$255,000	**166**
$255,000–$380,000	**167**
$380,000–$470,000	**168**
$470,000+	**169**

THE EVERGLADES

GETTING THERE

AIR No airlines fly directly to the Everglades or Naples from the UK, but there are a number of direct flights to Miami. American Airlines (0845 778 9789; www.aa.com) only flies directly to Miami from Heathrow, and from there offer connections to Naples and Fort Myers. British Airways (0870 850 9850; www.ba.com) flies directly into Miami from Heathrow and can organise connections to Naples and Fort Myers with American Airlines (see above). Continental Airlines (0845 607 6760; www.continental.com) flies via Newark to Miami, Fort Myers and Naples. Virgin Atlantic (0870 574 7747; www.virgin-atlantic.com) flies directly to Miami from Heathrow, and from there connections are available to Fort Myers and Naples.

RAIL There are no rail services in the region but Amtrak (+ 1 800 872 7245; www.amtrak.com) offers mainline services to Fort Myers and Miami. From there Greyhound offers bus services to Florida City and Homestead.

ROAD The US 41 runs directly from Miami into the Everglades and the 9336 turns off to head south to Homestead and Florida City. The I-75 also runs from Fort Lauderdale and Miami across the top of the Everglades to Naples.

COACH Greyhound buses (+1 800 231 2222; www.greyhound.com) serve Homestead, Immokalee and Okeechobee.

Area profile

THE EVERGLADES NATIONAL PARK COVERS 1.5 MILLION ACRES OF THE southern tip of Florida making it the largest remaining subtropical wilderness in the USA. The haven incorporates many different interdependent ecosystems from; open prairies to mangrove forests and both salt and freshwater areas. The most famous feature of the Everglades is the 80 kilometre wide River of Grass, which makes its slow progression from Lake Okeechobee to the ocean, nourishing the grass lands en route and providing a lifeline for the thousands of native plant and animal species that are found in the area.

One of the most extraordinary ecosystems in the world, the Everglades is a hotbed for tourist activity, drawing over a million visitors annually. Primarily these are nature lovers, hikers, bird watchers and eco tourists keen to catch a glimpse of alligators, panthers or manatees.

Sadly, the National Park is continually encroached upon by human development and pollution, and though measures have been taken to offer some protection, the threat to the Everglades future is still very real. Once a four million-acre wetland wilderness system, the Everglades has lost around two million of these acres and it's estimated that it will cost around $8 billion and take almost 20 years to readdress the situation. The problem centres around the disruption of the water flow through the river system, primarily due to human demand and competition for the commodity.

On the edge of this vast wilderness, just 50 kilometres south of Naples, are the 10,000 Islands which include the towns of Chokoloskee and Everglades City. These final frontiers of civilisation can be found at the southern terminus of Highway 29. Everglades City, though small (the population is less than a thousand), offers an excellent visitor centre and museum and serves as the western gateway to the Everglades National Park. The area is surrounded by State and Federal parks and preserves such as: Big Cypress National Preserve, Fakahatchee Strand State Preserve, Florida Panther National Wildlife Refuge, Picayune Strand State Park, Collier Seminole State Park and Corkscrew Swamp Sanctuary.

Many of the early pioneers in the Everglades built houses on stilts over water and cut mangroves to remove the mosquito habitat

THE EVERGLADES

The economy and housing market

The main industrial backbone of the Everglades area is tourism and eco-tourism, with many hotels, restaurants and shops thriving on the high visitor figures in the area. The economy also benefits from a healthy commercial fishing industry.

Due to the proximity of the Gulf of Mexico – just a few minutes by boat – and with plenty of backwaters nearby, sport fishing is also a big draw to the area. In fact, in their pursuit of the elusive largemouth bass on canal L-67A, anglers inject roughly $1,120,000 into the local economy over a six month period – that's an impressive $41,000 for every mile of canal.

The housing market in the Everglades offers a mixture of resale and new-build property, both of which have seen dramatic increases in value over the past few years. Prices are now quite high and on a similar level to those found in nearby resorts and on Marco Island. Though remote, the Everglades is one of the most popular house-buying areas in Florida, so market factors dictate that prices can only continue to rise. The strict building regulations should ensure that this is the case.

There is a wide variety of property types available in the region, from one–bedroom condos retailing at $150,000, to stunning houses starting from $1 million. A particular quirk of the market is the preponderance of mobile homes. Chokoloskee hosts many of them, while Plantation Island is zoned exclusively for them. Though you may not see the appeal of life in a mobile home, specification is very high and those on Plantation Island offer a wide stretch of canal front and are situated within minutes of the Gulf of Mexico. The price tags are also appealing: for a 540 square foot mobile home on a waterfront plot with a ramp and dock, expect to pay around $90,000.

Potential purchasers should be prepared for the remoteness of a home on any of the 10,000 Islands; Chokoloskee has a population of just 400 and Plantation Island around 200. There are few amenities – for example no bank or pharmacy – though Everglades City does boast the smallest kindergarten in the whole of Florida. However, the advantages are the clean and natural environment, so the area remains popular.

Social groups

Property purchasers in the Everglades are generally young couples who are looking for somewhere to retire in the future, and also people from the busy east and west coast areas who are looking for a change of pace in life.

Historically, few residents of the area were born elsewhere – the black and Hispanic populations are well below the state average – although the population is small in comparison with the large conurbations on the east coast. International interest is increasing though, and some realtors indicate that almost half of their sales are to overseas buyers and 'snowbirds' from the northern states and Canada, who regularly spend their winters here.

The Everglades are also popular with investors as there is no rental restriction on property and a steady flow of tourists guarantees tenants.

The Everglades National Park is only a small part of the Everglades ecosystem but much of it is inaccessible

The housing market in the Everglades has seen a dramatic increase in value over the past few years

Average monthly temperature °C (Celsius)

THE EVERGLADES:
Dec 19, Nov 22, Oct 25, Sept 27, Aug 28, July 28, June 27, May 25, April 22, March 20, Feb 19, Jan 18

LONDON:
Dec 7, Nov 10, Oct 14, Sept 19, Aug 21, July 22, June 20, May 17, April 13, March 10, Feb 7, Jan 6

Average monthly rainfall mm (millimetres)

THE EVERGLADES:
Dec 44, Nov 48, Oct 97, Sept 209, Aug 219, July 186, June 251, May 90, April 49, March 49, Feb 38, Jan 43

LONDON:
Dec 81, Nov 78, Oct 70, Sept 65, Aug 62, July 59, June 58, May 57, April 56, March 64, Feb 72, Jan 77

Florida Climate Center (www.coaps.fsu.edu/climate_center)

AVERAGE HOUSE SALE PRICES

Hotspot	2-bed	3-bed	4-bed	5-bed
Everglades City	$345K (£189K)	$353K (£193K)	$379K (£208K)	$478K (£261K)
Plantation Island	$150K (£120K)	$232K (£127K)	$292K (£160K)	$342K (£187K)
Chokoloskee Island	$358K (£196K)	$451K (£247K)	$– (£–)	$800K (£440K)

THE EVERGLADES

Property hotspots

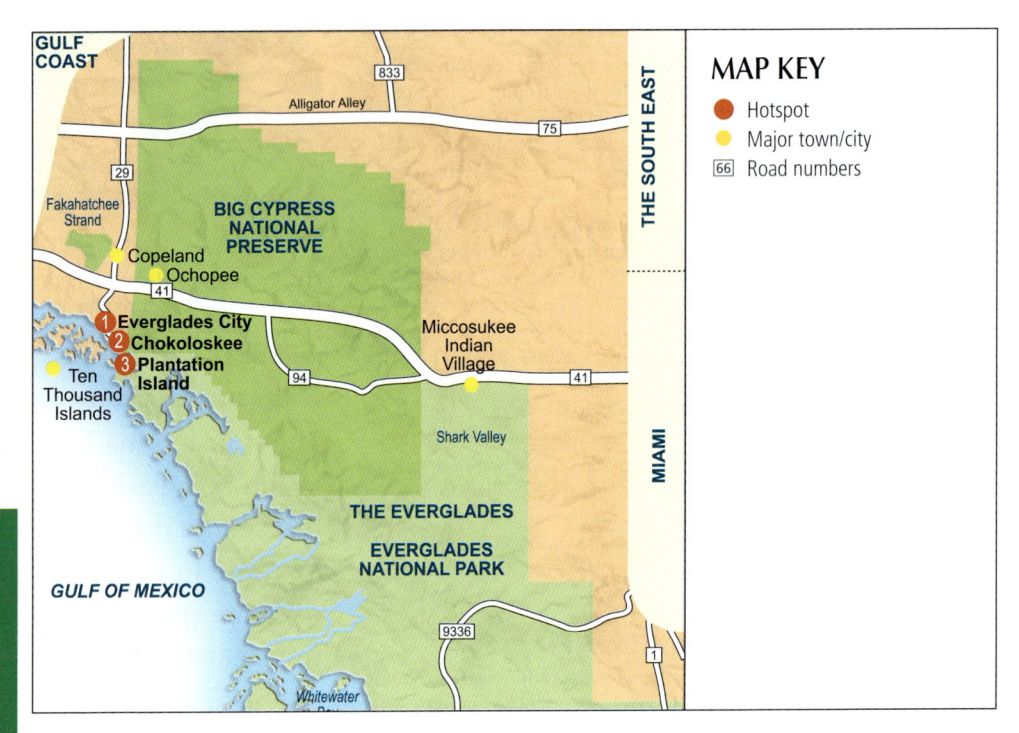

MAP KEY
- ● Hotspot
- ● Major town/city
- 66 Road numbers

1. Everglades City

ESSENTIALS ■ **Pop** 479 ■ **Airport** Naples Airport Tel:+1 239 643-171 ■ Southwest Florida International Airport, 16000 Chamberlin Pkwy Ste 8671, Fort Myers, FL 33901-8890, Tel: +1 239 768-1000 ■ **Tax** Property tax rate per $1,000: $4.25

KEY FACTS

■ **Schools** Everglades City School, 499 School Dr E, Everglades City, FL 34139, Tel: +1 239 695-2561
■ **Medical** The Willough At Naples, 9001 Tamiami Trl E, Naples, FL 34113-3304, Tel: +1 239 775-4500
■ **Rentals** This is primarily a resale and second homes market, and it is more expensive than neighbouring Plantation Island ■ A two-bedroom property will cost between $600 and $900 per week ■ There is a very strong rentals market driven by American snowbirds from the northern states who spend the winter here
■ **Pros** Snowbirds travel south to here in the winter for the mild climate, enlivening the city and boosting the population ■ You can enjoy fine dining, shopping and outdoor activities ■ This is a large, in-demand market from people from the northern states and Canada, and property is appreciating
■ **Cons** The weather in summer can be unpleasant, with high humidity and temperatures ■ There is a limited infrastructure and transport network ■ There is a small international presence here ■ Property is expensive starting at $300,000

Everglades City began expanding when the splendidly-named Barron Gift Collier, a wealthy railroader and speculator, made it his headquarters for building the Tamiami Trail across South Florida ('Tamiami' meaning Tampa to Miami). However, his vision of the city competing with Miami never came to fruition.

Today, Everglades City is a likeable, if somewhat sleepy, fishing village of around 500 inhabitants – hardly a 'city' in conventional terms – though in winter, the population is boosted by around 1,000 holiday-makers. It calls itself the 'Fishing and Stone Crab Capital of South West Florida' and there are a number of seafood restaurants stocked with shrimps, scallops and crabs, fresh from the city's docks.

Given its small population (and many retirees), real estate is hard to come by and the inventory is small, with often only two or three properties for sale at once. However, there have been a few new condominiums built recently, with prices for a one-bed place starting at $140,000 and rising to around $220,000. Newly built two and three-bedroom apartments cost between $385,000, while detached waterfront homes can sell for over $400,000, rising to the $1 million mark for larger plots. Expect to pay more than $500,000 for a two-bedroom home in this area simply because so few houses are available. ●

THE EVERGLADES

2. Chokoloskee Island

ESSENTIALS ■ **Pop** 404 ■ **Airport** Naples Airport, FL 34104, Tel:+1 239 643-171 ■ Southwest Florida International Airport, 16000 Chamberlin Pkwy Ste 8671, Fort Myers, FL 33901-8890, Tel: +1 239 768-1000 ■ **Tax** Property tax rate per $1,000: $4.25

Four miles south of Everglades City in the 10,000 Islands, Chokoloskee Island is home to around 400 inhabitants spread across its 150 acres, and regarded as one of the most desirable of the 10,000 Islands. It wasn't until 1956 that a causeway connected it to the mainland, as South Florida's coast was mainly wilderness at the end of the 19th century; only the small communities of Cape Sable, Chokoloskee and Flamingo existed. Most settlers were farmers and fishermen; sugar cane farming was popular, as was harvesting Buttonwood and red mangrove to make charcoal. Hurricanes were a frequent problem and many of the low-lying farm fields were hit by salted flood tides in the early 20th century.

Today, the sheltered water of the islands provides excellent fishing and the majority who visit do so because of the sports angling. The real estate market here is not dissimilar to Everglades City. Second homes are popular with northerners who want to take advantage of clement winters, and stilted and mobile homes are popular, but far more expensive than neighbouring Plantation Island. Mobile homes are the cheapest but those on a decent-sized lot sell for around $350,000. Houses range in price from between $400,000 and $800,000 and will continue to rise as demand outstrips supply. ●

KEY FACTS
■ **Schools** Everglades City School, 499 School Drive, Everglades City, FL 34139, Tel: +1 239 695-2561
■ **Medical** Cleveland Clinic Florida Hospital, 2950 Cleveland Clinic Blvd, Weston, FL 33331-3609, Tel: +1 954 689-5000
■ **Rentals** A popular tourist area with excellent rental potential ■ A two-bedroom property will bring in between $600 and $900 per week ■ There are no rental restrictions, and homes can be rented daily, weekly and monthly
■ **Pros** Between December and April, the weather is mild and pleasant ■ Situated at the entrance to the waterways there is an abundance of waterside property ■ Zoned for both homes and mobile homes ■ Less than 50 per cent of buyers are international and there is a lot of interest from the busy east and west coast areas ■ Fantastic waters for sports fishermen
■ **Cons** Prices in the area have constantly risen every year and there is limited space for development ■ The fragile ecosystem is under threat from expansion ■ Prices are expensive, with mobile homes costing from $349,000 and waterfront homes from $815,000

3. Plantation Island

ESSENTIALS ■ **Pop** 202 ■ **Airport** Naples Airport, FL 34104, Tel:+1 239 643-171 ■ Southwest Florida International Airport, 16000 Chamberlin Pkwy Ste 8671, Fort Myers, FL 33901-8890, Tel: +1 239 768-1000 ■ **Tax** Property tax per $1,000: $4.25

The community of Plantation Island lies on the waterfront less than two miles east of Everglades City. In an area zoned only for mobile homes, it's home to around 200 people. All homes front a man-made canal which is linked to the Gulf of Mexico by Halfway Creek – a boat ride of just five minutes. This makes it an excellent location for both sea and freshwater fishing, and the angling attractions ensure a healthy rental market in winter – the wet season is in summer, making it a far less desirable place to visit around this time. The residents' median age is around 50 and this is mainly a community of retirees. With very little real estate development, property is scarce, and a mobile home with a couple of bedrooms on a larger than average plot sells for around $250,000, although prices can differ by $100,000 either way. Smaller two-bed plots (often on stilts) can be picked up for $150,000. It's a quiet region compared with much of Florida, so those who demand amenities on the doorstep should look elsewhere. Conversely, because Plantation Island is surrounded by State and Federal land, there are strict development regulations, making it an excellent investment area. No new land will be made available for building, so the only way to improve on the original mobile homes is to replace them with similar sized, upgraded models. ●

KEY FACTS
■ **Schools** Everglades City School, 499 School Drive, Everglades City, FL 34139, Tel: +1 239 695-2561
■ **Medical** Cleveland Clinic Florida Hospital, 2950 Cleveland Clinc Blvd, Weston, FL 33331-3609, Tel: +1 954 689-5000
■ **Rentals** On average, a two-bedroom property will cost around $900 per week ■ This area has a healthy seasonal rentals market, particularly in the winter months ■ Summer here is the low season, owing to the weather, so bear that in mind if you want to buy-to-let
■ **Pros** Plantation Island is ideal for people who enjoy a quiet life ■ Sports fishing is a widespread activity and the National Park status mean that the wildlife is now better protected ■ This is a waterfront community where the average property costs $150,000 ■ The majority of properties are located on the waterfront
■ **Cons** The weather in summer can be quite unpleasant with temperatures averaging 28° Celsius and humidity at 90 per cent ■ Thunderstorms are common and mosquitoes are plentiful ■ This area is zoned for mobile homes only, restricting the type of home that you can purchase

■ THE EVERGLADES

$100,000–$145,000
(£55,000–£79,750)

With bargain prices for waterfront properties this is an excellent location

$120,000   CODE GLA
GLADE HAVEN RESORT
Offering excellent rental potential, a stunning cabin, set amidst the National Park
£66,000

- 1 | no garden, with a boat mooring | a short drive from the shops
- not located on a main road | room for parking

$139,900   CODE BWR
EVERGLADES CITY
With access to a private boat ramp, a spacious home with all mod cons available
£76,945

- 1 | with a large garden | close to amenities | not located on a main road
- room for parking, with a car port

$140,000   CODE EIP
PLANTATION ISLAND
Located on the waterfront this mobile home offers all amenities and a spacious garden
£77,000

- 2 | with a garden | situated close to the town centre | not located on a main road
- room for parking

$144,500   CODE EIP
EVERGLADES CITY
Only a stone's throw from the port, a comfortable mobile home with great views
£79,475

- 1 | with a small garden | within easy reach of amenities | not located on a main road
- room for parking

$145,000   CODE EIP
EVERGLADES CITY
A mobile home, partially furnished and located on the waterfront; with a boat slip
£81,950

- 1 | with a garden | situated close to town | not located on a main road
- room for parking

PRICE GUIDE

THE EVERGLADES

$145,000–$225,000
(£79,750–£123,750)

Ideal for family holiday homes, these properties offer excellent rental potential

$149,000
CODE EIP
PLANTATION ISLAND
Situated on the waterfront, a mobile home with all mod cons and furnishings
£81,950

- 1 | with a garden | close to shops and amenities | not located on a main road | room for parking

$150,000
CODE GLA
EVERGLADES CITY
With excellent rental potential, a stunning and spacious property with a large porch
£82,500

- 3 | with a large garden | within easy reach of the town centre | not located on a main road | room for parking

$154,900
CODE EIP
PORT OF THE ISLANDS
A fully furnished studio apartment, with a private dock and waterfront views
£85,195

- 1 | with small garden | close to amenities | not located on a main road | room for parking

$177,000
CODE EIP
EVERGLADES CITY
This villa is located in an active area of the town yet it remains a peaceful environment
£97,350

- 1 | with a garden | close to the shops | not located on a main road | room for parking

$224,000
CODE BWR
CHOKOLOSKEE ISLAND
A newly built, fully furnished property, on the waterfront, with a private boat dock
£168,000

- 2 | with a boat dock | within easy reach of amenities | not located on a main road | room for parking

PRICE GUIDE

■ THE EVERGLADES

$225,000–$255,000
(£123,750–£140,250)

Stylish wood-built properties, designed in the local style, make for a unique home

PRICE GUIDE

$225,000   CODE BWR
CHOKOLOSKEE ISLAND
A mobile home, set in an attractive landscape with fruit trees, close to the water,
£123,750

🛏 3   ❀ with a large garden   🔭 close to the town centre   🚷 not located on a main road   🚗 room for parking

---

$249,000   CODE EIP
EVERGLADES CITY
With a swimming pool and easy access to the coast an ideal family holiday home
£136,950

🛏 3   ❀ with a garden   🔭 situated close to the town centre   🚷 not located on a main road   🚗 room for parking

---

$250,000   CODE GLA
10,000 ISLANDS
With a swimming pool, private marina and boat dock, a unique property on stilts
£137,500

🛏 3   ❀ with a dock and small garden   🔭 within easy reach of shops and amenities   🚷 not located on a main road   🚗 room for parking

---

$250,000   CODE EIP
PLANTATION ISLAND
A fully furnished mobile home, located on the waterfront, ideal as a holiday home
£137,500

🛏 1   ❀ with a small garden   🔭 situated close to amenities   🚷 not located on a main road   🚗 room for parking

---

$252,000   CODE BWR
CHOKOLOSKEE ISLAND
Situated on raised ground with fabulous views and a separate one-bedroom flat
£138,600

🛏 3   ❀ with a large garden   🔭 situated close to amenities   🚷 not located on a main road   🚗 room for parking

THE EVERGLADES

$255,000 – $380,000
£140,250–£209,000)

Slightly more upmarket homes with great facilities, but at very affordable prices

$260,000   CODE EIP
EVERGLADES CITY
A spacious modern property, well located and ideal as a holiday home
£143,000

- 3 | with a large garden | situated close to the town centre | not located on a main road | room for parking

---

$325,000   CODE EIP
EVERGLADES CITY
A wooden home on stilts, with large rooms and a separate shop, ideal as a business
£178,750

- 3 | with a large garden | situated in the town centre | not located on a main road | room for parking

---

$349,000   CODE GLA
CHOKOLOSKEE ISLAND
Overlooking the water and with its own concrete dock, a spacious, modern property
£191,950

- 3 | with a large garden | situated close to amenities | not located on a main road | room for parking

---

$349,000   CODE GLA
PLANTATION ISLAND
This property comes with a separate guest quarter, an orchard, and is on the waterfront
£191,950

- 2 | with a spacious garden | situated close to the town centre | not located on a main road | room for parking

---

$375,000   CODE BWR
CHOKOLOSKEE ISLAND
A wooden property set on stilts, with beautiful views over the waterfront
£206,250

- 4 | with a large garden | situated close to amenities | not located on a main road | room for parking, with a car port

PRICE GUIDE

167

■ THE EVERGLADES

$380,000—$470,000
(£209,000–£258,500)

Luxurious properties, with fabulous amenities, many with water views

$389,000 — CODE GLA
EVERGLADES CITY
Newly constructed, a stunning property, tiled throughout, with a separate workshop
£213,950

3 | with a large garden | situated close to amenities | not located on a main road | room for parking for a boat, trailer and car

$395,000 — CODE GLA
EVERGLADES CITY
A fully restored property, with a sunroom, swimming pool and a plush interior
£217,250

2 | with a large garden | situated close to amenities | located on a main road | room for parking

$399,000 — CODE EIP
EVERGLADES CITY
Arranged over two floors, a historic home requiring some attention, close to the dock
£219,450

4 | with a small garden | situated close to amenities | not located on a main road | room for parking

$429,000 — CODE GLA
EVERGLADES CITY
A totally restored property, with a spa and enjoying a waterfront location
£235,950

3 | with a large garden | situated a mile from amenities and shops | not located on a main road | room for parking

$465,000 — CODE EIP
EVERGLADES CITY
A brand new home, with a separate workshop, located close to the attractions of town
£255,750

3 | with a large garden | situated close to the town centre | not located on a main road | room for parking

PRICE GUIDE

THE EVERGLADES

$470,000+
(£258,500+)

The most salubrious homes that the Everglades has to offer, many with docking

$529,000 CODE EIP

EVERGLADES CITY
Located on the waterfront with two covered boat ramps, a spacious resale property
£290,950

3 | with a garden | situated within easy reach of amenities | not located on a main road | room for parking

---

$749,000 CODE EIP

EVERGLADES CITY
A newly constructed property, complete with a motor home and a private port
£411,950

3 | with a garden | situated close to the town centre | not located on a main road | room for parking

---

$854,000 CODE EIP

EVERGLADES CITY
A prestigious riverside property, with a swimming pool, sauna and a separate laundry
£469,700

3 | 24,000 square metres | situated close to the town centre | not located on a main road | room for parking

---

$875,000 CODE BWR

CHOKOLOSKEE ISLAND
Located on a development, a stunning property with private dock space and an office
£481,250

2 | with a large garden | situated close to amenities | not located on a main road | room for parking

---

$875,000 CODE GLA

EVERGLADES CITY
A large home built on stilts, with a separate laundry room, workshop and storage area
£481,250

1 | with a large garden and direct ocean access | situated close to amenities | not located on a main road | room for parking

PRICE GUIDE

169

| BULGARIA | CYPRUS | FLORIDA | SPAIN |

ABBEY GLOBAL

OVERSEAS PROPERTY AGENTS

With a weak $ there has never been a better time to buy your home in FLORIDA

ABBEY GLOBAL can offer you beautiful Pool homes on the Gulf coast,
from Sarasota To Naples & Orlando Disney areas from approximately £146,000 including pool
We offer a complete service & one-to-one Inspection tours

GULF COAST USEPPA IV
3,311ft² Pool Home
4/5 bedrooms 4 bathrooms
Approx. £146,400 + lot price

ORLANDO, 192 VENITIAN BAY
Fully Furnished
Communal Pool, Clubhouse & Gym
3 bed/2 bath from $155,000
4 bed/3 bath from $180,000 (less than £100K)

ORLANDO THE WILTSHIRE
Furnished Pool Home
3 bedrooms 2 bathrooms
Approx. £279,000

**A GREAT INVESTMENT WITH EXCELLENT RENTAL POTENTIAL.
ABBEY GLOBAL CAN OFFER BEAUTIFUL HOMES IN
CYPRUS; COSTA DEL SOL; COSTA BLANCA AND NOW BULGARIA.**

Call ABBEY GLOBAL for a friendly and personal service 020 8460 9903 / 020 8464 5991 / 020 8249 1900
100 High Street, Beckenham, Kent BR1 1EB
info@abbeyvillas.com   www.abbeyglobal.com

CALL, E-MAIL OR WRITE FOR YOUR FREE INFORMATION PACK

CALABAY HOMES
FLORIDA

ORLANDO, FLORIDA
NEW HOMES FOR SALE AND FOR RENT
CLOSE TO DISNEY WORLD & CENTRAL ORLANDO

THINKING OF BUYING A PROPERTY IN CENTRAL FLORIDA?

AS HOMEOWNERS OURSELVES WE KNOW HOW DAUNTING IT CAN BE

NOT ANY MORE!

WE HAVE SET UP A NETWORK OF RELIABLE CONTACTS IN THE UK AND IN FLORIDA TO HELP WITH:
★ MANAGEMENT
★ MORTGAGES ★ BEST LOCATION FOR MAXIMUM RENTAL INCOME &
GUARANTEED RENTAL PLANS

★ Why not arrange a visit with no pressure sales?   ★ Book your inspection trip now
★ Already own a home? Looking to change your management? — We can help
★ If you decide to buy we will refund the cost of your flights — so what have you got to lose!

Contact us for friendly, helpful advice

Calabay Homes, 17 Meadow Lane Business Park, Ellesmere Port, Cheshire CH65 4TY
Tel **0151 355 7017**   Fax **0151 513 3453**   Email **calabay.homes@btopenworld.com**

www.calabayhomes.com

Miami

Lively South Beach, great nightlife and fabulous art deco

- **Population** 2.3 million
- **Population increase** Between 1990-2003 the population increased by 408,738
- **Migration** 56,058 people migrated to the Miami area in 2003
- **Median age** 29.5; the state average is 38.7
- **Median home price** $189,800, compared with the state average of $141,100
- **Cost of living** The ACCRA cost of living index rates Miami as 112.2/100

Profile 172

Hotspots 174

Price Guide

$199,000–$260,000	178
$260,000–$345,000	180
$345,000–$555,000	182
$555,000–$849,000	184
$849,000–$2,000,000	186
$2,000,000–$4,000,000	187

GETTING THERE

AIR A limited number of airlines fly directly into Miami International, but it remains the main gateway into the state of Florida. **American Airlines** (0845 778 9789; www.aa.com) flies directly into Miami from Heathrow. **British Airways** (0870 850 9850; www.ba.com) flies directly into Miami from Heathrow, while **American Airlines** (see above). **Continental Airlines** (0845 607 6760; www.continental.com) do not offer any direct flights to Florida but fly via Newark to Miami. **Virgin Atlantic** (0870 574 7747; www.virgin-atlantic.com) flies directly to Miami from Heathrow.

RAIL Amtrak (+ 1-800 872 7245; www.amtrak.com) offers a number of mainline services to Miami.

ROAD Public transport along the south-east coast is fairly limited, so it's essential to have a car. US 1 runs along the south-east coast through Miami, as does the I-95 and I-195. The A1A also runs south along the eastern coastline through Palm Beach, Delray Beach, Fort Lauderdale and on to Miami Beach.

COACH Greyhound buses (+1 800 231 2222; www.greyhound.com) serve Miami Amtrak, Miami International Airport, Miami Cutler Ridge, Miami Downtown and North.

Area profile

OVER EIGHT MILLION VISITORS FLOCK TO GREATER MIAMI EACH YEAR, lured by the promise of renowned beaches, a host of attractions and the vibrant, cosmopolitan city itself.

Miami began its modern life during the turn of the century land rush, as a tourist town, but then boomed in the 1920s. By the 1930s and 1940s it was the centre of the prolific art deco movement, and already had a reputation as a playground for the rich and famous. Today, hordes of people from all over the world have moved to the area, with as many as 6,000 arriving every day in peak times.

Miami Beach, the 12 mile-long island that lies opposite the city, is a fashionable and fast-growing place, particularly famous for its exciting nightlife. Divided into two distinct sections; South Beach (or 'SoBe' as it is dubbed by locals), which contains what is probably the world's largest collection of pastel-coloured, restored art deco buildings – some 800 crammed within a square mile – and then the less-fashionable, North Beach, which blends more subtle 1950s architecture with beautiful ocean views.

Biscayne Bay lies south of Miami Beach, lined by rows of tall condos and office buildings. The area was once dubbed 'Millionaires Row', earning this epitaph due to the wealthy residents who secured pieces of the bayfront realty as winter retreats. These days Biscayne Bay is a lot more grounded, though property still sells at a premium.

Miami itself is about as cosmopolitan and diverse as it gets. It is known as the gateway to Latin America, but don't allow memories of the criminal underworld, exaggerated by 1980s television show *Miami Vice* to distort your image of the city. Though undeniably colourful and full of adventure, Miami is a very liberated and peace-loving society, where throbbing samba beats and impromptu street parties reign supreme.

South Beach (SoBe) is home to the largest number of restored art deco buildings in the world. And one or two classic cars, as well

MIAMI

The economy and housing market

Greater Miami is one of the wealthier areas of Florida, though certain parts of the city itself are extremely depressed economically. Due to its strategic geographical location, Miami receives huge investment and is home to many US businesses seeking to tap into the lucrative Latin American market and vice versa. Vast steel and glass skyscrapers built by financial and commercial corporations stand as a testament to its prosperity. Tourism and trade conventions also help drive the economy.

Property prices are higher than those found in the rest of Florida; hotspots such as South Miami Beach, Bal Harbour and Biscayne Bay are particularly expensive. Here realtors report annual capital appreciation on some property of between 10 and 20 per cent as Europeans, Latin Americans and North Americans all vie for a piece of prime real estate.

In South Beach – the most exclusive and expensive area in this region of Florida – you can expect to pay between $300 and $450 per square foot. An oceanfront studio apartment will set you back around $300,000, and this is at the low end of the market.

More reasonable, are properties in North Miami Beach, an up-and-coming area located on the mainland, north of downtown Miami, traditionally inhabited by those who can't afford South Beach. Here a two-bed, one-bathroom house might cost $180,000 and still benefit from price rises of between five and 10 per cent per annum.

Greater Miami is an investor's dream as the rental market is strong and rents are high. A continuous influx of business persons, trade conference attendees and residents unable to yet afford their own home, guarantees both long and short-term lets.

Social groups

Miami is predominantly a US/Latin American city, although it is famous for its resident melting pot of ethnic communities. And, it is precisely this cultural diversity that appeals to many visitors and potential home-buyers.

Probably the largest community is Cuban, centred on Callé Ocho and known as 'Little Havana'. Here visitors can sample cups of café con leche, partake in colourful festivals and enjoy the finest Cuban cigars. 'Little Haiti' forms the focal point of the Caribbean population, who have created a fascinating fusion of cultures and architecture in their local environ. The city is also home to significant numbers of Puerto Ricans.

Realtors are reporting that increasing numbers of Europeans are buying here due to the strength of sterling and the euro. Estimates suggest between 20 and 50 per cent of all sales are to Europeans with the rest of the market made up of US and Latin American buyers.

In terms of age demographics, while residents were once ageing, wealthy business people, the trend has turned in favour of younger buyers, keen to take advantage of low interest rates in order to buy their first property. ●

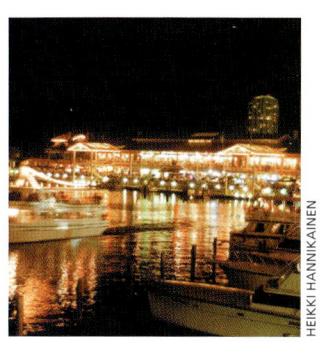

Miami is renowned for its exuberant nightlife and lively party atmosphere

A liberated and peace–loving society, Miami is colourful and full of adventure

MIAMI		LONDON		MIAMI		LONDON
21	Dec	7		55	Dec	81
24	Nov	10		87	Nov	78
26	Oct	14		157	Oct	70
28	Sept	19		213	Sept	65
29	Aug	21		219	Aug	62
29	July	22		147	July	59
28	June	20		217	June	58
26	May	17		140	May	57
24	April	13		85	April	56
22	March	10		65	March	64
21	Feb	7		53	Feb	72
20	Jan	6		48	Jan	77

Average monthly temperature °C (Celsius)

Average monthly rainfall mm (millimetres)

Florida Climate Center (www.coaps.fsu.edu/climate_center)

AVERAGE HOUSE SALE PRICES

Hotspot	2-bed	3-bed	4-bed	5-bed
South Beach	$600K (£330K)	$1M (£550K)	$– (£–)	$– (£–)
North Miami Beach	$199K (£109K)	$432K (£236K)	$521K (£284K)	$1.6M (£888K)
Biscayne Bay	$363K (£199K)	$639K (£349K)	$1.3 (£717K)	$5M (£3M)
Aventura	$326K (£179K)	$670K (£365K)	$776K (£423K)	$1.5M (£825K)
Bal Harbour	$677K (£372K)	$1.4M (£770K)	$2.09M (£1.14M)	$3.2M (£1.8M)
Surfside	$400K (£220K)	$706K (£385K)	$912K (£497K)	$2.9M (£1.6M)

■ MIAMI

Property hotspots

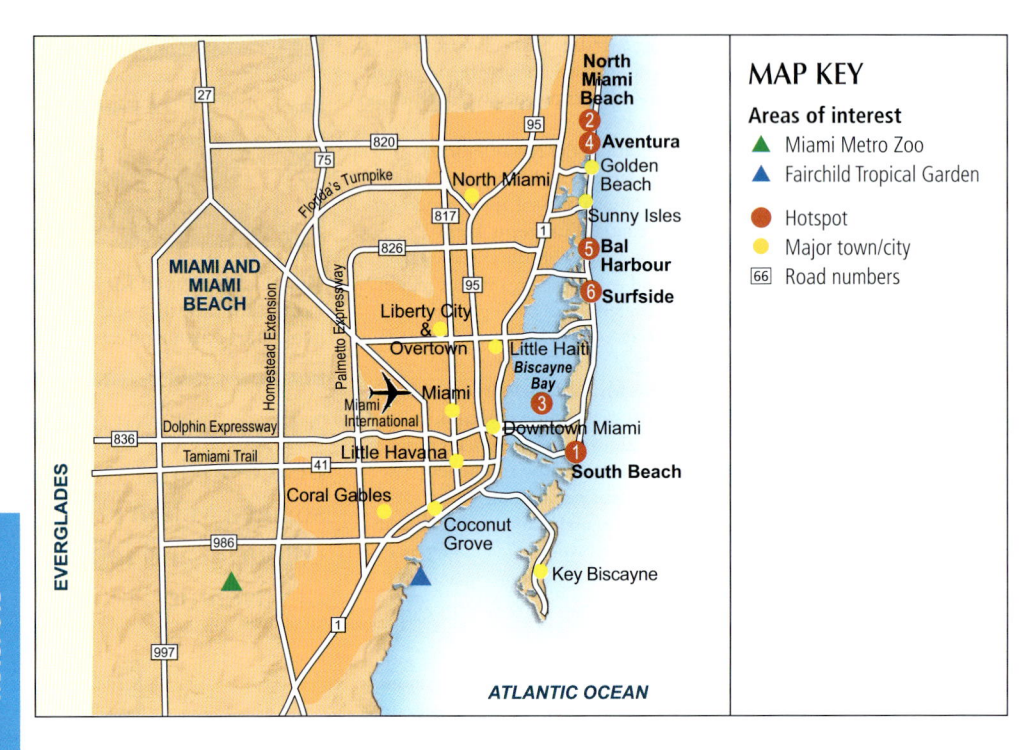

MAP KEY

Areas of interest
▲ Miami Metro Zoo
▲ Fairchild Tropical Garden
● Hotspot
● Major town/city
66 Road numbers

1. South Beach

ESSENTIALS ■ **Pop** 49,522 ■ **Airport** Miami International Airport, PO Box 592075, Miami, Florida 33159, Tel: +1 305 876 7000 ■ **Tax** Property tax rate per $1,000, $20

Miami Beach is a 12 mile-long island that lies adjacent to the city of Miami across Biscayne Bay, connected by the MacArthur Causeway. Development of the island only really began in 1913, while the 1920s saw a building boom in South Beach, the hub of the island. In the 1930s the art deco cult left South Beach with around 800 preserved buildings in the fabulous 'Art Deco Historic District'. Over the years, the area has seen good and bad times – in the 1980s it was down-trodden and drug-ridden – but after it was added to the National Register of Historic Places in 1979, South Beach has established itself as one of the most desirable resorts in the country. Ocean Drive is home to the finest array of art deco buildings in the world, as well as a wide, sandy beach, great restaurants, delis and chic boutiques. It's an incredibly trendy area, full of strutting fashion victims with expensive, flashy cars and motorcycles. Property is expensive here; the median house value in South Beach is well over $350,000. Luxury, new high-rise blocks offer prices ranging from $300,000 for small one-bedroom apartments, and up to $12 million for the finest penthouse. A two-bedroom townhouse will set you back around $1 million, while homes in protected areas are phenomenally expensive; renovated flats and lofts are desirable too, and don't stay on the market for long. ●

KEY FACTS

■ **Schools** Miami Beach Senior High School, 2231 Prairie Ave, Miami Beach, FL 33139-1517, Tel: +1 305 532-0846
■ **Medical** South Shore Hospital, 600 Alton Rd, Miami Beach, FL 33139, Tel: +1 305 674-8155
■ **Rentals** This is an area full of condos and holiday homes; rental demands are very high ■ A one-bedroom condo costs from $350 to $900 a week between the winter and summer months
■ **Pros** Prices range from $80,000 to $10M offering something for every budget ■ This is an exciting area in which to live with a blend of cultures, including large Latin, Jewish and gay communities ■ Has an excellent infrastructure ■ This is a top realty location, experiencing high levels of investment and strong appreciation; prices have increased from $300 per square foot to $400 in the last year ■ South Beach is one of the most well-recognised beaches in America attracting families, as well as singles and young couples
■ **Cons** An oceanfront property costs from $300,000 ■ There are tight building regulations in the area, and increasingly few renovation properties on the market ■ This is a poseurs' paradise, and not be to everyone's taste

MIAMI

2. North Miami Beach

ESSENTIALS ■ **Pop** 40,786 ■ **Airport** Miami International Airport, PO Box 592075, Miami, Florida 33159, Tel: +1 305 876 7000 ■ **Tax** Property tax rate per $1,000; $23

Confusingly, the city of North Miami Beach lies on the mainland, north-west of the island of Miami Beach. Development began in earnest in 1917, when newspaper baron, Lafe Allen, purchased 557 acres of land with the intention of building a city with wide boulevards and residential streets. Originally called Fulford-by-the-Sea, after Captain William H Fulford who initially owned the parcel of land, the name was changed in 1931 to take advantage of the growing popularity of nearby Miami Beach. After the completion of the North Miami Beach Boulevard in 1951, new residential areas were developed and businesses attracted; the city gradually expanded and it's now home to around 42,000 people. In 2000, a $17.5 million bond for neighbourhood improvements was approved and many residential areas have been upgraded. The central Hanford Boulevard has also been improved with a Super Wal-Mart opening at the end of the year. Real estate prices have been rising steadily and the city offers a good selection of housing. At the low end of the market, one-bed apartments start at $50,000 and single storey homes at just over $150,000. The Eastern Shores suburb with waterfront properties, is the most expensive area of the city. Further out of town, Sunny Isle and Golden Beach are phenomenally expensive. ●

KEY FACTS

■ **Schools** Beth Jacob High School Inc, 1110 NE 163rd St, North Miami Beach, FL 33162, Tel: +1 305 940-1172
■ **Medical** Parkway Regional Medical Centre, 160 NW 170th Street, North Miami Beach, FL 33169, Tel: +1 305 651-1100
■ **Rentals** This area primarily offers long-term lets ranging from $700 a week for a one-bedroom condo, to $1,025 for a three-bedroom condo
■ **Pros** Intensive redevelopment and regeneration has made this a more attractive neighbourhood, with plenty of amenities nearby ■ The city offers a variety of property, from starter homes for $30,000, to luxurious waterfront condos for $1.3 million ■ This is still an affordable neighbourhood compared with much of Miami, and the 2000 census states the average property price in 2000 was $93,000 – well below the state average
■ **Cons** Despite the variety of property and current affordability, prices are set to rise quite steeply ■ This is essentially still a fairly grotty area compared with many other parts of the region, despite the recent facelift

3. Biscayne Bay

ESSENTIALS ■ **Pop** – ■ **Airport** Miami International Airport, PO Box 592075, Miami, Florida 33159, Tel: +1 305 876 7000 ■ **Tax** Property tax rate per $1,000; $22

Biscayne Bay splits mainland Miami with the adjacent islands. It's the world's busiest cruise port, and the land that fronts the bay area on both sides provides some of the regions most desirable real estate. Key Biscayne is an exclusive playground island that lies five miles south-west of downtown Miami. In the early 20th century it became a favourite spot for the rich to gather at the start of the Miami 'winter season'. One-bedroom apartments start at just under $300,000, while detached properties can go for between $1 million and $20 million. On the other side of the bay, downtown Miami is full of high-rise blocks, dotted with historical, early 20th-century buildings. Brickell Avenue, which faces the bay, is home to a wealth of international banks, and in the past few years, thousands of new apartments have been built. Prices range from around $200,000 into the many millions. New shops and restaurants are springing up to cater for the influx of residents, and prices should rise steadily in the future. Adjacent to Brickell Avenue lies Brickell Key, a small island which houses a number of towering condos. Its history dates back to 1896 when Henry Flagler had a nine-foot-deep channel dug from the Miami River, creating two offshore islands in the process. In 1943 the islands were joined, making a 44 acre island. Condos here start at around £300,000. ●

KEY FACTS

■ **Schools** Coconut Grove Montessori School, 2850 SW 27th Ave, Miami, FL 33133, Tel: +1 305 444-4484
■ **Medical** Health South Doctors Hospital, 5000 University Dr, Miami, FL 33146-2008, Tel: +1 305 666-2111
■ **Rentals** Most rentals here are long term, and vary from $1,140 a month for a one-bedroom condo, to $1,535 a month for a two-bedroom condo
■ **Pros** An ideal location for those drawn to the fast-paced, urban lifestyle of Miami ■ Highly accessible for downtown Miami and all amenities ■ This area has developed a vibrant social life, with numerous places to shop and dine ■ This is the fastest growing area in Miami and an excellent investment prospect ■ Development has been huge, with 1,000 new apartments built in 2001 alone
■ **Cons** This is a phenomenally expensive part of Miami, known as the original 'Millionaires Row' ■ The average cost of buying a condo here varies from $200 per square foot, to $1,000 per square foot ■ Dominated by the Latin American bankers and businessmen, prices remain very high ■ 99 per cent of this area consists of condos

MIAMI

4. Aventura

ESSENTIALS ■ **Pop** 25,267 ■ **Airport** Miami International Airport, PO Box 592075, Miami, Florida 33159, Tel: +1 305 876 7000 ■ **Tax** Property tax rate per $1,000; $23

KEY FACTS

■ **Schools** Aventura Montessori School, 21058 W Dixie Hwy, Miami, FL 33180, Tel: +1 305 932-1716
■ **Medical** Aventura Hospital And Medical Center, 20900 Biscayne Blvd, Aventura, FL 33180, Tel: +1 305 682-7000
■ **Rentals** Aventura is more of a long-term rentals market ■ Monthly rental varies from between $1,199 and $1,799 a month for between a one-three-bedroom condo ■ This is an extremely expensive market to access
■ **Pros** Aventura is one of Miami's newest communities and has under-gone a facelift that has made it a very desirable place to live ■ There are a number of new amenities, including a $4 million recreation centre ■ This is a luxurious condo community, well located for the airports and other cities in the region ■ The average property is a luxurious waterfront home
■ **Cons** The average residents are extremely wealthy 50-somethings, and living costs are extremely high ■ The average property price is $225,900, considerably larger than the state average of $141,100

One of Miami's newest communities and a highly desirable place to live, the city of Aventura was incorporated as a residential community as recently as 1995. Essentially, it's an upmarket development of condominiums and homes, with many full-service communities in luxury, gated developments. Its population has risen rapidly and is now approaching 30,000. In recent years, almost $50 million has been spent on modernising the city's infrastructure, installing new drainage systems, pavements, lighting and parks. Nearby, the Aventura Mall is home to an impressive 200 shops, four of which are department stores, including the upmarket Macy's. Development continues apace and many new waterfront blocks are under construction. Some of the new communities such as; Porto Vita, Hamptons South and The Parc at Turnberry Isle are extremely exclusive, with prices rising as high as $10 million. Williams Island even has its own 55-man security department. Older, one-bed apartments can start as low as $150,000, while three-bed, single storey homes start at just under $300,000. The median age of residents is over 50 years old, and there are a number of communities exclusively constructed for Aventura's wealthy community of over 55s. If you're not keen on high rises, then Aventura is probably not for you. ●

5. Bal Harbour

ESSENTIALS ■ **Pop** 3,305 ■ **Airport** Miami International Airport, PO Box 592075, Miami, Florida 33159, Tel: +1 305 876 7000 ■ **Tax** Property tax rate per $1,000; $23

KEY FACTS

■ **Schools** Bay Harbor Elementary School, 1155 93rd St, Bay Harbor Islands, FL 33154, Tel: +1 305 865-7912
■ **Medical** Parkway Regional Medical Centre, 160 NW 170th Street, North Miami Beach, FL 33169, Tel: +1 305 651-1100
■ **Rentals** This is not a short-term rentals area but long term ■ Weekly rentals vary between $450 and $1,050, with a monthly rental costing between $1,150 and $1,500
■ **Pros** Recently $1.8 million has been spent on a facelift for Bal Harbour Beach ■ This is a small community, well-known as a destination for the rich and famous ■ There are a number of luxurious shops housed in Bal Harbour Village mall ■ Bal Harbour offers a number of apartment buildings, condos and single family homes ■ There are a number of quality restaurants offering a variety of different cuisines
■ **Cons** This is an extremely stylish and expensive community which is costly to invest in ■ The average house price is $664,300, $523,200 above the state average

Sitting on the northern tip of Miami Beach, Bal Harbour Village is an exclusive resort town of around 3,500 inhabitants. Formed in 1946, its first apartments were converted barracks left behind by the US Army at the end of the Second World War. It was also home to a prisoner of war camp, which is now the site of the area's exclusive shopping mall. Bal Harbour was the first planned community in Florida to have its utilities incorporated underground, which is certainly a pointer of what was to follow. Careful planning, restricted building practices and closely managed growth have ensured that Bal Harbour remains as charming as it was in the post-war years. Its most famous attraction is Bal Harbour Shops – an open-air mall with the finest stores and boutiques in Miami. Real estate is, as one might expect, phenomenally expensive; the median price for a home is around $700,000. Very few new buildings are permitted, although recently, two beachfront blocks sold out quickly and prices started at $1.2 million. At the lower end of the market, one-bed apartments start at just under $200,000, although the best penthouses on Collins Drive can hit the $4 million mark. Detached homes with a view of the water regularly sell for around $4.5 million. Prices will continue to rise due to the town's exclusivity and strictly imposed building restrictions. ●

6. Surfside

ESSENTIALS ■ **Pop** 4,909 ■ **Airport** Miami International Airport, PO Box 592075, Miami, Florida 33159, Tel: +1 305 876 7000 ■ **Tax** Property tax rate per $1,000; $23

Surfside is a small but pleasant resort town, situated just south of Bal Harbour at the northern end of Miami Beach. Founded in 1935, it was incorporated by members of a private surf club and it's now home to just over 4,500 inhabitants. The mile-long beach is the town's most popular attraction, and there are a healthy sprinkling of reasonably-priced hotels, restaurants, cafes and shops – particularly in comparison with its illustrious neighbours; South Beach and Bal Harbour. Surfside retains a great deal of small town charm and old-fashioned Miami feel; the beachfront hotels and condominiums are not permitted to exceed 12 storeys, and the rest of the town is low rise.

Consequently, the town hasn't suffered any of the over-development that other places have experienced, and its population remains at a stable level. Although less expensive than the neighbouring towns, property still sells at well above the state average because it is a prime location. Detached two-bedroom homes start at around $400,000, and larger plots can sell for well over $2 million. Apartments range from between $200,000 for a single-bed, up to $2 million for a beachfront penthouse. As in most Florida towns, prices are rising and demand is strong. For those with *very* deep pockets, neighbouring island, Indian Creek, offers a handful of homes in the $30 million bracket. ●

KEY FACTS

■ **Schools** Bay Harbor Elementary School, 1155 93rd St, Bay Harbor Islands, FL 33154, Tel: +1 305 865-7912
■ **Medical** Parkway Regional Medical Centre, 160 NW 170th Street, North Miami Beach, FL 33169, Tel: +1 305 651-1100
■ **Rentals** As with most of Miami, despite the occasional hotel rental, this market is primarily geared for long-term rentals and is very expensive
■ Not recommended for those seeking to buy for investment ■ For a week's rental expect to pay between $1,295 for a one-bedroom condo and $3,775 for a three-bedroom luxury condo
■ **Pros** Surfside is recognised as having a stunning beach, as well as the nudist beach of Haulover Beach Park ■ This is a family-orientated area with plenty for both parents and children to do ■ Collins Avenue has recently undergone expensive refurbishment, while Harding Avenue maintains the old-fashioned Miami feel
■ **Cons** With the average house price at $202,500, an expensive area in which to buy ■ Primarily a pre-construction market with prices varying from $350,000 to $2 million ■ A small community only nine blocks long and 10 blocks wide

Surfside is a pleasant resort town recognised for its stunning beach

■ MIAMI

$199,000 – $260,000
(£110,000–£142,300)

Comfortable family homes, close to all the attractions of Miami and the beach

$199,000   CODE IWM
BISCAYNE BAY
Minutes from South Beach, this condo has a huge balcony and access to all amenities
£108,860

1 | with a large balcony | situated close to the town centre | not located on a main road | room for parking

$199,000   CODE BTB
NORTH MIAMI BEACH
A large home with a huge lot where avocado and mango trees grow
£108,860

4 | with a large garden | situated close to the town centre | not located on a main road | room for parking

$229,000   CODE COL
MIAMI
With a lovely garden, this home is fully air conditioned with all mod cons
£125,950

4 | with a large garden | situated close to shops and attractions | not located on a main road | room for parking

$249,000   CODE MLR
MIAMI BEACH
A fully renovated property, located in an exclusive gated community with all mod cons
£136,950

1 | with a small garden | situated close to the beach and shops | not located on a main road | room for parking

$259,900   CODE COL
MIAMI
Arranged over two storeys, a fully air-conditioned fashionable home with all mod cons
£142,945

4 | with a small garden | situated close to all shops and attractions | located on a main road | room for parking

PRICE GUIDE

florida villa finders

Our staff in the UK and Florida will be please to assist you in the purchase of YOUR perfect vacation home in Orlando, Florida

We represent all major developers in **Central Florida** and can show you any resale home on the market

All homes are in areas that are zoned for **SHORT TERM RENTALS**

All homes have their own **PRIVATE, HEATED, SCREENED POOL**

We can assist you in choosing and organising the delivery of your **furniture**

We will help you arrange suitable **financing** with deposits as low as 20%

All the villas we show you will be within **10 to 15 minutes of DISNEY**

INSPECTION VISITS can be arranged

Our **AFTER SALES SERVICE** is second to none

PROPERTY MANAGEMENT services are available to purchasers. Use of our Management company is not a condition of the purchase - YOU make your own decision

The staff at Florida Villa Finders have years of experience of both owning and selling homes in Florida.

We have licensed REALTORS waiting to work with you!

Contact us now for a friendly informal chat about purchasing property in Central Florida

0845 2260611

info@floridavillafinders.com
www.floridavillafinders.com

LOCATIONS - FLORIDA: KISSIMMEE, MIAMI, ORLANDO & THE GULF COAST. CARIBBEAN: THE BAHAMAS

Do you dream of a holiday home in the sun or simply making an investment in property abroad?

If so, you could find your ideal property in our extensive portfolio of new build and resale apartments, townhouses and villas.

Would you like: an extensive choice of properties, guaranteed rentals, legal, financial and tax advice, full after sales service, property management and lettings?

If you are serious about purchasing property we will be serious about helping you find it. We will show you the best opportunities both for investment and for enjoyment now and in the future. Come and spend a few days in the sun with us and actually see first hand the property and the lifestyle that is available to you.

Call us now to arrange a stress free and no pressure trip from **just £299** per person. If you are serious, "seeing is believing" so what is stopping you?

GPG
THE GLOBAL PROPERTY GROUP

For more information visit www.thegpg.com
or call: 08707 52 56 52

■ MIAMI

$260,000 – $345,000
(£142,300–£190,000)

You will find some great investment opportunities in this mid-range market

$275,000 — CODE MLR

MIAMI
Located in the heart of Coconut Grove, this condo offers a gym, pool and attractions
£151,250

🛏 1 | 🌼 with a balcony | 🏙 situated in the centre of Miami | 🚫 not located on a main road | 🚗 room for parking

$275,000+ — CODE IWM

BRICKELL
A high-class new development with a private marina, fitness centre, pool and spa
£150,435

🛏 1 | 🌼 with a garden | 🏙 situated close to town | 🛣 located on a main road | 🚗 valet parking

$289,990 — CODE COL

MIAMI
With a communal swimming pool, this development property comes fully furnished
£159,495

🛏 4 | 🌼 with a small garden | 🏙 situated close to the town centre | 🚫 not located on a main road | 🚗 room for parking

$324,900 — CODE DRC

MIAMI BEACH
Open-plan condo with spectacular views from the large balcony and all amenities
£177,732

🛏 2 | 🌼 with a small garden and large balcony | 🏙 situated close to the town centre | 🚫 not located on a main road | 🚗 room for parking

$344,500 — CODE BTB

AVENTURA
An impressive condo, with a spacious balcony and views over the water and a golf course
£188,454

🛏 2 | 🌼 with a garden | 🏙 situated close to town | 🚫 not located on a main road | 🚗 room for parking, with a garage

Opening the door to your dreams

Thinking of purchasing a property in Florida?

Check with us first for truly independent advice. Unlike many companies offering similar advice, we are not linked to any specific property developer. We are specialists in the purchase of investment property in central Florida as we are ourselves homeowners there.

we offer

Friendly and practical guidance on seeking and selecting a property
Up to date information on the range of homes and locations available
The personal services of an independent Florida based real estate agent with 16 years experience
Escorted and informed tours of properties available
Information regarding regulations on property rental
The facility to arrange financial advice for an American mortgage
Help with selecting a management company to look after the property

Exclusively Florida

Do you want to realise your Florida dream? We did – so can you!
For further details please contact Chris and Fiona.
Tel/Fax: +44 (0) 1453 836150.   E-mail: enquiries@exclusivelyflorida.co.uk
Web: www.exclusivelyflorida.co.uk

★ *Miami Beach*
★ *Bal Harbour*
★ *Sunny Isles Beach*
★ *Aventura*
★ *Fisher Island*
★ *South Beach*
★ *Miami*

from $500,000 to over $50,000,000

Our Speciality
'Buying, Selling and Investment' of

Luxury Oceanfront & Waterfront Condominiums & Homes in South Florida

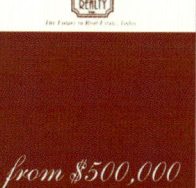

We assist you in finding that Special Holiday Residence, call today:
Magda S. (Hernandez) Saltzman
at **786-326-6048** or simply email: msaltz9708@aol.com
And visit our website for our complete Real Estate MLS listings at
www.MagdaSaltzman.com

Just Florida

- **Superb Villas with Pools**
- **Gated Communities**
- **Executive Houses**

with maximum income and capital growth potential available for purchase with 75% mortgages

- **Inspection trips available**
- **Rentals available**

at discounted rates for 2004, 2005 & 2006

'Oakwood', Appley Lane North, Appley Bridge, Lancashire, WN6 9AQ

Telephone 01257 251501 and 251471
Fax 01257 251502
Email: info@justflorida.com

www.justflorida.com

■ MIAMI

$345,000-$555,000
(£190,000-£301,000)

Gorgeous waterfront homes, fantastic balcony views and luxurious gardens

$365,000   CODE DRC
MIAMI BEACH
A luxurious condo situated directly on the waterfront with fantastic views
£199,668

2 | with a balcony | situated close to the town centre
not located on a main road | room for parking

$389,000   CODE IWM
BISCAYNE BAY
An ideal investment, this low-maintenance penthouse is fully furnished with an ocean view
£212,797

1 | with a large balcony | close to shops and amenities | not located on a main road | room for parking, with a two-car garage

$425,000   CODE BTB
BISCAYNE BAY
A spacious condo with a meditation garden and a water sculpture
£232,490

2 | with a small garden | situated close to the town centre | located on a main road | room for parking

$449,000   CODE DRC
MIAMI BEACH
This fabulous condo has a huge terrace directly overlooking the ocean
£245,619

2 | with a garden | close to shops and amenities | not located on a main road | room for parking

$555,000   CODE MLR
MIAMI BEACH
A beautifully renovated house, situated in landscaped gardens with a swimming pool
£305,250

3 | with a large garden | situated close to shops, amenities and the beach
not located on a main road | room for parking

PRICE GUIDE

182

The World of Florida

Luxury homes for sale and rent

from

F I Grey & Son UK • Florida Villa Rentals

Holidaying in Florida?

For your holiday in Florida we have over 100 luxury pool homes for you to choose from.

Just a few minutes from Disney and all the attractions of Orlando, or close to the sparkling blue waters of the Gulf Coast.

Villa prices from £395 a week plus tax.

Flights, car hire and travel insurance can be arranged.

Agents for ATOL holders.

For holiday information call our special
Florida Villa Rentals line: 01432 344417

Buying a home in Florida?

We have one of the largest selections of 3, 4 and 5 bedroom homes in Orlando and the Gulf Coast.

Mortgages arranged in the US and UK.

Deposits from as little as 20%.

Inspection trips in one of our luxury homes, just minutes from Disney of the Gulf Coast.

Full management and rental services.

St Ethelbert House • Ryelands Street • Hereford • HR4 0LA
Tel: 01432 265599 • Fax: 01432 845640
Email: homes@worldofflorida.co.uk • www.worldofflorida.co.uk

MEMBERS OF THE FEDERATION OF
OVERSEAS PROPERTY DEVELOPERS
AGENTS AND CONSULTANTS

www.worldofflorida.co.uk

■ MIAMI

$555,000 – $849,000
(£301,000–465,000

For great nightlife and fabulous art-deco surroundings, buy in lively South Beach

$589,000 CODE MSS

SOUTH MIAMI BEACH
A luxurious waterfront development, with a stunning view of downtown Miami
£323,950

2 | with a balcony | situated in the city centre | located on a main road
room for parking

$629,000 CODE MZI

SOUTH BEACH
An amazing condo with direct access to the garage and fantastic views of South Beach
£344,085

2 | with a garden | situated close to amenities | not located on a main road
room for parking.

$629,900+ CODE MZI

SOUTH BEACH
A furnished condo in a lively area with amazing views of the water and beach.
£344,085

2 | with a balcony | situated close to the town centre
not located on a main road | room for parking

$769,000 CODE COL

MIAMI BEACH
With a patio offering a garden view, a two-storey family home with all mod cons
£422,950

5 | with a small garden | situated close to amenities | not located on a main road | room for parking

---

$849,900 CODE MZI

SOUTH BEACH
A rare corner unit in one of the hottest buildings on South Beach, the Murano Grande
£464,433

2 | with 2 large balconies | situated close to amenities and shops
not located on a main road | room for parking

PRICE GUIDE

Classic
Florida Realty

Inspection Trips Departing Daily!

We are Florida's leading Real Estate company, specializing in the sale and management of freehold holiday homes for vacations and investment. We offer several guaranteed income programs where we pay the mortgage and running costs.

For more details and a complete information package, please call:

0800.298.7308 (UK)

Sales:
Largest selection of both new and resale properties in Florida.

Management:
Totally worry free professional service.

Income:
We have the best rental program under the Sun!

www.ClassicFloridaRealty.com

■ MIAMI

$849,000 – $2,000,000
(£465,000–£1,100,000)

Stunning, luxury properties in exclusive areas, with lots of added extras

$849,000   CODE MZI
SOUTH BEACH
A luxurious condo with oversized windows and dark wood flooring
£464,433

🛏 2   ❀ with 2 large balconies   🏙 situated in the town centre   🚧 located on a main road   🚗 room for parking.

$895,000   CODE COL
MIAMI BEACH
Overlooking a golf course, a two-storey property with a swimming pool and all mod cons
£492,250

🛏 4   ❀ with a garden   🏙 situated close to the city centre   🚧 not located on a main road   🚗 room for parking

---

$999,000   CODE COL
MIAMI BEACH
A single family home, with all mod cons, air conditioning and a separate laundry room
£549,450

🛏 4   ❀ with a garden   🏙 situated close to all shops and amenities   🚧 not located on a main road   🚗 room for parking

---

$1,375,000   CODE HOM
SAN SOUCI VILLA
A luxurious waterfront home in an exclusive area with a pool and private boat dock
£757,232

🛏 3   ❀ pool, deck and indoor jacuzzi   🏙 situated in exclusive San Souci area   🚧 five minutes from Bal Harbour shops   🚗 room for parking, with a two-car garage

$1,995,000   CODE MZI
SOUTH BEACH
Luxury condo featuring flow-through design. Completely furnished, with private elevator
£1,091,335

🛏 2   ❀ with 2 large balconies   🏙 situated close to amenities   🚧 located on a main road   🚗 room for parking

PRICE GUIDE

$2,000,000–$4,000,000
(£1,100,000–£2,200,000)

Those with more than $1 million to spend will discover a wealth of opportunities

$ 2,750,000   CODE HOM
NORMANDY SHORES VILLA
A fabulous bayfront home with a large wood deck, a pool and great city views
£1,514,486

- 4 | with a large garden, pool and deck | close to shops and amenities
- located in a golf community | room for parking, with a two-car garage

$3,700,000   CODE SUS
MIAMI
Superb luxury home at Sabal Lake with swimming pool and waterfront views
£2,037,045

- 5 | with pool and garden on good-sized plot | situated close to amenities, two miles from downtown | not located on a main road | circular driveway, with a garage

$3,750,000   CODE HOM
MIAMI
Luxury new-build home with eight bathrooms, huge gardens and large pool
£2,064,574

- 6 | five acres, swimming pool, BBQ area | eight miles from downtown Miami
- not located on a main road | circular drive, with a large garage

$3,900,000   CODE GRL
FISHER ISLAND, MIAMI
Located on the waterfront, this fabulous townhouse has a swimming pool and spa
£2,133,436

- 4 | with a garden | situated close to the beach and amenities | not located on a main road | room for parking

$3,950,000   CODE HOM
SOUTH MIAMI
Expansive newly built, eight-bath home with pool, balcony, patio and high ceilings
£2,174,355

- 6 | 1 acre plot with pool | situated close to amenities, around eight miles from downtown Miami | not located on a main road | large garage and further parking

---

MIAMI

PRICE GUIDE

187

SAVE THOUSANDS! / BUY A RE-SALE / SAVE THOUSANDS

FLORIDA
FREE BUYERS' SERVICE!

FROM KISSIMMEE'S 'NO 1' SHORT TERM RENTAL HOME SPECIALIST

PRE-OWNED

Homes Starting At £70,000

Condos Starting At £35,000

- Pre-owned Freehold Furnished Pool Homes from £70,000
- Re-sale Condos / Town Homes from only £35,000
- 1997 - 2004 Over $65 Million in sales

INCLUDES POOL & FURNISHINGS

or

NEW

Homes Starting At £110,000

Condos Starting At £60,000

- New Freehold Homes with Pool from £110,000-£500,000
- Furniture Packages, Financing & Award Winning Management

COMMUNITY POOLS, GOLF ETC.

- Windward Cay • Hamilton's Reserve • Lindfields • Chatham Park
- Buenaventura Lakes • Meadow Woods • Creekside • Country Creek Estates

Appointed Agent for • Sunset Lakes • Indian Point • Formosa Gardens
• Eagle Point • Rolling Hills • Indian Ridge • Jade East Condos • Indian Creek

Interested?

Call Mark Alexander - Licensed Florida Real Estate Broker
Suite 'J', 1400 W. Oak St. Kissimmee, Florida
Tel 001 407 932 0088   Fax 001 407 870 2060
E-mail: Markatafm@aol.com - Web: www.floridasunshine.com
UK for brochure 0161 975 5315
New website: www.realtor.com/Orlando/MarkAlexander

AFM INC.
WE SELL SHORT TERM RENTAL HOMES
MARK R. ALEXANDER
Lic. Real Estate Broker

FLORIDA KEYS

Florida Keys

Sport fishing, scuba diving and the historic town of Key West

- **Population** 80,995
- **Population increase** Between 1992-2002 the population grew by 29.1%
- **Migration** 1,448 people migrated to the Monroe area in 2003
- **Median age** 40.3; the state average is 38.7
- **Median home price** $241,200, compared with the state average of $141,100
- **Cost of living** The ACCRA cost of living index rates in Monroe County as 109.63/100

Profile 190
Hotspots 192

Price Guide

$300,000–$400,000	196
$400,000–$625,000	198
$625,000–$750,000	199
$750,000–$890,000	200
$890,000–$1,290,000	201
$1,290,000–$1,400,000	202
$1,400,000–$2,200,000	204
$2,200,000 +	205

FLORIDA KEYS

GETTING THERE

AIR Key West airport is the main gateway to the Florida Keys. **American Eagle Airlines** (run by American Airlines) (0845 778 9789; www.aa.com) runs a service from Miami International to Key West, as do **US Airways** (0845 600 3300; www.usairways.com) and **Continental Airlines** (www.continental.com; 0845 607 6760). **American Airlines** (0845 778 9789; www.aa.com) and **British Airways** (www.ba.com; 0870 850 9850) both fly direct from Heathrow to Miami. There is also an airport in Marathon situated in the middle of the Overseas Highway. Connecting flights from Fort Lauderdale land here with **Florida Coastal Airlines** (www.flyfca.com; +1 772 468 2255) and **Paradise Air** (www.flyparadiseair.com; +1 305 743 4222). Flights are available with **American Airlines** from Heathrow to Fort Lauderdale, connecting in Chicago, Boston or New York.

RAIL Amtrak (+ 1 800 872 7245; www.amtrak.com) offers no mainline services to the Florida Keys, but does provide Thruway connecting bus services to Key West and Key Largo.

ROAD As there are no rail services in the region, having a car is extremely useful. The Overseas Highway, US1, runs south west from Florida City and through the Keys ending at Key West. Directions and addresses in the Keys are often given in Mile Markers, which refer to the small green and white signs at the roadside indicating the distance from Key West. An alternative approach to the Keys is on Route 997 (the Card Sound Road) which has less traffic and better views.

COACH Greyhound buses (+1 800 231 2222; www.greyhound.com) serves Key Largo, Tavernier, Islamorada, Marathon and Key West.

Area profile

THE FLORIDA KEYS IS A NECKLACE OF TROPICAL AND MANGROVE ISLANDS jutting some 120 miles into the sea south of the Florida peninsula. It's surrounded by 220 miles of North America's only living coral reef.

Incorporating over 800 islands, covering 1,034 square miles and with a population of just 80,995 the Keys can be roughly divided into five main areas. The northernmost – just 30 minutes drive from Miami Airport – is Key Largo, the self–proclaimed 'Dive Capital of the World'. Tourists flock here to experience the delights of the John Pennekamp Coral Reef State Park, the 78 square mile marine protection area that currently boasts around 600 species of tropical fish and around 40 species of coral.

Next down the chain is Islamorada, famed for its sport fishing. With the highest concentration of charter boats in Florida and azure seas teaming with tuna, marlin, tarpon and sailfish, this is a must for angling lovers.

Marathon is the most developed area, and the heart of the Keys in both a commercial and geographical sense. It boasts its own airport, a nine hole golf course, a sizeable luxury resort area and wonderful shopping facilities.

All of the Keys are known for their tropical and unspoiled landscape, but the least developed is the Lower Keys, just south of Marathon. A huge draw for eco-tourists and nature lovers is the National Key Deer and Great White Heron Wildlife refuge, home to migratory birds, rare and endangered species, and tiny deer that stand just two feet off the ground.

The last part of the Florida Keys island chain is Key West, which occupies a position just 90 miles north of Cuba. The cosmopolitan party capital of the Florida Keys, Key West's principal bars and night-clubs are centred on the main thoroughfare of Duval Street.

The Florida Keys are linked by US 1, the Overseas Highway, which replaced Henry Flagler's Overseas Railroad. Beginning in Key Largo and running all the way to Key West, the full drive takes around one-and-a-half hours and is one of America's most renowned road trips.

The John Pennekamp Coral Reef State Park attracts many thousands of scuba divers every year

FLORIDA KEYS

The economy and housing market

This lovely archipelago draws much of its income from the tourists and weekenders who enjoy the tropical, laidback lifestyle experienced on the Keys. Relaxation comes at a price though, with the Florida Keys bearing the highest cost of living in the whole of the Sunshine State.

House prices are very expensive, having risen exponentially over the past seven years. The high rate of demand means the market moves very quickly, so potential buyers need to make their decisions fast. The most expensive area is Key West, slightly cheaper are the Middle Keys (from Long Key to south of Marathon), less pricey again are the Upper Keys (from Key Largo to Long Key), while any bargains are likely to be found in the Lower Keys (from Sunshine Key south). On average, a two-bed condo will costs upwards of $300,000, an average single family home $350,000, a house on the canal front with a mooring $700,000 and an oceanfront property $1.5 million. Supply is limited due to strict building and planning regulations, which naturally means that investing in a property on the Keys will allow for excellent capital appreciation, currently estimated at around 20 per cent annually. Rental demand is high, too, and in peak season prices can reach $275 per night for a large, well-located villa in Key West.

Key West is one of the most desirable places to live in Florida… as you can see!

Social groups

Although the Keys is a hugely popular tourist destination, there are relatively few European home-owners; in fact, around 90 per cent of property sales are to Americans. The high cost of both living and property is prohibitive to all but the reasonably wealthy, and most residents are owner occupiers as opposed to investors. Very few actually rent out their property when they are not in situ.

The islands have a reputation as a playground for the rich and beautiful but don't be put off by these apparent pretensions. Florida Keys inhabitants have an incredibly relaxed 'live and let live' attitude and pride themselves on their diversity, with many originally hailing from the Carolinas, the Bahamas, the Caribbean or nearby Cuba. It is precisely this attitude that has allowed Key West to become one of the best-known gay resorts in all of Florida, even describing itself in some literature as 'the original gay destination'. This might well be true; it is rumoured that Captain Tony's Saloon was a gay bar even in 1928 when it was the favoured watering hole of the young Ernest Hemingway.

Welcoming people from all walks of life, the Keys have also become home to many artists, painters, creative thinkers and writers. Once installed on the islands, residents quickly become part of the community and a great sense of cohesiveness prevails. Life on the archipelago could be described as village life with a cosmopolitan air. There truly is nowhere else quite like it, and many are soon smitten by the relaxed tropical lifestyle.

FLORIDA KEYS		LONDON		FLORIDA KEYS		LONDON
Dec	22	7	Dec	54	81
Nov	25	10	Nov	67	78
Oct	27	14	Oct	110	70
Sept	28	19	Sept	138	65
Aug	29	21	Aug	137	62
July	29	22	July	83	59
June	29	20	June	116	58
May	27	17	May	88	57
April	25	13	April	52	56
March	23	10	March	47	64
Feb	22	7	Feb	38	72
Jan	21	6	Jan	56	77

Average monthly temperature °C (Celsius) — Florida Climate Center (www.coaps.fsu.edu/climate_center)

Average monthly rainfall mm (millimetres)

AVERAGE HOUSE SALE PRICES

Hotspot	2-bed	3-bed	4-bed	5-bed
Islamorada	$350K (£193K)	$606K (£333K)	$1M (£550K)	$2.2M (£1.2M)
Key West	$300K (£165K)	$432K (£236K)	$521K (£284K)	$1.6M (£888K)
Key Largo	$350K (£193K)	$450K (£248K)	$– (£–)	$2M (£1.1M)
Tavernier	$320K (£176K)	$670K (£365K)	$776K (£423K)	$– (£–)
Layton	$547K (£299K)	$900K (£495K)	$2.09M (£1.14M)	$– (£–)
Marathon	$638K (£348K)	$706K (£385K)	$912K (£497K)	$– (£–)

191

■ FLORIDA KEYS

Property hotspots

MAP KEY

Areas of interest
▲ John Pennekamp Coral Reef
▲ Looe Key Marine Sanctuary
● Hotspot
● Major town/city
66 Road numbers

1. Islamorada

ESSENTIALS ■ **Pop** 6,846 ■ **Airport** The Florida Keys Marathon, 9400 Overseas Highway 200, FL 33050, Tel: +1 305 289-6060 ■ **Tax** Property tax rate per $1,000; $14

KEY FACTS

■ **Schools** Island Christian School, 83400 Overseas Highway, Islamorada, FL 33036, Tel: +1 305 664 4933
■ **Medical** Mariners Hospital, 91500 Overseas Highway, Tavernier, FL 33070, Tel: +1 305 852-4418
■ **Rentals** A weekly rent for a two-bedroom property is typically $1,000 out of season and $1,800 during peak season ■ Monthly rates vary from $1,600 to over $4,100
■ **Pros** Offers the finest big game fishing in the region ■ The average house price is $263,500, cheap compared with many areas of the Keys ■ There is plenty to keep watersport fanatics busy with lots of excellent diving areas off the Islamorada coastline ■ This is a stunning area, with fantastic weather ■ A superb area for investment
■ **Cons** Despite offering cheap housing within the Keys region, the average house price is significantly above the Florida average ■ The average property price is $263,500, $122,400 more than the average Floridian house price ■ Houses have appreciated by 28 per cent over the last year

Islamorada is a small resort town of around 7,000 inhabitants that sits 40 miles from the mainland to the south of Key Largo. Islamorada, rather confusingly, is also the collective name for the strip of islands that stretch for 20 miles, including Upper and Lower Matecumbe, Windley and Plantation. It was incorporated as a town in 1907, but in 1935, a huge hurricane destroyed buildings and killed more than 400 people, many of them war veterans employed by the government to build the new highway that would later link Miami with Key West. Today, its marinas are full of bobbing charter boats that cater for the thousands of anglers who visit every year – Islamorada proudly proclaims itself to be the 'Sport Fishing Capital of the World' due to its bountiful waters. Good shops and restaurants are plentiful, and it's a popular spot for snorkelling and scuba diving. The Keys real estate market is currently booming and 2003 saw the average sale price in the Upper Keys increased 16 per cent to $407,000. At the lower end of the market, a single storey, two-bed home starts at around $350,000, but detached homes in prime positions can sell for over $3 million. Lower Matecumbe Key, which Islamorada also incorporates, provides prime real estate – plots of building land can sell for around $400,000, and the finest private estate, $8 million. ●

FLORIDA KEYS

2. Key West

ESSENTIALS ■ **Pop** 25,478 ■ **Airport** Key West International, 3491 S Roosevelt Blvd., FL 33040, Tel: +1 305 296-5439
■ **Tax** Property tax rate per $1,000: $14

Key West sits at the southern tip of the Lower Keys, just 90 miles from Havana. Originally developed as a naval base in the 1820s, it's now a popular, bohemian resort of around 25,000 inhabitants. Its most famous resident, Ernest Hemingway, lived here throughout the 1930s and his house is now one of the city's biggest tourist attractions. The influx of Key West's large artistic community can be traced back to the same period, around the time of the Great Depression, and remains home to many artists, performers and writers, as well as a sizeable and influential gay community. The old town is full of carefully restored historic buildings, bars and restaurants, as well as home to a host of great and often eccentric characters.

As more people have been attracted to the area, so the price of property has steadily risen. Apartments in marinas and small, two-bed, single storey homes start at around $200,000. Small homes in the Bahamian Village, just west of the old town start at well over $250,000, although prices are expected to continue rising in this area as developers move in and refurbish properties. At the top end of the market, large detached homes in the old town sell for between $3 and $7 million. Agents have recently reported slowing trends, as prices have risen beyond the means of many of the inhabitants. ●

KEY FACTS

■ **Schools** Key West High School, 2100 Flagler Ave, Key West, FL 33040, Tel: +1 305 293-1549
■ **Medical** Immediate Medical Care, Flagler Ave & 7th St, Key West, FL 33040, Tel: +1 305 295-7550
■ **Rentals** A two-bedroom property costs an average of $847 off season and $1,137 during peak season ■ Key West has a huge tourist industry making it ideal for those seeking to buy-to-let ■ Rentals of less than 30 days are not allowed in Key West unless the property has a transient rental occupational licence
■ **Pros** Famous for the laidback lifestyle, with a huge number of restaurants, bars and a party atmosphere every night ■ Known for its fabulous sunsets, history and famous residents such as; Ernest Hemingway and Tennessee Williams
■ **Cons** Huge demand, a stunning location and short supply due to building regulations makes for an expensive housing market ■ The average property price is $376,000 and it takes a deep pocket to afford to buy here ■ With over two million tourists every year, Key West can get extremely overcrowded ■ The cost of living for Key West is astronomical, with an ACCRA rating of 136.2/100, and the housing rate of 198.1/100

3. Key Largo

ESSENTIALS ■ **Pop** 11,886 ■ **Airport** Miami International Airport, P.O Box 592075, Miami, FL 33159, Tel: +1 305 876-7077
■ **Tax** Property tax rate per $1,000; $14

Key Largo is both the name of the largest Key island – around 30 miles long – and the town itself of around 12,000 inhabitants. Key Largo is the most visited island of the Keys due to its location; it's just over 50 miles south of Miami, and is a popular destination for weekenders from the mainland who are attracted to its wealth of snorkelling, diving and fishing opportunities and party atmosphere. Although not nearly as fashionable as Key West, Key Largo does have some excellent cafes and restaurants, and they're considerably cheaper than those further south.

For those looking for a house on the Keys, but who wish to be within striking distance of the mainland, Key Largo offers a good selection of properties at reasonable prices, albeit within a less historical setting than Key West. At the lowest end of the market to the north of the centre, single storey homes start at just under $200,000 and there are plenty of decent homes in the $350,000-$400,000 bracket. Waterfront apartments with docking facilities start at around $400,000, and at the top end of the market, oceanfront homes in exclusive Linderman Key and around Mutiny Place and South Ocean shores sell for between $2 million and $7 million. As the towns further south become more expensive, Key Largo is expected to rise in price. ●

KEY FACTS

■ **Schools** Key Largo School, 104801 Overseas Highway, Key Largo, FL 33037, Tel: +1 305 453-1248
■ **Medical** Mariners Hospital, 91500 Overseas Highway, Tavernier, FL 33070, Tel: +1 305 852-4418
■ **Rentals** A typical two-bedroom property costs $812 out of season and $1,000 during peak season ■ Rentals are available on a weekly basis
■ **Pros** Only an hour's drive from Miami airport and close to mainland Florida ■ This is a well-renowned area for diving, located as it is by the John Pennekamp Coral Reef State Park ■ It's popular with eco-tourists, birdwatchers and artists who take advantage of its proximity to the mainland with weekend visits
■ **Cons** This area is undergoing extensive protection in order to maintain its ecosystem and consequently this impacts on the property market by increasing the prices ■ The median property price is $174,200, with prices ranging from $90,000 to $1 million ■ Those seeking a waterfront property will be looking at paying a premium ■ At weekends Key Largo is packed with visitors from the mainland and it can get quite rowdy

■ **FLORIDA KEYS**

4. Tavernier

ESSENTIALS ■ **Pop** 2,173 ■ **Airport** The Florida Keys Marathon, 9400 Overseas Highway 200, FL 33050, Tel: +1 305 289-6060 ■ **Tax** Property Tax rate per $1,000; $14

KEY FACTS

■ **Schools** Coral Shores High School, 89901 Old Highway, Tavernier, FL 33070, Tel: +1 305 853-3222 ■ Plantation Key School, 100 Lake Road, Tavernier, FL 33070, Tel: +1 305 853-3281
■ **Medical** Mariners Hospital, 91500 Overseas Highway, Tavernier, FL 33070, Tel: +1 305 852-4418
■ **Rentals** Monthly rates for a three-bedroom house range from $2,000 to $4,000 ■ You are only allowed to rent property for a minimum of one month, which restricts the number of rentals you can secure per year ■ There is a much smaller tourist industry operating in Tavernier which means that this area does not yield high rental returns
■ **Pros** An excellent location to enjoy diving and wildlife ■ This is a cheaper market to buy into in comparison with the majority of the Keys
■ **Cons** The average house price is around $226,700 ■ This is not the most inviting of locations and there is very little of interest here, apart from the collection of historical buildings, ■ Those looking for restaurants and other facilities would be better off looking elsewhere

Tavernier began to expand as a town when Henry Flagler's railroad arrived around 1910, and it soon became an important link to the mainland for the Keys. However, once the line had been completed all the way to Key West, it became little more than a stopping off point for travellers to the furthest Key, and its population has settled down at just over 2,000.

The town's best feature is its collection of around 60 historic buildings, which the Old Tavernier Town Association fought to save over 20 years ago. Opened in 1928, the Tavernier Hotel and its Copper Kettle restaurant are popular with tourists attracted by the abundant watersports and diving, together with the Florida Keys Wild Bird Rehabilitation Center. Because it's such a small and comfortable community, property is expensive and little of note is available for under $300,000 apart from mobile homes. The limited amount of property, coupled with high demands has pushed prices out of the reach of most buyers. Many of the smaller, single storey homes sell for up to $400,000, while four-bedroom townhouses in new marina communities cost upwards of $2 million. South of the old town at Tavernier Creek, large, modern detached homes with oceanfront views can fetch over $3 million. ●

5. Layton

ESSENTIALS ■ **Pop** 186 ■ **Airport** The Florida Keys Marathon, 9400 Overseas Highway 200, FL 33037, Tel: +1 305 289-6060 ■ **Tax** Property Tax rate per $1,000; $14

KEY FACTS

■ **Schools** Island Christian School, 83400 Overseas Highway, Islamorada, FL 33036, Tel: +1 305 664-4933 ■ Coral Shores High School, 89901 Old Highway, Tavernier, FL 33070, Tel: +1 305 853-3222
■ **Medical** Mariners Hospital, 91500 Overseas Highway, Tavernier, FL 33070, Tel: +1 305 852-4418
■ **Rentals** There is a one month minimum on rentals in this area, and because of the size of the town, very few rental properties are available, which means that the market is strong
■ **Pros** This is an extremely small community, untouched by the tourism that dominates the rest of the Keys ■ Home to the Keys Marine Lab, this is a great diving and fishing spot ■ Its proximity to the Channel 5 bridge means that you can reach the ocean or bay by boat in under 15 minutes
■ **Cons** A strong seller's market exists here ■ This is an expensive area where a two-bedroom home, fronting a canal will set you back around $600,000 ■ As with much of the Keys, there are a limited number of properties available ■ Layton is tiny, with only a post office, so if you want to eat out or go shopping you'll have to travel the 15 miles or so to Islamorada or Marathon

With a small population of around 200 – mainly retirees, Layton is Florida Keys' smallest city. It lies on Long Key at the southern end of the Upper Keys, 15 miles from both Islamorada and Marathon. Long Key was a very fashionable resort in the early 19th century. Its 75-room hotel attracted many well-known figures of the time including; William Hearst, Herbert Hoover and Franklin Roosevelt. The exclusive Long Key Fishing Club, formed by author Zane Grey, included President Hoover as an honorary member. In 1935, a devastating hurricane hit Long Key destroying most of the buildings in the process. In the late 1950s, a Miami grocer named Del Layton bought 40 acres of land on the Key and built the canals that the majority of homes now front. Apart from a post office, the city is entirely residential, but it does have a major attraction in Long Key State Park. Opened in 1969 and covering 965 acres, it is a popular area for camping, swimming, canoeing and cycling. With a dearth of properties and little new development in such a desirable location, real estate in Layton is expensive. Adjacent to the Overseas Highway, two and three-bed homes built in the 1950s and 1960s sell for between $1 and $2.5 million. With easy access to the mainland and a strong rental market, Layton's prices should rise steadily in the future. ●

FLORIDA KEYS

6. Marathon

ESSENTIALS ■ **Pop** 10,255 ■ **Airport** The Florida Keys Marathon, 9400 Overseas Highway 200, FL 33037, Tel: +1 305 289-6060 ■ **Tax** Property Tax rate per $1,000; $14

Marathon lies on the centre of the string of islands on Key Vaca. The town itself was named after the Key until railroad workers renamed it Marathon, during the lengthy construction of the Seven Mile Bridge between 1908 and 1912 (the previous bridge had been destroyed by a hurricane in 1906). After the railroad was completed, hotels and small businesses were attracted to the area and today it's a busy town of around 10,000 inhabitants. Fishing and snorkelling are the area's main attractions. Scuba diving is popular around Sombrero Reef, as is its historic, 142-foot lighthouse which was completed in 1858. The area is also home to the Sombrero Resort and Lighthouse Marina. While it's certainly less historical in terms of its architecture than other island towns, Marathon has great shops and restaurants, as well as a hospital and an airport. North east of the town is Crane Point Hammock, a 64-acre site with tropical forest, wetlands and trails that are fronted by two museums. Real estate prices are increasing with local agents reporting huge growth this year. The cheapest homes in town are inland, single storey, fixed mobile units, and they start at just under $200,000. A one-bed, waterfront apartment in one of the area's few high-rises, costs around $300,000. As in most Key towns, premium properties can sell for many millions. ●

KEY FACTS

■ **Schools** Marathon High School, 350 Sombrero Beach Rd, Marathon, FL 33050, Tel: +1 305 289 2486
■ **Medical** Fishermen's Hospital, 3301 Overseas Highway, Marathon, FL 33050, Tel: +1 305 743-5533
■ **Rentals** During peak season a two-bedroom house costs between $950 and $1,600 a week ■ Monthly rents for a two-bedroom house vary from $3,200 to $4,500 ■ During the Lobster Dive sport season on the last Wednesday and Thursday of July, many rentals increase by as much as $200 per week
■ **Pros** Marathon is an ideal base for families; it's fairly quiet with a limited amount of nightlife ■ Marathon has a good infrastructure with an airport in the heart of town, and it's located only 50 miles from Key West ■ Marathon remains a good investment with strong predicted appreciation
■ **Cons** The average house price is $222,500 ■ This area is highly developed and prone to be over-run by tourists in the summer months ■ This is primarily a tourist destination and only a serious relocation prospect for those with deep pockets

The Florida Keys is a unique chain of islands connected by long bridges, a great feat of engineering

■ THE FLORIDA KEYS

$300,000 – $400,000
(£165,000–£220,000)

Despite the pricey nature of Keys property, there are some bargains to be found

$329,900   CODE MAR
KEY LARGO
Built on stilts this property, with a private marina, is set in a beachfront community
£181,445

2 | with a small garden | situated close to the town centre | not located on a main road | room for parking

---

$345,000   CODE MAR
ISLAMORADA
A charming 'conch' style home, well appointed and close to the oceanfront
£189,750

2 | with a garden | close to shops and attractions | not located on a main road | room for parking

---

$359,000   CODE MAR
ISLAMORADA
Constructed on stilts, this modern house has a balcony from which it enjoys great views
£197,450

2 | with a garden | situated close to the beach and amenities | not located on a main road | room for parking

---

$379,000   CODE MAR
KAWAMA
Spacious and well maintained, a fully furnished home, set on the beach, with a tennis court
£208,450

2 | with a large garden | located in the town centre | not on a main road | room for parking

---

$399,000   CODE MAR
TAVERNIER
A 'conch' style property, just a short walk to the canal and close to the beach
£219,450

2 | with a small garden | situated close to amenities | not located on a main road | room for parking

IRM
Investments, Real Estate & Management

Buying in Florida?
IRM makes it possible!

Featuring
- Great Locations
- Various Floor Plans and Models
- Mortgage Plans for U.S. and Foreign Investors
- Investment and Business Opportunities
- Businesses for Sale
- Immigration Services
- New Villas, Town Homes and Condos
- Property Management

Book your inspection visit now and receive a 2 night 3 day complimentary stay.

Orlando
Phone: (407) 903-0134
Toll Free: (866) 476-6752
Fax: (407) 903-0688

Caracas
Phone: (58212) 265-0313
Fax: (58212) 267-5651

South Florida
Phone: (305) 792-9987
Toll Free: (877) 792-9987
Fax: (305) 792-4687

United Kingdom
Phone: (44) 01425-653540
Fax: (44) 01425-656305

SUNTRUST
Glenn Hight: 407-667-7505
www.suntrustmortgage.com/ghight

Financial services available through SunTrust Bank.
Equal Housing Lender

www.irm-usa.com
E-mail: info@irm-usa.com

■ THE FLORIDA KEYS

$400,000—$625,000
(£220,000–£343,750)

This price bracket will buy you a little slice of paradise in historic Key Largo

$400,000   CODE MAR
KEY LARGO
With a private boat ramp and a large porch, this home comes with all mod cons
£165,000

🛏 2   🌼 with a garden   🏬 within easy reach of the shops and beach   🚸 not located on a main road   🚗 room for parking

$459,000   CODE MAR
KEY LARGO
Set in a gated development, an oceanfront condo, with a private marina and beach
£252,450

🛏 2   🌼 with a communal garden   🏬 situated close to the town centre   🚸 not located on a main road   🚗 room for parking

$549,000   CODE MAR
KEY LARGO
With a boat ramp this waterfront home is the height of luxury and a perfect retreat
£301,950

🛏 3   🌼 with a garden   🏬 a short walk to the schools and shops   🚸 not located on a main road   🚗 room for parking

$599,000   CODE MAR
KEY LARGO
An oceanside condo, with a swimming pool and hot tub, an ideal investment opportunity
£329,450

🛏 1   🌼 with a communal garden   🏬 close to shops and amenities   🚸 not located on a main road   🚗 room for parking

$625,000   CODE MAR
KEY LARGO
With a private dock and boat ramp, this home has magnificent bay views and beach access
£343,750

🛏 3   🌼 with a patio   🏬 within easy reach of amenities   🚸 not located on a main road   🚗 room for parking

THE FLORIDA KEYS

$625,000–$750,000
(£343,750–£412,500)

The Upper Keys offer wonderful waterfront properties for less than £500,000

$659,000
CODE MAR

KEY LARGO
Renovated to high standards, this oceanfront property is well located in a popular area

£362,450

3 | with a garden | within easy reach of shops and attractions | not located on a main road | room for parking

---

$675,000
CODE ACR

UPPER MATECUMBE KEY
A small cottage, arranged over two floors, with a separate workshop in the grounds

£371,250

2 | with a large garden | situated close to shops | not located on a main road | room for parking

---

$689,000
CODE MAR

KEY LARGO
Enjoying bay views, this property has been recently extended; ideal for the family

£378,950

3 | no garden | within easy reach of shops and attractions | not located on a main road | room for parking

---

$699,000
CODE MAR

KEY LARGO
A recently renovated home, located on the waterfront, with a private dock

£384,450

3 | with a small garden and private dock | situated close to amenities | not located on a main road | room for parking

---

$750,000
CODE EXI

KEY COLONY BEACH
This duplex offers the buyer a wealth of opportunities; an ideal investment home

£412,500

4 | with a garden | close to the town centre | not located on a main road | room for parking

PRICE GUIDE

■ THE FLORIDA KEYS

$750,000 – $890,000
(£412,500–£489,500)

More fantastic properties in Key Largo and the surrounding area

$789,000   CODE MAR
KEY LARGO
Built on stilts, this fully furnished home is conveniently located on the bay, with views
£433,950

- 2 | no garden | situated close to amenities | not located on a main road
- room for parking

$799,000   CODE MAR
KEY LARGO
With views overlooking the bay, this home has a private dock, ideal for keen sailors
£439,450

- 2 | with a small garden and marina | situated close to amenities | not located on a main road | room for parking

---

$825,000   CODE MAR
KEY LARGO
With magnificent bay views and a private dock, a modern home in a glorious setting
£453,750

- 3 | with a marina | close to the port and shops | not located on a main road
- room for parking

$849,000   CODE MAR
PLANTATION KEY
A luxurious waterfront home, recently renovated, with a balcony overlooking the canal
£466,950

- 3 | with a garden and marina | close to amenities and attractions
- not located on a main road | room for parking

$889,000   CODE MAR
KEY LARGO
Located in a gated community, a dazzling townhouse, set on the oceanfront, with a pool
£488,950

- 3 | with a marina | close to all amenities | not located on a main road
- room for parking

PRICE GUIDE

THE FLORIDA KEYS

$890,000 — $1,290,000
(£489,500–£709,500)

The historic resort towns of Marathon and Islamorada are ideal for families

$899,000   CODE MAR
PLANTATION KEY
In pristine condition, a modern home with beautiful ocean views, and a private dock
£494,450

- 2 | with a garden | close to shops and the port | not located on a main road | room for parking

$995,000   CODE EXI
ISLAMORADA
Recently renovated this stylish bay side home comes complete with a swimming pool
£547,250

- 3 | with a garden | within easy reach of shops and attractions | not located on a main road | room for parking

$999,000   CODE MAR
KEY LARGO
A stunning custom-built home, overlooking the ocean, with a private boat dock
£549,450

- 4 | with a garden | close to amenities | not located on a main road | room for parking

$1,200,000   CODE EXI
MARATHON
Located on the canal, this duplex property has fantastic lagoon views
£660,000

- 6 | with a garden | situated close to amenities | not located on a main road | room for parking

$1,260,000   CODE FLK
MARATHON
A spacious modern property located in a much sought-after area, with waterfront access
£639,000

- 6 | with well maintained gardens | situated close to amenities | not located on a main road | room for parking

PRICE GUIDE

■ THE FLORIDA KEYS

$1,290,000—$1,400,000
(£709,500–£770,000)

When you have more than $1,000,000 to spend, there is no shortage of properties

$1,295,000   CODE FLK
MARATHON
A fantastic home with fabulous views over the water, located in a peaceful area
£712,250

- 3 | with a large, well-maintained garden | within easy reach of the town centre
- not located on a main road | room for parking

$1,300,000   CODE FLK
MARATHON
Situated on Key Haven, a newly built, open-plan property, on the waterfront
£715,000

- 3 | with a large garden | close to amenities | not located on a main road
- room for parking

$1,300,000   CODE MAR
PORT LARGO
Located on the canal and overlooking the ocean, a stunning, modern property
£715,000

- 3 | with a small garden | situated close to all amenities and attractions
- not located on a main road | room for parking

$1,350,000   CODE FLK
KEY WEST
A luxurious family home with a fully fitted kitchen, located on the oceanfront
£742,500

- 2 | almost 1/4 acre | situated close to the town centre | not located on a main road
- room for four cars to park

$1,395,000   CODE FLK
MARATHON
A newly constructed waterfront home with a spa, enjoying ocean views from its balcony
£767,250

- 3 | with a large maintained garden | situated close to the beach and shops
- not located on a main road | room for parking

PRICE GUIDE

"Use our years of Experience . . . to Benefit yours"

"It all makes Cents with HOMES OF AMERICA"
"We Lead the way in Florida Real Estate"

★ Min 20% deposit with 80% USA or UK Mortgage
★ Let us show you how to self finance your home
★ Homes of America UK & USA Offices
★ Free Services of Licensed Realtors ★ Buyers Representation
★ Relaxed yet Professional Company ★ Member of the N.A.E.A & N.A.R
★ Homes of America Property Management Company
★ Try & Buy Programme / Inspection Accommodation
★ Homeowner Referrals available
★ We help you buy a home. . . . not sell you one!

UK Office: **01244 579076**
US Office: **14758 East Orange Lake Blvd, Town Center, HWY 192**
Email: **florida@homesofamerica.co.uk**
Real Estate: **www.homesofamerica.co.uk**
Rental: **www.floridavipvacationc.com**

Exclusive Development starting from $270,000 (approx 150,000 UK sterling)
Upgraded furniture as standard, tiled roof, 14 x 28 private pool, extended deck as standard, etc......

■ THE FLORIDA KEYS

$1,400,000 – $2,200,000
(£770,000–£1,210,000)

Homes for those with deep pockets in the most sought-after areas in the Keys

$1,425,000   CODE MAR
KEY LARGO
Situated directly on the oceanfront a stunning modern villa, with a pool and a dock
£783,750

🛏 4   ❀ with a small garden   🏙 situated close to the town centre   🚫 not located on a main road   🏠 room for parking

---

$1,675,000   CODE MAR
KEY LARGO
A private gated home, fronting directly onto the ocean, with a separate guest house
£921,250

🛏 3   ❀ with a large garden   🏙 situated close to the town centre   🚫 not located on a main road   🏠 room for parking

---

$2,150,000   CODE FLK
KEY WEST
On the harbour front, a townhouse with all mod cons and great views from its balcony
£1,182,500

🛏 3   ❀ with a pool and patio   🏙 situated close to amenities   🚫 not located on a main road   🏠 room for parking, with a garage

$2,150,000   CODE ACR
PLANTATION KEY
With private dockage space, a fabulous home with a two-bedroom guest quarter
£1,182,500

🛏 2   ❀ with a landscaped garden   🏙 situated close to the shops   🚫 not located on a main road   🏠 room for parking

---

$2,195,000   CODE FLK
KEY WEST
This townhouse has an ocean view from its balcony, and comes fully furnished
£1,207,250

🛏 4   ❀ with 1/4 of an acre   🏙 situated a short distance from amenities   🚫 not located on a main road   🏠 room for parking

PRICE GUIDE

THE FLORIDA KEYS

$2,200,000+
(£1,210,000+)

With no expense spared, luxury homes in Florida really don't come any better

$3,200,000 — CODE ACR
LOWER MATECUMBE KEY
A bayfront estate, with a private dock and a boat included in the price
£1,760,000

- 5 | with a small garden | situated close to the town centre | not located on a main road | room for parking

---

$3,675,000 — CODE ACR
KEY LARGO
A recently built home, designed to the highest standards, with fantastic ocean views
£2,021,250

- 4 | with a large garden | situated close to shops and attractions | not located on a main road | room for parking

---

$4,700,000 — CODE ACR
KEY LARGO
A newly constructed home with a pool and spa, fronting onto a lagoon, with a dock
£2,585,000

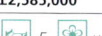

- 5 | with two acres | situated close to amenities | not located on a main road | room for parking

---

$5,700,000 — CODE ACR
KEY LARGO
A Polynesian-style secluded property, newly built, with a dock and beachfront access
£3,135,000

- 4 | with a large garden | situated in the village centre | not located on a main road | room for parking

---

$15,000,000 — CODE ACR
MARATHON
A nine-acre island, offering a salt water lagoon, private dock, swimming pool and views
£8,250,000

- 5 | with nine acres | situated a short distance from mainland amenities | not located on a main road | room for parking

PRICE GUIDE

■ BUYER'S REFERENCE INTRO

There's more to Florida than just hustle and bustle; there is also peace and tranquillity

Buyer's Reference

Directory of Useful Contacts
Index and Index to Agents
Average price matrices

Average house sale prices **208**
Average apartment prices **210**
Average lettings prices **212**
Glossary **214**
Directory of useful contacts **218**
Index of agents **232**
Index **236**
Contributors **240**
Index to Ads **242**

■ BUYER'S REFERENCE

House price matrix

Hotspots	2-bed	3-bed	4-bed	5/6 bed
The Panhandle				
Fort Walton Beach	$195,888 (£107,157)	$283,500 (£154,400)	$482,000 (£262,500)	$775,000 (£422,150)
Pensacola	$142,650 (£77,700)	$287,000 (£156,300)	$440,600 (£240,000)	$1,010,000 (£550,160)
Destin	$567,400 (£310,387)	$1,130,000 (£615,500)	$1,470,000 (£800,700)	$3,185,000 (£1,735,000)
Panama City Beach	$494,000 (£269,000)	$645,500 (£351,600)	$1,060,000 (£577,400)	$1,630,000 (£888,000)
The North East				
Daytona Beach	$147,500 (£80,350)	$305,000 (£166,000)	$447,000 (£243,500)	$739,725 (£404,655)
New Smyrna	$217,500 (£118,500)	$508,000 (£277,000)	$639,000 (£348,000)	$917,000 (£499,500)
St Augustine	$342,000 (£186,300)	$550,000 (£299,600)	$1,125,000 (£612,800)	$1,532,333 (£838,239)
Ormond Beach	$132,550 (£72,509)	$295,550 (£161,676)	$467,000 (£254,400)	$612,733 (£335,186)
Ponte Verda Beach	$247,320 (£135,292)	$388,240 (£212,380)	$902,760 (£493,841)	$2,872,983 (£1,571,622)
The Gulf Coast				
Clearwater	$230,200 (£125,400)	$364,100 (£198,330)	$530,000 (£288,700)	$920,000 (£501,100)
St Petersburg	$224,550 (£122,300)	$420,870 (£229,250)	$568,000 (£309,400)	$1,220,000 (£664,500)
Sarasota	$373,400 (£203,400)	$801,200 (£436,400)	$1,790,000 (£975,000)	$3,300,000 (£1,797,500)
Englewood	$545,000 (£297,000)	$707,000 (£385,100)	$1,206,000 (£657,000)	$2,219,800 (£1,214,308)
Venice	$294,000 (£160,150)	$360,800 (£196,500)	$780,000 (£425,000)	$1,880,000 (£1,024,000)
Naples	$215,660 (£117,973)	$863,000 (£470,000)	$2,650,000 (£1,443,500)	$3,700,000 (£2,015,400)
Fort Myers	$430,000 (£234,200)	$590,000 (£321,400)	$457,280 (£250,148)	$2,030,000 (£1,106,000)
Bradenton	$280,000 (£152,500)	$645,000 (£351,300)	$867,000 (£472,300)	$1,480,000 (£806,200)
Punta Gorda	$241,500 (£131,500)	$500,000 (£272,350)	$619,000 (£337,200)	$945,500 (£515,000)
Cape Coral	$155,715 (£85,181)	$608,000 (£331,200)	$816,000 (£444,500)	$1,750,000 (£953,200)
Central Florida				
Orlando	$287,000 (£156,300)	$303,000 (£165,000)	$660,000 (£359,500)	$912,000 (£497,000)
Kissimmee	$146,500 (£79,800)	$236,650 (£129,000)	$401,300 (£218,600)	$551,100 (£300,200)
Davenport	$165,600 (£90,200)	$265,000 (£144,350)	$131,966 (£72,190)	$177,700 (£97,208)

BUYER'S REFERENCE

Hotspots	2-bed	3-bed	4-bed	5/6 bed
The South East				
Palm Beach	$651,400 (£355,000)	$822,000 (£448,000)	$3,040 000 (£1,656,000)	$5,300,000 (£2,887,000)
Fort Lauderdale	$365,300 (£199,000)	$423,600 (£230,740)	$573,362 (£313,649)	$1,276,650 (£698,372)
Port St Lucie	$219,376 (£120,006)	$234,400 (£128,000)	$294,750 (£160,550)	$533,760 (£291,985)
Hollywood	$520,300 (£283,400)	$539,000 (£293,600)	$586,000 (£319,200)	$1,195,000 (£651,000)
Boca Raton	$375,600 (£204,600)	$1,218,000 (£663,460)	$1,442,500 (£786,000)	$2,868,000 (£1,562,000)
The Everglades				
Everglades City	$345,000 (£188,727)	$353,000 (£193,103)	$379,333 (£207,509)	$478,000 (£261,482)
Plantation Island	$219,660 (£120,165)	$231,666 (£126,730)	$292,000 (£159,734)	$342,256 (£187,222)
Chokoloskee Island	$357,833 (£195,747)	$451,000 (£246,712)	$ – (£–)	$ – (£–)
10,000 Islands	$155,000 (£84,790)	$300,000 (£164,110)	$ – (£–)	$ – (£–)
Miami				
South Miami	$384,000 (£209,200)	$432,600 (£235,600)	$502,333 (£274,793)	$1,100,000 (£599,000)
North Miami Beach	$198,600 (£108,641)	$432,300 (£235,500)	$520,500 (£283,500)	$1,630,000 (£888,000)
Biscayne Bay	$363,000 (£198,573)	$638,800 (£349,446)	$1,310,600 (£716,944)	$4,984,750 (£2,726,832)
Aventura	$326,660 (£178,694)	$670,000 (£365,000)	$776,000 (£422, 700)	$1,539,400 (£842,105)
Bal Harbour	$676,700 (£370,178)	$1,133,800 (£620,228)	$2,085,000 (£1,136,000)	$3,150,000 (£1,723,160)
Surfside	$502,700 (£274,994)	$706,000 (£384,500)	$912,000 (£496,800)	$2,960,000 (£1,612,000)
The Florida Keys				
Islamorada	$606,300 (£331,667)	$1,220,000 (£664,550)	$1,780,000 (£970,000)	$2,825,000 (£1,539,000)
Key West	$950,000 (£517,500)	$1,187,000 (£646,500)	$1,946,000 (£1,060,000)	$2,813,000 (£1,532,000)
Key Largo	$495,000 (£270,000)	$1,130,000 (£615,500)	$2,864,000 (£1,560,000)	$2,237,000 (£1,218,500)
Tavernier	$606,300 (£331,667)	$696,000 (£379,100)	$1,405,000 (£765,300)	$2,440,000 (£1,334,765)
Layton	$547,000 (£299,228)	$1,274,750 (£697,332)	$ – (£–)	$ – (£–)
Marathon	$638,000 (£347,500)	$568,200 (£310,825)	$1,393,000 (£759,000)	$2,061,000 (£1,122,600)

PRICE MATRIX

■ BUYER'S REFERENCE

Apartment price matrix

Hotspots	1-bed	2-bed	3-bed	4-bed
The Panhandle				
Fort Walton Beach	$205,960 (£112,667)	$377,880 (£206,713)	$566,360 (£369,818)	$804,780 (£440,242)
Pensacola	$262,783 (£143,751)	$292,060 (£159,767)	$623,800 (£341,240)	$1,397,800 (£764,645)
Destin	$331,483 (£181,332)	$609,800 (£333,581)	$1,165,780 (£637,722)	$1,681,800 (£920,003)
Panama City Beach	$259,780 (£142,108)	$736,225 (£402,740)	$709,600 (£388,176)	$1,030,800 (£563,883)
The North East				
Daytona Beach	$69,133 (£37,818)	$204,646 (£111,948)	$354,140 (£193,726)	$822,750 (£450,073)
New Smyrna	$169,997 (£92,994)	$256,700 (£140,423)	$486,960 (£266,384)	$1,883,333 (£1,030,249)
St Augustine	$160,660 (£87,886)	$260,740 (£142,633)	$352,260 (£192,698)	$549,633 (£300,668)
Ormond Beach	$78,914 (£43,168)	$219,873 (£120,278)	$342,194 (£187,192)	$795,195 (£434,999)
Ponte Verda Beach	$259,200 (£141,791)	$239,880 (£131,222)	$721,107 (£394,470)	$1,232,999 (£674 494)
The Gulf Coast				
Clearwater	$124,485 (£68,097)	$291,550 (£159,488)	$874,620 (£478,447)	$1,430,725 (£782,656)
St Petersburg	$142,433 (£77,916)	$310,433 (£169,817)	$976,480 (£534,168)	$1,259,860 (£689,187)
Sarasota	$82,973 (£209,500)	$1,063,485 (£581,763)	$1,801,242 (£985,342)	$2,608,980 (£1,427,203)
Englewood	$292,400 (£159,953)	$413,460 (£226,177)	$623,000 (£340,802)	$584,633 (£319,814)
Venice	$133,640 (£73,105)	$229,160 (£125,358)	$558,160 (£321,744)	$587,666 (£321,474)
Naples	$91,740 (£50,184)	$239,940 (£131,255)	$523,280 (£286,252)	$1,687,500 (£923,121)
Fort Myers	$121,320 (£66,366)	$237,916 (£130,148)	$660,671 (£361,410)	$610,340 (£333,877)
Bradenton	$63,550 (£34,764)	$278,975 (£152,609)	$442,125 (£241,857)	$621,175 (£339,804)
Punta Gorda	$144,633 (£79,119)	$438,980 (£240,137)	$504,760 (£276,121)	$619,475 (£338,874)
Cape Coral	$82,300 (£45,020)	$258,540 (£141,430)	$425,740 (£232,894)	$821,500 (£449,389)
Central Florida				
Orlando	$111,460 (£60,972)	$274,342 (£150,075)	$416,633 (£227,913)	$740,283 (£404,960)
Kissimmee	$124,560 (£68,138)	$134, 450 (£73,548)	$160,060 (£87,558)	$222,760 (£121,857)
Davenport	$47,250 (£25,847)	$115,675 (£63,278)	$192,780 (£105,457)	$172,200 (£94,199)

PRICE MATRIX

BUYER'S REFERENCE

Hotspots	1-bed	2-bed	3-bed	4-bed
The South East				
Palm Beach	$131,475 (£71,921)	$224,200 (£122,645)	$487,600 (£266,734)	$2,128,800 (£1,164,528)
Fort Lauderdale	$89,700 (£40,069)	$179,060 (£97,952)	$345,560 (£189,033)	$811,400 (£443,864)
Port St Lucie	$116,633 (£63,802)	$154,380 (£84,451)	$183,320 (£100,282)	$269,133 (£147,225)
Hollywood	$85,550 (£46,798)	$190,883 (£104,419)	$365,616 (£200,005)	$237,883 (£130,130)
Boca Raton	$89,340 (£48,872)	$304,316 (£166,471)	$1,315,780 (£719,777)	$2,590,560 (£1,417,126)
The Everglades				
Everglades City	$85,980 (£47,034)	$150,000 (£82,055)	$219,135 (£119,874)	$– (£–)
Plantation Island	$68,725 (£37,594)	$160,000 (£87,525)	$191,259 (£104,625)	$– (£–)
Chokoloskee Island	$125,359 (£68,575)	$210,382 (£115,086)	$– (£–)	$– (£–)
10,000 Islands	$112,798 (£61,704)	$120,000 (£65,644)	$183,421 (£100,337)	$– (£–)
Miami				
South Miami	$169,800 (£92,913)	$184,500 (£100,927)	$427,466 (£233,839)	$745,800 (£407,978)
North Miami Beach	$122,214 (£66,855)	$189,633 (£103,736)	$573,600 (£313,779)	$794,382 (£434,554)
Biscayne Bay	$366,000 (£200,214)	$424,100 (£231,997)	$427,450 (£233,830)	$795,375 (£435,097)
Aventura	$189,000 (£103,389)	$449,580 (£245,935)	$1,152,600 (£630,512)	$1,509,975 (£826,009)
Bal Harbour	$301,400 (£164,876)	$818,333 (£447,656)	$1,877,800 (£1 027 222)	$3,250,000 (£1,777,863)
Surfside	$343,760 (£188,048)	$472,133 (£258,273)	$787,780 (£430,943)	$971,595 (£531,496)
The Florida Keys				
Islamorada	$452,193 (£247,365)	$614,800 (£336,317)	$974,800 (£533,249)	$2,359,000 (£1,290,455)
Key West	$438,200 (£239,710)	$618,600 (£338,395)	$846,600 (£463,119)	$1,489,000 (£814,535)
Key Largo	$274,450 (£150,133)	$600,580 (£328,538)	$1,341,760 (£733,989)	$711,500 (£389,215)
Tavernier	$294,000 (£160,828)	$512,250 (£280,218)	$662,162 (£362,225)	$1,066,000 (£583,139)
Layton	$284,419 (£155,587)	$621,812 (£340,152)	$984,193 (£538,388)	$1,088,582 (£593,851)
Marathon	$282,975 (£154,797)	$485,500 (£265,585)	$749,666 (£410,093)	$608,333 (£332,779)

PRICE MATRIX

■ BUYER'S REFERENCE

Letting price matrix

Hotspots	1-bed	2-bed	3-bed	4-bed	5/6 bed
The Panhandle					
Fort Walton Beach	$977 (£534)	$2,312 (£1,265)	$3,703 (£2,026)	$4,934 (£2,699)	$5,940 (£3,249)
Pensacola	$2,694 (£1,474)	$2,489 (£1,362)	$5,040 (£2,757)	$4,590 (£2,511)	$7,440 (£4,070)
Destin	$1,890 (£1,034)	$3,042 (£1,664)	$4,440 (£2,429)	$5,560 (£3,042)	$11,396 (£6,234)
Panama City Beach	$1,880 (£1,028)	$2,633 (£1,440)	$4,720 (£2,582)	$7,409 (£4,053)	$13,919 (£7,614)
The North East					
Daytona Beach	$2,060 (£1,127)	$3,100 (£1,696)	$3,490 (£1,909)	$5,467 (£2,990)	$8,600 (£4,705)
New Smyrna	$1,831 (£1,002)	$2,120 (£1,160)	$2,670 (£1,461)	$5,060 (£2,768)	$7,617 (£4,167)
St Augustine	$1,438 (£787)	$1,999 (£1,094)	$3,160 (£1,729)	$6,400 (£3,501)	$8,149 (£4,458)
Ormond Beach	$1,450 (£793)	$1,520 (£831)	$3,288 (£1,798)	$5,050 (£2,763)	$5,345 (£2,924)
Ponte Vedra Beach	$1,560 (£853)	$3,050 (£1,668)	$3,800 (£2,079)	$4,400 (£2,407)	$6,740 (£3,687)
The Gulf Coast					
Clearwater	$2,819 (£1,542)	$1,666 (£911)	$2,356 (£1,289)	$9,280 (£5,076)	$7,725 (£4,226)
St Petersburg	$1,970 (£1,078)	$2,180 (£1,193)	$2,265 (£1,239)	$6,108 (£3,341)	$7,960 (£4,355)
Sarasota	$2,148 (£1,175)	$2,425 (£1,327)	$3,380 (£1,849)	$5,175 (£2,831)	$– (£–)
Englewood	$1,350 (£738)	$1,850 (£1,012)	$2,720 (£1,488)	$4,400 (£2,407)	$– (£–)
Venice	$1,560 (£853)	$2,389 (£1,307)	$3,340 (£1,827)	$3,740 (£2,046)	$5,174 (£2,830)
Naples	$2,380 (£1,302)	$3,080 (£1,685)	$3,760 (£2,057)	$6,010 (£3,288)	$– (£–)
Fort Myers	$1,620 (£886)	$2,340 (£1,280)	$3,252 (£1,789)	$4,133 (£2,261)	$6,946 (£3,800)
Bradenton	$1,262 (£691)	$2,120 (£1,160)	$2,918 (£1,596)	$3,418 (£1,870)	$– (£–)
Punta Gorda	$1,375 (£752)	$1,770 (£968)	$2,160 (£1,182)	$3,138 (£1,716)	$– (£–)
Cape Coral	$1,467 (£802)	$2,140 (£1,170)	$2,920 (£1,597)	$4,940 (£2,702)	$– (£–)
Central Florida					
Orlando	$1,050 (£574)	$1,678 (£918)	$2,580 (£1,411)	$3,160 (£1,729)	$4,860 (£2,659)
Kissimmee	$1,493 (£816)	$2,316 (£1,267)	$2,940 (£1,608)	$3,440 (£1,882)	$6,236 (£3,411)
Davenport	$2,078 (£1,137)	$2,600 (£1,422)	$3,060 (£1,674)	$3,384 (£1,851)	$4,267 (£2,334)

BUYER'S REFERENCE

Hotspots	1-bed	2-bed	3-bed	4-bed	5/6 bed
The South East					
Palm Beach	$1,587 (£868)	$3,540 (£1,936)	$5,437 (£2,974)	$7,000 (£3,829)	$– (£–)
Fort Lauderdale	$2,400 (£1,313)	$2,290 (£1,253)	$10,100 (£5,525)	$11,790 (£6,449)	$13,625 (£7,453)
Port St Lucie	$723 (£395)	$1,672 (£915)	$2,620 (£1,433)	$4,255 (£2,327)	$– (£–)
Hollywood	$2,980 (£1,630)	$2,480 (£1,357)	$3,250 (£1,778)	$7,589 (£4,151)	$– (£–)
Boca Raton	$1,544 (£844)	$3,660 (£2,002)	$5,500 (£3,009)	$6,813 (£3,727)	$– (£–)
The Everglades					
Everglades City	$1,677 (£917)	$1,937 (£1,059)	$2,230 (£1,220)	$3,872 (£2,118)	$– (£–)
Plantation Island	$675 (£369)	$1,023 (£560)	$– (£–)	$– (£–)	$– (£–)
Chokoloskee Island	$1,191 (£652)	$1,473 (£806)	$– (£–)	$– (£–)	$– (£–)
10,000 Islands	$1,920 (£1,050)	$2,500 (£1,368)	$4,020 (£2,199)	$7,050 (£3,857)	$– (£–)
Miami					
South Miami	$2,120 (£1,160)	$3,420 (£1,871)	$4,233 (£2,316)	$7,834 (£4,285)	$10,458 (£5,721)
North Miami Beach	$725 (£397)	$1,020 (£558)	$1,238 (£677)	$3,785 (£2,071)	$– (£–)
Biscayne Bay	$3,733 (£2,042)	$4,720 (£2,582)	$8,100 (£4,431)	$10,563 (£5,778)	$12,381 (£6,773)
Aventura	$1,168 (£639)	$1,500 (£821)	$2,086 (£1,141)	$4,978 (£2,723)	$– (£–)
Bal Harbour	$1,800 (£985)	$3,238 (£1,771)	$3,700 (£2,024)	$8,248 (£4,512)	$– (£–)
Surfside	$2,560 (£1,400)	$2,416 (£1,322)	$4,120 (£2,354)	$8,080 (£4,420)	$11,440 (£6,258)
The Florida Keys					
Islamorada	$1,684 (£921)	$2,490 (£1,362)	$6,480 (£3,545)	$8,235 (£4,505)	$10,960 (£5,995)
Key West	$3,210 (£1,756)	$3,660 (£2,002)	$5,300 (£2,899)	$9,038 (£4,944)	$5,933 (£3,246)
Key Largo	$1,736 (£950)	$1,760 (£962)	$2,880 (£1,575)	$6,840 (£3,742)	$5,650 (£3,091)
Tavernier	$1,460 (£799)	$2,590 (£1,417)	$4,040 (£2,210)	$7,200 (£3,939)	$5,900 (£3,228)
Layton	$1,899 (£1,039)	$2,600 (£1,422)	$3,414 (£1,868)	$7,120 (£3,895)	$– (£–)
Marathon	$2,510 (£1,373)	$3,444 (£1,884)	$3,920 (£2,144)	$9,100 (£4,978)	$13,250 (£7,248)

PRICE MATRIX

BUYER'S REFERENCE

Glossary

A

Acceleration clause
A clause that allows the lender to demand payment of the outstanding loan for certain reasons.

Ad valorem tax
A tax based upon the assessed value of the property.

Adjustable rate mortgage (ARM)
This mortgage offers a fixed interest rate and initial monthly repayment, for a period of between six months and five years, after which both will adjust to reflect current market interest rates.

Affidavit
A sworn statement made under oath reduced to writing.

Agent
One who is authorised to represent and act on behalf of another.

Amortization
Payment of a debt in instalments.

Annual percentage rate (APR)
The cost of credit expressed as a yearly rate. The APR includes the interest rate, points, broker fees and certain other credit charges that the borrower is required to pay.

Appraisal
An estimate of value of a property by a professional third party.

Appreciation
An increase in the worth of a property.

ASHI
American Society of Home Inspectors

Assessed value
The value placed on property by a tax assessor.

B

Balloon mortgage
A mortgage loan that requires the remaining balance to be paid at an agreed time after an agreed amount of monthly payments.

Broker
An intermediary who assists in negotiating contracts between two or more parties, one who is licensed to assist in the purchase, selling, rental or managing of real estate.

Business broker
An intermediary who assists in negotiating contracts between parties; licensed to assist in the purchase and selling of businesses.

C

Cap
A limit placed on an adjustable rate mortgage as to how much the interest rate or mortgage payments may increase or decrease.

Chain of title
An analysis of the past transfers of title to a property.

Clear title
A title free of liens or legal questions of ownership.

Closing
The final stage of a transaction, when a seller delivers the title to the buyer in exchange for the purchase price.

Closing costs
Expenses of the sale, which must be paid by the buyer or deducted from the proceeds of the sale in the case of seller's expenses.

Comparable market analysis
A comparison of prices of similar houses in the same area. A CMA is used to determine the value of a property.

Condo
An apartment, often with community facilities, e.g. a swimming pool.

Contingency
A condition that must be met before a contract is legally binding.

Contract
An oral or written, often legally binding, agreement between two parties.

Conveyance
The transfer of title to real property by means of a written instrument.

Curtailment
A payment that shortens or ends a mortgage, thereby paying off the entire debt.

D

Deed
A written document that conveys the ownership of real estate from one person or party to another.

Deposit
Money offered by a prospective buyer in entering into a contract to purchase.

Depreciation
A decline in the value of a house due to a change in the conditions of the market (i.e. a significant rise in interest rates), decline of the neighbourhood or lack of upkeep/wear and tear on a home.

Down payment
A portion of the price of a home, usually between three and 20 per cent, not borrowed and paid up front.

YOUR DREAM HOME IN ORLANDO, FLORIDA CAN PAY FOR ITSELF!

Holiday Homes in the Orlando, Florida Area

- **Commitment to Professional, Honest & Ethical Representation!**

- **Thorough Knowledge of the Home Buying Process!**

- **Experts in Investment Properties Close to the Disney Area!**

- **Access to Hundreds of New or Existing Resale Properties!**

ORLANDO VACATION REALTY

101 Polo Park Blvd., Suite 1 • Davenport, FL 33897
(863) 424-3580 • 877-850-3580 (toll free) • UK 020-8421-8375
E-mail: info@orlandovacationrealty.com

WWW.ORLANDOVACATIONREALTY.COM

■ BUYER'S REFERENCE

E

Easement
A right of way giving persons other than the owner access to or over a property.

Equity
The difference between the fair market value of the property, and the amount still owed on its mortgage.

Escheat
Property that reverts to state ownership when an individual dies without a will and without heirs.

Escrow
Money deposited with a third party until the transaction is closed.

Estate
An individual's possessions and property, relevant particularly at the time of death.

F

FIRPTA
A tax on foreign persons selling a home in the United States, thus ensuring US tax gains realised on the disposition of property interests.

Fixed rate mortgage
The interest is fixed at the time of the loan and remains constant for its duration.

Flow through amount
For people buying in a group or corporation, tax cannot be avoided but instead will flow through to the US or UK tax returns of the individuals involved. There are forms which must be filled in annually.

FNMA (Fannie Mae)
The Federal National Mortgage Association. The largest supplier of home mortgage funds in the US.

Foreclosure
A legal action that terminates all ownership rights in a home when the homebuyer fails to make the mortgage payments or is otherwise in default under the terms of the mortgage.

Frontage
The length of a property abutting a street, or, as in many cases in Florida, the oceanfront, canal, or Intracoastal Waterway.

G

Good faith deposit
A sum of money to show the seller that your interest in the property is serious.

Good faith estimate
An estimate of charges a borrower is likely to incur in connection with a mortgage closing.

Graduated payment mortgage (or GPM)
A mortgage with an interest rate that starts out low and increases gradually according to a predetermined rate.

Grandfather clause
Something which was once permissible and continues to occur despite changes in the law.

Gross area
The total floor area measured from the exterior of the walls.

H

Home inspection
The equivalent of a UK survey.

HUD-1 statement
The document used in closing a real estate transaction which itemises the funds payable and provides a summary of the seller's net proceeds and the buyer's net payment.

I

Inflation
An increase in the general level of prices.

IRS
Inland Revenue Service.

ITIN no.
Individual Taxpayer Identification Number, issued by the IRS for tax processing.

J

Joint tenancy
Each involved party owns the entire property. In the event of death, the survivor owns the entire property.

L

Leasehold
The right to hold or use a property for a fixed period of time.

Lien
A legal claim or charge allowed to a creditor against a debtor's property that must be paid when the property is sold to transfer title.

Lock-in
An agreement in which the lender guarantees a specified interest rate for a certain amount of time.

M

Market value
The current value of your home based on what a willing purchaser would pay. The value determined by an appraisal is sometimes used to determine market value.

Mortgage
A legal document that pledges a property to the lender as security for the payment of a loan or debt.

N

Notary
An individual authorised by law to certify documents and signatures.

O

Off–plan
Buying off–plan means buying a house or condo which has not yet been built, but for which plans have been made.

P

Points
One per cent of the amount of the mortgage loan. For example, if a loan is made for $50,000, one point equals $500.

Preapproval
A commitment from a lender to loan a certain amount of money to a buyer at a designated interest rate and for a specified period of time.

Principal
The amount borrowed, not including interest or other charges.

Private mortgage insurance (PMI)
Mortgage insurance that protects lenders from a loss if the buyer defaults.

R

Real estate agent
Someone who is licensed to both negotiate and transact the sale of property.

Real property
Land and appurtenances permanently on it, including buildings, trees, minerals, and the interest, benefits, and inherent rights thereof.

Realtor
A real estate professional who holds active membership in a local real estate board that is affiliated with the National Association of Realtors.

S

Secured loan
A loan backed up by collateral, i.e. the property.

Security
When property is used as an assurance as collateral for a loan.

Survey
A document showing the legal boundaries of a property.

T

Tenancy by entirety
Joint ownership of property between husband and wife with the right of survivorship.

Tenancy in common
A version of joint tenancy of a property, but without any right of succession by survivorship among the owners.

Title
A legal document that evidences a person's ownership of and right to possess a property.

Title examination
An examination of property information in public records to determine that a seller is the legal owner and to find any other claims or encumbrances on the property title.

Title insurance
Insurance that protects the owner or mortgagee against loss arising from disputes over, or defects in the title to, a parcel of real estate arising after the ownership has been transferred.

W

Walkthrough
The seller invites the buyer to inspect the property and a list of items to be repaired or replaced will be agreed. Normally takes place after the home inspection.

Warranty
A guarantee by the seller, covering the title as well as the physical condition of the property.

Will
A written document stating how an individual wishes to have his or her property distributed after his or her death.

Z

Zoning
A regulation by local government of the use and development of private land.

Directory of useful contacts

ACCOUNTANTS

Accounting Staff Services, Inc.
10832 Tea Olive Lane
Boca Raton
Florida 33498
Tel: +1 561 558 9100
www.AccountingStaffServices.com

ATI Professional Services, Inc.
1802 Janice Avenue
Orlando
Florida 32803
Tel: +1 407 896 1553
Fax: +1 407 898 1458

British American Tax
8 Forest View
London E11 3AP
Tel: 020 8989 0088
E-mail: liz@britishamericantax.com

Byck Financial Services
7285 Morocca Lake Drive
Delray Beach
Florida 33446
Tel: +1 561 638 1980
www.byck.com

C & E Financial Services, Inc.
5446 Oak Branch Drive
Lake Worth
Florida 33463
Tel: +1 561 433 5885
www.cefinancialservices.com

CPA Miami
215 Romano Avenue
Coral Gables
Florida 33134
Tel: +1 305 567 3152
www.cpamiami.com

David A. Freidin CPA
3499 NW 97th Blvd, Suite 14
Gainesville
Florida 32606
Tel: +1 352 332 8066
Fax: +1 352 332 7966

Dennis A Newman CPA/PFS
Mary Tamburello
33 SE 7th Street, Suite N
Boca Raton
Florida 33432
Tel: +1 561 361 1958

Dunlap Tax & Accounting Services
1737 West Oakridge Road
Orlando
Florida 32809
Tel: +1 407 851 3075
Fax; +1 407 851 0602

Francisco Garcia de Quevedo, CPA
9270 Bay Plaza Blvd, Suite 609
Tampa
Florida 33619
Tel: +1 813 623 5588
www.qbcenter.com

LMercado Accounting Services, Inc.
5301 Taylor Street
Hollywood
Florida 33021
Tel: +1 954 967 0070

Morgan's Accounting Solutions, Inc.
143 Yacht Club Drive, Suite 16
North Palm Beach
Florida 33408
Tel: +1 561 371 1153
www.morgansaccountingsolutions.com

Peggy A. Gatliff, CPA
128 Palmetto Lane
Largo
Florida 33770
Tel: +1 727 709 5383
www.peggygatliffcpa.com

Phyllis D. Smith, CPA
1555 US 1
Sebastian
Florida 32958
Tel: +1 772 589 2939

Piña Accounting & Tax Service, Inc.
555 East 25th Street, Suite 111
Hialeah
Florida 33013
Tel: +1 305 836 0166

Rachlin, Cohen & Holtz LLP
One SE Third Ave, Tenth Floor
Miami
Florida 33131
Tel: +1 305 377 4228

Rachlin, Cohen & Holtz LLP
(Fort Lauderdale office)
450 E Las Olas Blvd
Suite 950
Fort Lauderdale
Florida 33301
Tel: +1 954 525 1040

Rachlin, Cohen & Holtz LLP
(West Palm Beach office)
777 South Flagler Drive
Suite 150 East
West Palm Beach
Florida 33401
Tel: +1 561 833 0002

Robert E. Long MA, CPA, PA
11555 Heron Bay Blvd
Suite 200
Coral Springs
Florida 33076
Tel: +1 954 603 0480
www.rlongcpa.com

ARCHITECTS

Arango Architects
4180 Loquat Avenue
Miami
Florida 33133
Tel: +1 305 663 0870
E-mail: utopia@shadow.net

ArchitecturePlus International
2709 Rocky Point Dr, Suite 201
Tampa
Florida 33607
Tel: +1 813 281 9299
E-mail: api@architectureplus.com

Architects Design Group, Inc..
P.O. Box 1210
Winter Park, Florida 32790
Tel: +1 407 647 1706
kristinem@architectsdesigngroup.com

DIRECTORY

LJ Cano Architects
PA. 5040 NW 7th Street, Suite 670
Miami
Florida 33133
Tel: +1 305 445 1952
E-mail: LJC@mail.usa.com

Julian J. Garcia, Architect-Engineer-Planner
737 West Central Avenue
Winter Haven
Florida 33880
Tel: +1 863 294 4780
E-mail: jjgarcia@engineer.com

John Henry Design International, Inc.
7491 Conroy Windermere Rd
Orlando
Florida 32835
Tel: +1 407 539 0359
E-mail: jchenry@ctinet.net

Jonnatti Architecture Incorporated
21021 US Highway
19 North Clearwater
Florida 33765
Tel: +1 727 725 2724

J Mikael Kaul Architects Inc.
P.O Box 222
501 Hollywood
Florida 33022
Tel: +1 305 681 8999
E-mail: mikaelkaul@yahoo.com

Prescott Architects, Inc.
625 E. Highway 98
Suite 6
Destin
Florida 32541
Tel: +1 850 837 6494
E-mail: goodsontl@gnt.net

Raymond and Associates Architects
917 11th Street
Palm Harbor
Florida 34683
Tel: +1 727 786 1937
E-mail: Mosad@rayarch.com

Seibert Architects PA
325 Central Avenue
Sarasota
Florida 34236
Tel: +1 941 366 9161
E-mail: saparch@gate.net

BANKS AND FINANCIAL SERVICES

The 4less Group PLC
160 Brompton Road
Knightsbridge
London, SW3 1HW
Tel: 020 7594 0525
www.the4lessgroup.com
E-mail: ah@currencies4less.com

Bank of Florida
110 East Broward Boulevard
Fort Lauderdale
Florida 33301
Tel: +1 954 653 2000

Bank of Naples
4099 Tamiami Trail North
Naples
Florida 34103
Tel: +1 239 430 2500

Bank of St. Petersburg
777 South Pasadena Avenue
St. Petersburg
Florida 33707
Tel: +1 813 347 3132

British Homes Group
2960 Vineland Road, Suite D
Kissimmee
Florida 34746
E-mail: info@britishhomesgroup.com
www.britishhomesgroup.com

Conti Financial Services
Kevin Fleury
204 Church Road
Hove
East Sussex BN3 2DJ
Tel: 01273 772811
E-mail: kevin@contifs.com

Equitable Bank
633 S. Federal Highway,
Ft. Lauderdale
Florida 33301
Tel: +1 954 524 2265

Florida Mortgage Partners Inc.
2511 Edgewater Drive
Orlando
Florida 32804-4405
Tel: +1 407 999 2566

First Community Bank of Southwest Florida
1565 Red Cedar Drive
Fort Myers
Florida 33907
Tel: +1 941 939 4100

First Florida Bank
8850 Tamiami Trail North
Naples
Florida 34107 1449
Tel: +1 941 597 8989

First Southern Bank
7301 W Palmetto Park Rd
Boca Raton
Florida 33434
Tel: +1 561 479 2100

First State Bank
22 South Links Avenue
Sarasota
Florida 34276
Tel: +1 941 929 9000

First State Bank of Fort Lauderdale
424 West Sunrise Blvd
Fort Lauderdale
Florida 33311
Tel: +1 954 764 8300

First State Bank of the Florida Keys
1201 Simonton Street
Key West
Florida 33040
Tel: +1 305 296 8535

DIRECTORY

International Mortgages
PO BOX 118
Elan House
Berwick-upon-Tweed TD15 1XA
Northumberland
Tel: 08707 875 100

LynxBanc Mortgage Corporation
1650 S Dixie Highway
Suite 110
Boca Raton
Florida 33432
Tel: +1 561 392 8044

Merchants & Southern Bank
3631 North Main Street
Gainesville
Florida 32602
Tel: +1 352378 6227

My USA Loan
1975 Englewood Road
Englewood
Florida 34223
Tel: +1 877 380 7128
www.myUSAloan.com

Old Harbor Bank
2605 Enterprise Road East
Clearwater
Florida 33759 1067
Tel: +1 727 451 2265

PanAmerican Bank
3400 Coral Way, Suite 700
Miami
Florida 33133
Tel: +1 954 985 3900

Pointe Bank
21845 Powerline Road
Boca Raton
Florida 33498
Tel: +1 954 437 2265

Premier Community Bank of South Florida
1451 Northwest 62nd Street
Suite 212
Ft Lauderdale
Florida 33309 1953
Tel: +1 954 343 1644

Premier Community Bank of Southwest Florida
4959 South Cleveland Avenue
Fort Myers
Florida 33907,
Tel: +1 941 415 7566

Prosperity Bank
790 North Ponce De Leon Street
St. Augustine
Florida 32085
Tel: +1 904 824 9111

Union Bank of Florida
1580 Sawgrass Corp. Parkway
Suite 310
Sunrise
Florida 33323
Tel: +1 954 514 1800

TIB Bank of the Keys
99451 Overseas Highway
Key Largo
Florida 33037
Tel: +1 305 451 4660

BUILDERS AND DECORATORS

Aaron Alexis Corporation
18800 Northwest 2nd Avenue
Miami
Florida 33301
Tel: +1 954 895 0101

Advance Restoration & Construction
P.O. Box 4443
Miami
Florida 33160
Tel: +1 305 956 5866
E-mail: info@advancecr.com

AG Pifer Construction Co. Inc.
3629 Old Deland Road
Daytona Beach
Florida 32124
Tel: +1 386 257 4448

American Roofing Enterprises Inc.
13680 Southwest 55th Lane
Miami
Florida 33175
Tel: +1 305 226 7026

Commercial Construction USA
14225 60th St N
Clearwater
Florida 33760
Tel: +1 727 524 9788
www.ccusainc.com

Gardner Plumbing
Daytona Beach
Florida 32114
Tel: +1 386 761 6049

Green Construction Management Inc.
111 Nw 183rd St, Ste 105
Miami
Florida 33056
Tel: +1 305 620 2220
www.greenconstructionmgt.com

Grenier Construction
Daytona Beach
Florida 32114
Tel: +1 386 672 3610

Henry Company Homes
4229 Hwy. 90,
Pace
Florida 32571
Tel: +1 800 424 3679

Kyle Plumbing II Inc.
Palm Beach
Florida 33480
Tel: +1 561 393 1400

CAR HIRE

Avis Car Rentals
700 Catalina Drive
Daytona Beach
Florida 32114-3827
Tel: +1 386 252 6826
www.avis.com

DIRECTORY

Alamo Rent-A-Car
Jacksonville International Airport
Jacksonville
Florida 32202
Tel: +1 904 741 4428
www.alamo.com

Dollar Rent-A-Car
3670 NW South River Drive
Miami
Florida 33142-6206
Tel: +1 305 894 5020
www.miami.dollar.com

Dollar Rent-A-Car
1805 Hotel Plaza Boulevard
Orlando
Florida 32830
Tel: +1 407 583 8000
www.dollar.com

Enterprise Rent A Car
2200 Bee Ridge Road
Sarasota
Florida 34239
Tel: +1 941 926 8780
www.enterprise.com

Hertz Car Rental
Tampa International
Tampa
Florida 33602
Tel: +1 813 874 3232
www.hertz.com

CURRENCY EXCHANGE

Currencies4less
160 Brompton Road
Knightsbridge
London, SW3 1HW
Tel: 020 7228 7667

Currencies Direct
Hanover House
73/74 High Holborn
London WC1V 6LR
Tel: 020 78130332
www.currenciesdirect.com

Custom House Currency Exchange
20002 Gulf Blvd Ph 5
Indian Rocks Beach
Florida 33785
Tel: +1 727 517 8999

Foreign Currency Exchange
4200 Conroy Road
Orlando
Florida 32839
Tel: +1 407 345 5111

Foreign Currency Exchange Corp.
5750 Major Blvd Ste 200
Orlando
Florida 32819
Tel: +1 407 226 2649

Foreign Currency Exchange Corp.
12801 W Sunrise Blvd
Fort Lauderdale
Florida 33323
Tel: +1 954 846 7068

HIFX
59-60 Thames Street
Windsor
Berkshire SL4 1TX
www.hifx.co.uk

Miami Currency Exchange
101 Lenape Drive
Miami
Florida 33166
Tel: +1 305 887 520

TTT Moneycorp Limited
2 Sloane Street
London SW1X 9LA
Tel: 020 7823 7700
www.ttt.co.uk

SGM FX
Prince Rupert House
64 Queen Street
London EC4R 1AD
Tel: 020 77780234
www.sgm-fx.com

EDUCATION

Florida Department of Education
Office of the Commissioner
Turlington Building
Suite 1514
325 West Gaines Street
Tallahassee
Florida 32399
Tel: +1 850 245 0505

EXHIBITIONS

Destinations Holiday and Travel Show
Clarion Events Ltd
Earls Court Exhibition Centre
London SW5 9TA
Tel: 020 7370 8296
www.DestinationsShow.com

GARDENERS

Acorn Landscaping & Maintenance
1346 N Haverhill Rd
West Palm Beach
Florida 33417
Tel: +1 561 689 2439

Alan's Affordable Lawn Care Inc.
Sebastian
Florida 32958
Tel: +1 772 589 7273

American Maintenance
3416 Shader Road
Orlando
Florida 32808
Tel: +1 407 298 0911
www.americanmaint.com

Beta's Lawn Maintenance & Landscape
22171 Birr Court
Mount Dora
Florida 32757
Tel: +1 52 383 4496

DIRECTORY

Bladecutters Lawn Service & Landscaping Co
400 Pomont Avenue
Saint Augustine
Florida 32084
Tel: +1 904 829 8237

Clean & Green Lawn Service
Key West
Florida 33040
Tel: +1 305 296 1795

Creative Cultivation Lawn & Garden
73 Isle Of Saint Thomas
Naples
Florida 34114
Tel: +1 239 775 4442

Delarbre's Lawn Landscaping & Nursery
East Mail
McIntosh
Florida 32664
Tel: +1 352 591 2079

Ecology Landscape & Yard Maintenance
2091 Oakford Road
Sarasota
Florida 34240
Tel: +1 941 921 2879

Florida Gold Coast Property Maintenance
10291 Northwest 43rd Street
Coral Springs
Florida 33065
Tel: +1 954 346 6634

Foster Landscaping Service
2670 Solo Dos Familiaf
Pensacola
Florida 32534
Tel: +1 850 944 7200

Greater Outdoors Lawn Care
3821 Springlake Village Court
Kissimmee
Florida 34744
Tel: +1 407 348 6479

Jr Sodding & Lawn Care
4613 Yarmouth Avenue South
Saint Petersburg
Florida 33711
Tel: +1 727 327 3315

MIA Lindsay Lawn Service
15255 Southwest 103rd Place
Miami
Florida 33157
Tel: +1 305 278 2020

Michelle Nash's Lawn Care & Pressure Cleaning
Port Saint Lucie
Florida 34952
Tel: +1 772 834 9620

RENZ & Son Quality Landscaping
1640 North Hercules Avenue
Suite A
Clearwater
Florida 33765
Tel: +1 727 420 4061

Roy's Landscape Maintenance Inc.
15021 North Pebble Lane
Fort Myers
Florida 33912
Tel: +1 239 482 1363

Tropic Care Landscaping
305 15th Avenue
Indian Rocks Beach
Florida 33785
Tel: +1 727 596 2881

Valentine's Lawn & Shrub Care Inc.
1601 Christa Court
Saint Cloud
Florida 34772
Tel: +1 407 891 9245

Winn's Landscaping & Technical Design
Punta Gorda
Florida 33950
Tel: +1 941 637 8900
www.winnslandscaping.com

GOVERNMENT BODIES

British Consulate
1001 Bricknell Bay Drive
Suite 2800
Miami
Florida 33131
Tel: +1 305 374 1522

Florida Chamber of Commerce,
512 N.E Third Ave
Fort Lauderdale
Florida 33301
Tel: +1 954 462 6000
www.eflorida.com

Florida Department of Citrus
P.O Box 148,
Lakeland
Florida 33802 0148
Tel: +1 863 499 2500

Florida Department of Community Affairs
2555 Shumard Oak Boulevard
Tallahassee
Florida 32399 2100
Tel: +1 877 352 3222

Florida Department of Education
Office of the Commissioner
Turlington Building
Suite 1514
325 West Gaines Street
Tallahassee
Florida 32399
Tel: +1 850 245 0505

Florida Department of Financial Services
200 East Gaines Street,
Tallahassee
Florida 32399 0300
Tel: +1 850 413 3100

Florida Department of Transport
Jose Abreu, Secretary of Transportation
605 Suwannee Street
Tallahassee
Florida 32399 0450
Tel: +1 850 414 4100
www.dot.sate.fl.us

DIRECTORY

Florida Fish and Wildlife Conservation Commission
620 South Meridian Street
Tallahassee
Florida 32399-1600

HEALTHCARE

Department of Health
Orlando
Florida 32801
Tel: +1 407 836 2600

HOME INSPECTORS

AA Certified Home Inspectors
7758 Mystic Point
Jacksonville
Florida 32277
Tel: +1 904 744 3396

Chaparro Home Inspection Services
2503 Logandale Drive
Orlando
Florida 32817
Tel: +1 407 963 3781

Homesouth Inspections Inc.
14100 River Road
Pensacola
Florida 32507
Tel: +1 800 329 4037

Miami Property Inspection
10620 Killan Drive, Suite B
Miami
Florida 33176
Tel: +1 305 972 7189

Prestige Home Inspection
1128 Castle Woods Terrace
Casselberry
Florida 32707
Tel: +1 407 699 9991

Universal Home Inspection
Orlando
Florida 32869
Tel: +1 407 390 1689

HOME SECURITY

American Home Security Ctr
8951 Bonita Beach Road
Suite 665
Bonita Springs
Florida 34135
Tel: +1 239 992 8006

Auto & Home Security Inc.
330 Myrtice Ave Ste 63,
Merritt Island, Florida 32953
Tel: +1 321 454 4784

Brink's Home Security Inc.
6171 Mid Metro Drive
Suite 9
Fort Myers
Florida 33912
Tel: +1 239 275 5085

Edison Home Security
750 North Drive
Melbourne
Florida 32934
Tel: +1 321 259 9898

Florida Home Security & Iron
14025 NW 19th Avenue
Opa Locka
Florida 33054
Tel: +1 305 687 3338

Home & Land Security Inc.
17694 122nd Drive N,
Jupiter
Florida 33478
Tel: +1 561 309 3631

Protect-A-Home Security Alarm
214 Quail Ave,
Sebring
Florida 33872
Tel: +1 863 382 2436

Safe Home Security Inc.
13965 Collier Blvd
Naples
Florida 34119
Tel: +1 239 455 1193

Southern Home Security
26 Adams Ave,
Kissimmee
Florida 34744
Tel: +1 407 933 1399

INSURANCE

A H & L Insurance
6650 Southpoint Parkway
Jacksonville
Florida 32216 8023
Tel: +1 804 281 4699

All Purpose Insurance
1206 N Mills Avenue
Orlando
Florida 32803
Tel: +1 407 855 5992

Michael Lea
10025A N Dale Mabry
Tampa
Florida 33618
Tel: +1 866 315 5291
www.allstate.com

Sihle Insurance Group
871 Douglas Avenue
Altamonte Springs
Florida 32714
Tel: +1 407 869 0962

Steve Rahal
3675 N Country Club Drive
Miami
Florida 33180
Tel: +1 305 918 0633

Troy Fain Insurance
1147 E Tennessee Street
Tallahassee
Florida 32308
Tel: +1 850 224 3156

DIRECTORY

INTERIOR DESIGN

Accessible Interiors
120 NE 51st Street
Fort Lauderdale
Florida 33334
Tel: +1 954 491 6075

Cabral Design Associates
847 4th Avenue
S Naples
Florida 34102
Tel: +1 239 649 5001

Eagle Rock Design
3650 N 36th Avenue 38
Hollywood
Florida 33021
Tel: +1 954 964 2449

Florida Villa Interiors Inc.
5495 Irlo Bronson Highway
Kissimmee
Florida 34746
Tel: +1 407 396 1277

Gables Interiors
Collins Avenue
Miami Beach
Florida
Tel: +1 305 865 8150
www.gablesinteriors.com

Inside Interiors
7829 Front Beach Road
Panama City Beach
Florida 32407
Tel: +1 850 234 7868

Marive King Interiors
10603 SW 116 Street
Miami
Florida 33176
Tel: +1 305 255 0936

Micheline Laberge
4834 Rockinghorse Lane
Sarasota
Florida 34241
Tel: +1 941 924 1778

Lifestyle Interior Decorating
1721 Mapleleaf Blvd
Oldsmar
Florida 35241
Tel: +1 727 488 1698

Elizabeth Lindholm Interiors
2804 Casa Wy.
Delray Beach
Florida 33445
Tel: +1 561 573 5277

Montanna & Associates
733 W Smith Street
Orlando
Florida 32804
Tel: +1 407 425 7444

Riehl Designs
Palm Beach
Florida
www.riehldesigns.com
E-mail: shelly@riehldesigns.com

Sandcastle Designs
109 N Central Avenue
Flagler Beach
Florida 32136
Tel: +1 386 517 0507

LAW FIRMS

Baker & Hostetler
SunTrust Center
Suite 2300
200 South Orange Avenue
Orlando
Florida 32801 3432
Tel: +1 407 649 4000
E-mail: info@bakerlaw.com

Beggs & Lane
P.O. Box 12950
501 Commendencia Street
Pensacola
Florida 32591 2950
Tel: +1 850 432 2451
Fax: +1 850 469 3330

Bennetts & Co Solicitors
High Street
Wrington
Bristol BS40 5QB
Tel: 01934 862786
info@bennettlaw.co.uk

Paul A. Blucher, P. A.
434 S. Washington Boulevard
Second Floor
Sarasota
Florida 34236
Tel: +1 941 955 4019
Fax: +1 941 955 4889

Paul A. Blucher
109 North Brush Street
Suite 510
Tampa
Florida 33602
Tel: +1 813 221 9007
Fax: +1 941 955 4889

Carnal & Mansfield,
6528 Central Ave
Suite B
St. Petersburg
Florida 33707
Tel: +1 727 381 8181
Fax: +1 727 381 8783
E-mail: carnal.mansfield@verizon.net

Conti Financial
Conti Financial Services
204 Church Road
Hove
East Sussex BN3 2DJ
United Kingdom
Tel: +44 (0)1273 772 811
Fax: +44 (0)1273 321 269
E-mail: enquiries@contifs.com

De la O & Marko
3001 S.W. 3rd Avenue
Miami
Florida 33129
Tel: +1 305 285 2000
Fax: +1 305 285 5555

Conti Financial Services
Overseas Mortgage Specialists

FINANCING A PROPERTY OVERSEAS?

Conti Financial Services offers you:

- Choice of products
- Competitive terms
- Preferential rates
- Proven experience

Contact the UK's leading overseas mortgage specialists, who arrange finance in more than 20 countries.

Conti Financial Services are available at:
FREEPHONE: 0800 970 0985 or
TEL: + 44 (0) 1273 772811
FAX: + 44 (0) 1273 321269
E-Mail: enquiries@contifs.com
or visit www.mortgagesoverseas.com

Head Office: 204 Church Road, Hove, Sussex, England BN3 2DJ

STATUTORY NOTICES
YOUR HOME IS AT RISK IF YOU DO NOT KEEP UP REPAYMENTS ON A MORTGAGE OR OTHER LOAN SECURED ON IT. BE SURE YOU CAN AFFORD THE REPAYMENTS BEFORE ENTERING INTO ANY CREDIT AGREEMENT.

THE STERLING EQUIVALENT OF YOUR LIABILITY UNDER A FOREIGN CURRENCY MORTGAGE MAY BE INCREASED BY EXCHANGE RATE MOVEMENTS.

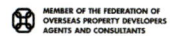

MEMBER OF THE FEDERATION OF OVERSEAS PROPERTY DEVELOPERS AGENTS AND CONSULTANTS

Thinking of buying property in Florida?

Buying a home in Florida should be a dream come true. But the legal implications of house-buying in the US are very different from the UK, so it's important to take the best advice as early as possible.

As one of only a few law firms in England and Wales with a partner qualified as both an American Attorney at Law and practising English Solicitor, Bristol-based Bennetts Solicitors specialise in Florida. Our extensive knowledge and experience of this State and overseas property transactions can help you make the purchase of your dreams become reality, smoothly, quickly and at an affordable price.

For a no obligation conversation, ring us today and ask to speak to Kevin Burke.

Tel: +44 (0) 1934 862786
www.bennettlaw.co.uk

Bennetts
Solicitors & Attorneys
Partnership in Law

FLORIDA VILLA INTERIORS INC

FURNITURE PACKAGES
FOR VACATION VILLAS & PRIVATE HOMES

LET US TAKE THE STRESS OUT OF FURNISHING YOUR VACATION PROPERTY.
DISCUSS YOUR NEEDS AND YOUR BUDGET WITH OUR ASSOCIATES

(001) 407 396 1277

5495 WEST IRLO BRONSON HIGHWAY, KISSIMMEE, FLORIDA 34746
EMAIL: INFO@FLORIDAVILLAINTERIORS.COM

British American Tax

- London-based US Tax firm.
- Advice on both US and UK issues.
- Three packages of services at fixed prices to suit any budget
- Referral discount programme.

We ensure that you proactively reduce your taxes not only now — but over the life of the property.

Knowing both UK and US tax legislation means our clients pay the lowest tax on purchase, during ownership and on sale of any US property.

8 Forest View
London E11 3AP
Tel: 020 8989 0088   Fax: 020 8530 3828
FloridaHouseGuide@BritishAmericanTax.com

www.BritishAmericanTax.com

DIRECTORY

Dobson and Brown, P. A.
66 Cuna Street
Suite A
St. Augustine
Florida 32084
Tel: : +1 904 824 9032
Fax : +1 904 824 9236

Law Office of Gary Ferman
27 Bruton Street
London W1J 6QN
Tel: 020 7499 5702
Fax: 020 7236 2533
info@fermanlaw.com
www.fermanlaw.com

Gunster Yoakley
One Biscayne Tower
Suite 3400
2 South Biscayne Boulevard
Miami
Florida 33131
Tel: +1 800 615 1980

James W. Martin, P.A
Plaza Tower
Suite 703
111 Second Avenue Northeast
St. Petersburg
Florida 33701
Tel: +1 727 821 0904
www.jamesmartinpa.com
E-mail: jim@jamesmartinpa.com

Marcell Felipe
The Old Glass Works
22 Endell Street
Covent Garden
London WC2H 9AD
Tel: 020 7420 4166
Fax: 020 7836 3626
E-mail: info@uslawinlondon.com
www.uslawinlondon.com

McCarthy, Summers, Bobko & McKey
Monterey Triangle
2400 SE Federal Highway
Fourth Floor
Stuart, Florida 34994
Tel: +1 772 286 1700
Fax: +1 772 283 1803
E-mail: info@mcsumm.com

MORTGAGE LENDERS

Florida Mortgage Partners
4473 Fox Street
Orlando
Florida 32814
Tel: +1 407 999 0060
www.floridamortgagepartners.com

International Mortgages
PO Box 118
Elan House
Berwick-upon-Tweed
Northumberland TD15 1XA
Tel: 08707 875 100
www.internationalmortgages.net

MyUSALoan.com
1975 Englewood Road
Englewood
Florida 34223
Tel: +1 877 380 7128
www.myusaloan.com

NOTARIES

Debra J Romano
P.O. Box 721303
Orlando
Florida 32872
Tel: +1 407 737 7739
Fax: +1 407 737 4745
E-mail: dromano@
mobilenotaryorlando.com

Hilda Luisa Diaz-Perera
1510 9th Street SW
Naples
Florida 34117
Tel: +1 239 455 8407
Fax: +1 775 655 3054
E-mail: hilda@jose-marti.org

Jay B. Davis
PO Box 149043
Orlando
Florida 32814 9043
Tel: +1 407 399 2400
E-mail: JDavis@Natlogic.net

Jennifer L. Perez
2055 SW 122nd Avenue
Suite 509
Miami, Florida 33175
Tel: +1 305 487 4854
Fax: +1 305 675 9213
E-mail: notaryfl@bellsouth.net

Joan J Myers, Certified Notary Signing Agent
923 NW 12th Terrace
Cape Coral
Florida 33993
Tel: +1 239 458 0159
fax: +1 239 458 1875
E-mail: Diggy86@aol.com

PET TRANSPORTATION

Air Animal Pet Moving Services
4120 West Cypress Street
Tampa
Florida 33607-2358
Tel: +1 813 879 3210
Toll free: +1 800 635 3448
Fax: +1 813 874 6722
E-mail: petmover@airanimal.com
E-mail: petsfly@aol.com
www.airanimal.com

Air Pets Oceanic
Willowslea Kennels
Spout Lane North
Stanwell Moor
Staines
Middlesex TW19 6BW
Tel: +44 01753 685571
FreeTel: 0800 371554
(if calling from the UK)
Fax: +44 01753 681655

Animal Airlines
Adlington
Cheshire
United Kingdom
Tel: +44 01625 827 414
Fax: +44 01625 827 237

FLORIDA MORTGAGE PARTNERS, INC

- FINANCING UK TO FLORIDA SINCE 1989
- 20% DEPOSITS, NO VERIFICATION OF INCOME
- INTEREST ONLY & CAPITAL REPAYMENT
- 0$ OUT OF POCKET RE MORTGAGES AVAILABLE FOR YOUR FLORIDA HOME
- WE SHOP DOZENS OF LENDERS SO YOU DON'T HAVE TO!
- FREE PRE APPROVALS WITHIN 48 HOURS

SEAN DEPASQUALE
MORTGAGE BROKER FEATURED ON ITV'S 'I WANT THAT HOUSE'
WWW.FLORIDAMORTGAGEPARTNERS.COM
001-407-999-0060x101 OFFICE
SDMONEY@AOL.COM E-MAIL

MyUSALoan.com
Billion$ to Lend

- Buying or Refinancing any USA Property.
- NO US Social Security Number . . . ok !!
- NO DOC Loans, easy and simple financing.
- Condo, single family home or commercial.
- Lowest interest rates and fees around.
- GET CASH OUT! Lower your interest rate.
- Fixed, ARM, Interest Only, Jumbo Loans.
- APPLY ONLINE ... www.MyUSALoan.com

USA Telephone/Fax: **001-877-380-7128**
Email 'English' Jan: **jan@MyUSALoan.com**

We Buy Houses.
Holding a Mortgage?
We buy 1st and 2nd Mortgages

MyUSALoan

---

internationalmortgages.net

Looking to buy a property in Florida?

Buoy, oh buoy, oh buoy
- have we got a deal for you...

- Mortgages can be arranged in both US dollars and Sterling
- Maximum loan to value of 90% in US dollars and 80% in Sterling
- Mortgages can be arranged with "no proof of income" to a maximum of 75% loan to value

www.internationalmortgages.net
Elan House, PO Box 118, Berwick Upon Tweed TD15 1XA UK
Telephone: +44 (0) 8707 875 100 • Fax: +44 (0) 8707 875 101
Email: info@internationalmortgages.net

STATUTORY NOTICES
Your home is at risk if you do not keep up repayments on a mortgage or other loan secured on it. Be sure you can afford the repayments before entering into any credit agreement. The Sterling equivalent of your liability under a foreign currency mortgage may be increased by exchange rate movements.

DIRECTORY

Overhill Kennels and Exports
Norton Lane
Pensford
Bristol BS39 4EY
Tel: +44 01275 832489
Fax: +44 01275 831991
E-Mail: k9meg@overhill.co.uk

PHONE COMPANIES

Bellsouth Residential Services
Tel: +1 888 757 6500
www.bellsouth.com

Nextel
4500 Carillion Point
Kirkland
Washington State 98033
Tel: +1 425 576 3600
Fax: +1 425 576 3650
www.nextel.com

Sprint
Tel: +1 800 877 7746
www.sprint.com

PROPERTY MANAGERS

All American Management
PO Box 3056
Winter Park
Florida 32790
Tel: +1 407 834 7600
Fax: +1 407 834 8987
E-mail: aam@aampm.com
www.aampm.com

Choice Properties
542 Rayleigh Road
Eastwood
Leigh–on–Sea
Essex SS9 5HX
Tel: 01702 529 600
www.floridachoice.com

Minorca Property Manager's Ofc.
2601 N Peninsula Ave
New Smyrna Beach, Florida 32169
Tel: +1 386 427 7510

Property Managers
1627 S 21st Avenue
Hollywood
Florida 33020
Tel: +1 954 922 3133

Property Manager
10175 Collins Avenue
Miami
Florida 33154
Tel: +1 305 861 9938

Renaissance Property Managers
9731 N Oak Knoll Cir
Fort Lauderdale
Florida 33324
Tel: +1 954 693 9989

Sarasota Management and Leasing
3234 S. Tamiami Trail,
Sarasota
Florida 34239
Tel: +1 941 953 5200
Tel: +1 866 953 5200
Fax: +1 941 953 9056

PROPERTY SEARCH

New Skys
Warwick Road
London SW5 9TA
Tel: 0845 330 1449
www.newskys.co.uk

RELOCATIONS AND REMOVALS

Arrowpak International Head Office
National and International Operations Centre
Sherwood House
Norwood Road
Brandon
Suffolk IP27 0PB
Tel: 01842 812165
Fax: 01842 813051
E-mail: sales@arrowpak.co.uk
apk.ops@arrowpak.co.uk

Arrowpak International
National and International Sales
12 Roman Way
Godmanchester
Huntington
Cambridgeshire PE29 2LN
Tel: 01480 453115
Fax: 01480 414633
E-mail: sales@arrowpaksl.com

Excess International Removals
4 Hannah Close
Great Central Way
London NW10 0UX
Tel: 020 8324 2066
Fax: 020 8324 2095
E-mail sales@excess baggage.com
www.excess baggage.com
National Freephone: 0800 783 1085
USA Toll Free number 1 800 260 8098
Aberdeen: 01224 590333
Birmingham:0121 643 3533
Cardiff: 01222 226662
Dundee: 01382 201 144
Dublin: 01 676 7300
Edinburgh: 0131 220 2266
Glasgow: 0141 226 4300
Leeds: 0113 243 3444
Manchester: 0161 834 1117
Newcastle: 0191 232 3323
Norwich: 01603 763215

1st Move International Removals Limited
International House
Unit 5B
Worthy Road
Chittening Industrial Estate
Avonmouth
Bristol BS11 0YB
Tel: +44 0117 9828123
Fax: +44 0117 9822229
E-mail: info@shipit.co.uk

F+N International Removals
Unit 14
Autumn Park
Dysart Road, Grantham
Lincolnshire NG31 7DD
UK Head Office
Tel: +44 01476 579210
Fax: +44 01476 573715

DIRECTORY

PSS International Removals
1-3 Pegasus Road
Croydon
Surrey CR9 4PS
Tel: 020 8686 7733
Fax: 020 8686 7799
E-mail: sales@p-s-s.co.uk

SURVEYORS

All South Surveyors Inc.
9245 SW 44th Street
Miami
Florida 33165
Tel: +1 305 553 1410

Alpha Surveyors Inc.
7421 SW 163rd Pl
Miami
Florida 33193
Tel: +1 305 382 9390

Banks Engineering & Surveying
1144 Tallevast Road
Suite 115
Sarasota
Florida 34243
Tel: 1 941 360 1618
Fax: 1 941 360 6918
E-mail: mevukoder@bankseng.com

Barraco & Associates
2271 McGregor Blvd
Fort Myers
Florida 33901
Tel: +1 239 461 3170
Fax: +1 239 461 3169

Jeffrey C. Cooner & Associates, Inc.
3900 Colonial Blvd
Fort Myers
Florida 33912
Tel: +1 239 277 0722
Fax: +1 239 277 7179

Meridian Surveying & Mapping
5245 Ramsey Way, Suite 2
Fort Myers
Florida 33907
Tel: +1 239 275 8575
Fax: +1 239 275 8457

SWIMMING POOLS

A B Swimming Pools
9621 Boca Gardens Cir N
Boca Raton
Florida 33496
Tel: +1 561 488 9145

All Year Swimming Pool Service
10470 SW 26th Street
Miami
Florida 33165
Tel: +1 305 553 3882

Aps Swimming Pool Svc.
3311 Europa Drive
Apt. 316
Naples
Florida 34105
Tel: +1 239 514 7971

Aquamarine Swimming Pool Co
13217 Automobile Blvd,
Clearwater
Florida 33762
Tel: +1 727 299-9600

Becky's Swimming Pool Service
Sebring
Florida 33870
Tel: +1 863 214 1704

Blake Morton Swimming Pool
8515 Tourmaline Blvd
Boynton Beach
Florida 33437
Tel: +1 561 736 9061

Bob La Gasse Jr Swimming Pool
Sarasota
Florida 34231
Tel: +1 941 925 4429

Cecil T Hunter Swimming Pool
200 E Blount Street
Pensacola
Florida 32503
Tel: +1 850 436 5197

Central Florida Swimming Pools
711 SW 1st Avenue
Ocala
Florida 34474
Tel: +1 352 622 8787

Cushing Swimming Pool Const.
13833 Wellington Trce Ste E15
West Palm Beach
Florida 33414
Tel: +1 561 798-1441

Eugene J Butler Swimming Pool
900 Acorn Street
Jacksonville
Florida 32209
Tel: +1 904 630 0322

Fletcher Swimming Pool
700 Seagate Avenue
Neptune Beach
Florida 32266
Tel: +1 904 247 6327

Fruitland Park Swimming Pool
201 W Berckman Street
Fruitland Park
Florida 34731
Tel: +1 352 323 1653

Gary Nucci Swimming Pool Svc
1125 SW 54th Ln
Cape Coral
Florida 33914
Tel: +1 239 945 8449

Jackson's Swimming Pools
12720 E Wheeler Road
Dover
Florida 33527
Tel: +1 813 655 9886

Keys Swimming Pools
1472 74th Street Ocean
Marathon
Florida 33050
Tel: +1 305 743 5506

Miami Custom Swimming Pool
10830 NW 22nd Street
Miami, Florida 33172
Tel: +1 305 592 8066

DIRECTORY

Ream Swimming Pool Svc
PO Box 1664
Key West
Florida 33041
Tel: +1 305 294 6757

Sunburst Swimming Pools
490 North Street
Longwood
Florida 32750
Tel: +1 407 332 7946

Swimming Pools By John Wright
6830 SW 42nd Ct
Fort Lauderdale
Florida 33314
Tel: +1 954 581 7665

Swimming Pools By Ike Jr
3660 NW 126th Avenue
Pompano Beach
Florida 33065
Tel: +1 954 346 4100

West Coast Swimming Pool Supp.
1578 N Meadowcrest Blvd
Crystal River
Florida 34429
Tel: +1 352 564-0220

TAX SERVICES

British American Tax
8 Forest View
London E11 3AP
Tel: 020 8989 0088
E-mail: liz@britishamericantax.com

Gutta, Koutoulas & Relis LLC
8211 West Broward Blvd
Suite 350
Plantation
Florida 33324
Tel: +1 954 452 8813
Fax: +1 954 452 8359

Florida Department of Revenue
Taxpayer Services
1379 Blountstown Hwy
Tallahassee, Florida 32304-2716
Tel: +1 850-488-6800

TOURIST OFFICES

Central Florida Tourist Information Center
4838 W Irlo Brosn Memorial Highway
Kissimmee
Florida 34746-5334
Tel: +1 407 396 1883

The Florida Tourist Information Bureau
1980 N Atlantic Avenue
Suite 620
Cocoa Beach
Florida 32931 3274
Tel: +1 321 784 0616

Miami Beach Visitor Information Center
920 Meridian Avenue
Miami Beach
Florida 33139
Tel: +1 305 672 1270

South West Florida International Airport
Visitor Information
16000 Chamberlain Parkway
Suite 8071
Fort Myers
Florida 33901 8890
Tel: +1 239 768 4374

TRAVEL – AIR

American Airlines
Miami International Airport
Miami
Florida 33159
Tel: +1 800 433 7300

British Airways Travel Shops
213 Piccadilly
London, W1J 9HQ

Clearwater/St Petersburg International Airport
3192 Montrose Place
Clearwater
Florida 33755
Tel: +1 727 453 7850

Continental Airlines
5501 Spruce Street
St Petersburg
Florida 33701
Tel: +1 727 822 6430

Florida Coastal Airlines
9400 Overseas Highway
Marathon
Florida 33050 3303
Tel: +1 305 743 1940

Fort Lauderdale Hollywood International Airport
320 Terminal Drive
Fort Lauderdale
Florida 33315
Tel: +1 954 359 1200

Jacksonville International Airport
N Ocean Street
Jacksonville
Florida 32202
Tel: +1 904 741 277

Key West International Airport
S Roosevelt Boulevard
Key West
Florida 33040
Tel: +1 305 296 5439

Miami International Airport
PO BOX 592075
Miami
Florida 33159
Tel: +1 305 876 7000

Orlando International Airport
Orlando
Florida 32801
Tel: +1 407 825 2001

Panama City International Airport
Panama City
Florida 32401
Tel: +1 850 763 6751

Paradise Air
Key West
Florida 33040
Tel: +1 305 743 4222

DIRECTORY

Sarasota Bradenton International Airport
Sarasota
Florida 34231
Tel: +1 941 359 5200

Southwest Florida International Airport
Fort Myers
Florida 33901
Tel: +1 239 225 6100

Tallahassee International Airport
Tallahassee
Florida 32301
Tel: +1 850 575 4028

Tampa International Airport
Tampa Park
Tampa
Florida 33602
Tel: +1 863 767 8882

Virgin Atlantic Airways
6025 NW 18th Street
Miami
Florida 33126
Tel: +1 305 743 1940

TRAVEL – COACH

Greyhound Buses
10 N Pearl Street
Jacksonville
Florida 32202
Tel: +1 800 231 2222
www.greyhound.com

TRAVEL – RAIL

Amtrak
Tel: +1 800 872 7245
www.amtrak.com

Tri-rail
South Florida Regional Transportation Authority
800 NW 33rd Street
Suite 100
Pompano Beach

Florida 33064
Tel: +1 800 874 7245
www.tri-rail.com

Metro Rail Miami
Tel: +1 305 638 6700

TRAVEL – ROADS

American Automobile Assistance
1000 AAA Drive
Heathrow
Florida 32746
Tel: +1 407 444 7000

TRAVEL – SEA

Carnival Cruise Lines
10440 SW 48th Street
Miami
Florida 33165 5648
Tel: +1 305 554 5954

Celebrity Cruises
1080 Caribbean Way
Miami
Florida 33132 2028
Tel: +1 305 262 6677

Windjammer Barefoot Cruises
1122 Port Boulevard
Miami
Florida 33132 2009
Tel: +1 305 329 3742

UTILITY COMPANIES

Florida Power and Light Co.
(Electricity)
PO Box 025576
Miami
Florida 33102
Tel: +1 561 994 8227
www.fpl.com

Florida Public Utilities Company
(Gas, electricity, water)
401 S. Dixie Highway
West Palm Beach

Florida 33401
Tel: +1 561 832 0872

Progress Energy Florida
(Electricity and energy)
PO Box 1551
Raleigh
NC 27602-1551
Tel: +1 800 700 8744
www.progress-energy.com

VISAS

Immigration Visas
Devlin House
86 St George Street
Mayfair
London
Tel: 020 7529 1423
www.immigrationvisas.com

US Visa Consultants
Consular Services
27 York Street
London W1U 6PE
Tel: 020 7224 3629

Visa Plus Relocation Limited
100 Pall Mall
London, SW1Y 5HP
Tel: 0207 724 5556
info@visaplus.co.uk

British American Tax
8 Forest View
London E11 3AP
Tel: 020 8989 0088
E-mail: liz@britishamericantax.com

Law Office of Gary Ferman
27 Bruton Street
London W1J 6QN
Tel: 020 7499 5702
Fax: 020 7236 2533
info@fermanlaw.com
www.fermanlaw.com

231

Index of agents

Code	Name and address	Contact details
ACR	American Caribbean Real Estate 81800 Overseas Highway Islamoroda, FL 33036	Tel: +1 305 664 4966 www.americancaribbean.com
ABG	Abbey Global 100 High Street Beckenham Kent BR3 1EB	Tel: 020 8464 5991 info@abbeyvillas.com
BAL	Balistreri Realty 2281 East Sample Road Lighthouse Point, FL 33441	Tel: +1 954 254 8426
BER	Berry & Co Real Estate 330 Highway A1A 200 Ponte Vedra Beach, FL 32082	Tel: +1 904 273 4800
BHG	British Homes Group 2900 Vineland Road, Suite D Kissimmee, FL 34746	Tel: 0800 096 5959
BTB	Buy the Beach Realty Inc 800 West Avenue Miami Beach, FL 33139	Tel: +1 305 531 6929 www.buybeach.com
CAR	Carol Gabriel RE/MAX 100 Realty 1690 US 1 South St Augustine, FL 32084	Tel: +1 904 501 4568
CEN	Century 21 Atkins Realty 11516 San Jose Blvd Jacksonville, FL 32223	Tel: +1 904 262 2121 info@c21atkinsrealty.com www.c21atkinsrealty.com
COL	Coldwell Banker Realty Miami Beach 411 901 Collins Avenue, Suite 302 Miami Beach, FL 33139	info@miamibeach411.com
DRC	Drew Cashmere 10420 SW 77 Avenue Miami, FL 33156	Tel: +1 305 256 5967
DRV	Dream Villas Orlando 27 Exeter Vale Road Exeter Devon EX2 6LF	Tel: 01392 278230 chantvilla@btopenworld.com

INDEX OF AGENTS

Code	Name and address	Contact details
EIP	**Everglades Island Properties** PO Box 5008 102 S. Buckner Avenue Everglades City, FL 34139	Tel: +1 239 695 2277 office@evergladesislandproperties.com
ERA	**ERA American Realty** 1270 N Eglin Parkway Shalimar, FL 32579	Tel: +1 850 678 1196 Debbie@uniquepanhandleproperties.com
ESC	**Escapes 2** 228 Bury New Road Whitefield Manchester M45 8QN	Tel: 01613 512160 sales@escapes2.com
EXI	**Exit Realty** 5800 Overseas Highway, Suite 17 Marathon, FL 33050	Tel: +1 305 743 9292
FLC	**The Florida Connection** 151 Three Bridges Road Crawley West Sussex RH10 1JT	Tel: 01293 615034 floridaconnection@talk21.com
FRE	**Freedom Homes USA** Penthouse Suite, Riverside House 31 Cathedral Road Cardiff South Glamorgan CF1 9HB	Tel: 02920 383453 steve@freedomhomesusa.co.uk www.freedomhomesusa.co.uk
GLA	**Glades Realty** 207 West Broadway Everglades City, FL 34139	Tel: +1 239 695 4299 gladesrealty@aol.com
GRL	**Gary Lynn Broker Reciprocity** 97 Arthur Godfrey Road, Suite 409 Miami Beach, FL 33140	Tel: +1 305 532 8000 garylynn@garylynn.com www.garylynn.com
HOM	**Homesearch Overseas** The Greenway Donnington Newbury RG14 2LG	Tel: 01635 550365 info@homesearch-overseas.com
IWM	**I Want Miami**	Tel: +1 305 788 6605 www.iwantmiami.com
JAT	**Jarrod Thompson** 2401 PGA Blvd Palm Beach Gardens, FL 33410	Tel: +1 561 346 9100

INDEX OF AGENTS

Code	Name and address	Contact details
JJM	**Joanne and Jack McGann**	Tel: +1 800 245 0320
	RE/MAX Heritage Realty 1240 Palm Coast Parkway Palm Coast, FL 32137	jarrod@jarrodthompson.com
JUF	**Just Florida**	Tel: 01257 251501
	Oakwood, Appley Lane North Appley Bridge Wigan WN6 9AQ	Jmatbeach782@aol.com/info@justflorida.com
LIN	**Linda L Griffin**	Tel: +1 386 439 5151
	Beachside Sodi Real Estate Inc 1399 N Oceanshore Boulevard Flagler Beach, FL 32136	
MAK	**Mark Zilbert**	Tel: +1 305 674 4151
	Esslinger Wooten Maxwell Realtors Inc 419 Arthur Godfrey Road Miami Beach, FL 33140	realtor.mark@markzilbert.com
MAR	**Marr Properties Inc**	Tel: +1 305 451 4078
	99900 Overseas Highway Key Largo, FL 33037	www.marrproperties.com
MED	**Med Property Shop**	Tel: 0870 334 3343
		www.medpropertyshop.com E-mail: sales@medpropertyshop.com
MIS	**Michael Saunders**	Tel: +1 941 366 9250
	307 S Orange Avenue Sarasota, FL 34236-6803	www.michaelsaunders.com
MFJ	**Marilyn F Jacobs**	Tel: +1 561 988 0070
	Lang Realty 17500 Via Capri Boca Raton, FL 33496	marilynfjacobs@aol.com www.marilynjacobs.com
MLR	**Miami Lodge Realty**	Tel: +1 305 673 3303
	542 Washington Avenue Miami beach, FL 33139	info@miamilodgerealty.com
MSS	**Magda S Saltzman**	Tel: +1 305 868 2141
	2124 NE 123 Street Miami, FL 33181	Msaltz9708@aol.com
PAN	**Panhandle Realty**	Tel: +1 850 836 4825
	PO Box 178 1566 Highway 90 Ponce de Leon, FL 32455	PanhandleFLA@yahoo.com

INDEX OF AGENTS

Code	Name and address	Contact details
PAR	**Parson International** 9 Mavery House, Victoria Road Diss Norfolk IP22 4EX	Tel: 01379 650 680 E-mail: Kevin@parson.ltd.uk
REX	**Realty Executives of Ponte Vedra** 503B Centre Street Fernandina Beach, FL 32034	Tel: +1 904 261 1013
SOT	**Sothebys International Realty** 340 Royal Poinciana Way Palm Beach, FL 33480	Tel: +1 561 659 3555 Tel: 0207 598 1600
SUS	**Sunshine State Properties** 19 Leith Close Crowthorne Berkshire RG45 6TD	Tel: 01344 752358 sales@sunshinestateproperties.co.uk
TAV	**Tavolacci Realty** Flagler Beach, FL 32136	Tel: +1 386 439 1777
TED	**Taylor Edwards** 53175 Fletcher Avenue PO Box 193 Amelia Island, FL 32035-0193	Tel: +1 904 261 8433
TFS	**The Florida Store** Florida House 35 High Street County Durham DL16 6AA	Tel: 0800 1696247 info@floridastore.uk.com www.floridastore.uk.com
ULV	**Ultra Villas** Clarendon House, 42 Clarence Street Cheltenham Gloucestershire GL50 3PL	Tel: 01242 221500 post@ultravillas.co.uk www.ultravillas.com
WAT	**Watson Realty Group** 7821 Deerneck Club Road Suite 200 Jacksonville FL 32256	Tel: +1 800 257 5143
WCO	**William A Collins** World View Inc	Tel: +1 904 247 2865 E-mail: bill@wvi.us
WOF	**World of Florida** St Ethelbert House Ryelands Street Hereford HR4 0LA	Tel: 01432 845645 www.worldofflorida.co.uk

BUYER'S REFERENCE

Index

A

accountants 27, 48, 53, 64
  useful contacts 218
  see also tax advisors
agents 28, 37–8, 45, 47
  see estate agents; realtors
air travel 30
  Central Florida 126
  Everglades 160
  Florida Keys 190
  Gulf Coast 108
  Miami 172
  North East Florida 94
  Panhandle 82
  South East Florida 144
  useful contacts 230
airports 30
airports see individual hotspots
alimony, taxation 63
Amelia Island 96
American Society of Home Inspectors (ASHI) 44
angling
  Everglades 161, 162, 163
  Florida Keys 190, 192, 193, 194, 195
  Gulf Coast 112
  Lake Kissimmee 126
  Panhandle 84, 85
  South East Florida 145
  West Coast 73
Apalachicola 83, 84
Apalachicola National Forest 82, 84
apartments
  prices 210–11
  see also condominiums
architects, useful contacts 218
architecture
  Boca Raton 148
  Miami 172, 174
  Naples 108
  North East Florida 94
  Panhandle 82
  Pensacola 85
  Venice 112
art-deco architecture 172, 174
artist communities
  Florida Keys 191, 193
  New Smyrna Beach 97
Atlantic Beach 96
attorneys 29
  see also legal advisors
Aventura 174, 176
aviation industry 22

B

Bal Harbour 173, 174, 176
bank accounts 39, 51, 67, 75
banks 37, 39
  useful contacts 219
baseball 146
beaches
  Gulf Coast 108, 111, 112
  Miami 172, 174, 177
  North East Florida 94, 96, 99
  Panhandle 82, 84, 85
  South East Florida 144, 148
Better Business Bureau 69
Big Cypress National Preserve 60, 162
Biscayne Bay 173, 174, 175
Blackwater River State Forest 84
boating see water sports
Boca Raton 144, 145, 146, 148
Bonita Springs 110
Bradenton 73, 110, 115
Brandon 110
Brickell Key 175
brokers 28, 37, 52
Brooksville 110
builders 69
  useful contacts 220
building code 45, 69
Bureau of Citizenship and Immigration Services 56
Busch Gardens 108
buses
  Central Florida 126
  Everglades 160
  Florida Keys 190
  Gulf Coast 108
  Miami 172
  North East Florida 94
  Panhandle 82
  South East Florida 144
  useful contacts 231
business
  taxation 61, 63
  visas 56–60
buyer's estate agents see realtors
buying a business 39
buying a property 24–5, 28–9, 33–51
  additional costs 21, 35, 38, 44
  buy-to-let 21, 26–7, 38–9, 54–7

buying off-plan 39
case studies 52–5, 72–5
closing the sale 35, 44, 46–8, 53
contracts 34, 35–6, 40–2, 45, 46
deeds 46–7
deposits 21, 28, 36, 42, 46, 47
finding a property 20–1, 25, 28, 38–9
home inspections 44–5, 70
independent advice 41
joint purchase 29, 35
property appraisals 28, 42
realtors 25, 38, 52, 72, 75
typical bill of costs 40
see also estate agents; mortgages; prices

C

camping 126, 194
canals and waterways
  Central Florida 126
  Everglades 161, 163
  Gulf Coast 112, 115, 116
  Layton 194
  South East Florida 144, 147
  see also Intracoastal Waterway
Canaveral 30
Canaveral National Seashore 94
canoeing see water sports
Cape Coral 110, 116
capital gains tax 63
cars
  hire 220
  insurance 67
case studies 52–5, 72–5
Cedar Key 82
Celebration 129
Central Florida 125–41
  getting there 126
  hotspots 128–9
  price guides 127, 130–41
  profile 126–7
tourist attractions 20, 26
certificates of occupancy (COs) 46
chambers of commerce 69
Chiefland 84
Chokoloskee Island 160, 161, 162, 163
Clearwater 108, 109, 110, 110
  rental properties 27

rental prospects 27
Clermont 128
Clewiston 146
climate 15, 20, 21
  see also hurricanes
climate charts
  Central Florida 127
  Everglades 161
  Florida Keys 191
  Gulf Coast 109
  Miami 173
  North East Florida 95
  Panhandle 83
  South East Florida 145
closing the sale 35, 44, 46–8, 53
coaches see buses
Coconut Grove 174
Collier Seminole State Park 160
commercial opportunities 55, 73
completion see closing the sale
condominium associations 38
condominiums 34, 38, 41–2
  prices 210–11
  renovation 69
  waterfront 83, 95, 96, 112, 175, 176
construction permits 43
contacts 218–31
contingency clauses 42
contracts 34, 35–6, 40–2, 45, 46
  property renovation 69
conveyancing 46–8
Copeland 162
Coral Gables 174
coral reefs 147, 190
costs
  closing 44
  typical bill of 40
  see also outgoings and additional costs
Crane Point Hammock 195
credit cards 67, 75
credit rating 43–4, 75
Crestview 84
culture
  Palm Beach County 144
  Sarasota 72, 108
currency, exchange rates 33
currency exchange
  rates 20, 25, 26–7
  useful contacts 221
cycling 194

236

BUYER'S REFERENCE

D

Davenport 126, 128, 129
Daytona Beach 94, 95, 96, 96
  rental properties 27
Daytona Speedway 96
De Funiak Springs 84
decorators, useful contacts 220
deeds 46–7
  community restrictions 28–9
defence industries 22
Delray Beach 146
deposits 21, 28, 36, 42, 46, 47
Destin 83, 84, 85
Disney World 26, 126–7, 127, 128
dividends, taxation 63
diving and snorkelling 146
  Florida Keys 190, 192, 193, 194, 195
Dog Island 84
driving
  insurance 67
  licences 67, 75

E

economy 15, 22–3
  Central Florida 127
  Everglades 161
  Florida Keys 191
  Gulf Coast 109
  Miami 173
  North East Florida 95
  Panhandle 82–3
  South East Florida 145
education 66
  see also individual hotspots
  useful contacts 221
Eglin Air Force Base 82, 84
emigration
  checklist 51
  see also relocation
employment 22–3, 74–5
  taxation 63
  visas 56–60
Englewood 110, 112
equity 28
escrow
  agents 45, 47
  payments in 35
estate agents 21, 24, 25, 33, 34, 37–8, 40–1
  index of 232–5

see also realtors
Everglades 30, 159–69
  getting there 160
  hotspots 162–3
  price guides 161, 164–9
  profile 160–1
Everglades City 161, 162, 162
Everglades National Park 160, 162
exchange rates 20, 25, 26–7, 33

F

Fairchild Tropical Garden 174
Fakahatchee Strand State Preserve 160
Federation of Overseas Property Developers, Agents and Consultants (FOPDAC) 37
festivals 147
finance 28, 34–5, 46
  see also banks; mortgages; taxation
financial services, useful contacts 219
FIRPTA withholding tax 24, 48, 65
fishing see angling
Flagler Beach 96
flooding 45
Florida Adventure Museum 115
Florida Aquarium 108
Florida Gulf Coast Technology and Research Park 109
Florida Gulf Coast University 109
Florida Keys 189–205
  getting there 190
  hotspots 192–5
  price guides 191, 196–205
  profile 190–1
Florida Keys Wild Bird Rehabilitation Center 194
Florida Panther National Wildlife Refuge 160
Florida Real Estate Commission 38
FOPDAC see Federation of Overseas Property Developers, Agents and Consultants (FOPDAC)
Foreign Investment in Real Property Tax Act see FIRPTA withholding tax
forms

I-94W 53
  tax 64
  visas 56–60
  W7 24, 40
  W8ECI 48
Fort de Soto Park 108
Fort Lauderdale 144, 145, 146, 147
Fort Meade 110
Fort Myers 108, 109, 110, 114
Fort Walton Beach 83, 84, 84
furniture, removals 50–1

G

gardeners, useful contacts 221–2
gay communities 174, 191, 193
geography 15, 20
gift tax 65
glossary 214–17
Gold Coast 144–5
Golden Beach 174
golf 20, 21
  Central Florida 127, 128, 129
  Florida Keys 190
  Gulf Coast 112, 114
  North East Florida 97, 99
  Panhandle 83
  South East Florida 144, 146, 148
government bodies, useful contacts 222
Gulf Breeze 84, 85
Gulf Coast 107–22
  getting there 108
  hotspots 110–16
  price guides 109, 117–22
  profile 108–9
Gulf Place 83

H

Haines City 128
health care 51, 66
  useful contacts 223
hiking see walking
historic buildings
  Manatee Village Historical Park 115
  New Smyrna Beach 94
  Pensacola 85
  South Beach 174
  St Augustine 94, 97
  Tavernier 194

historic properties 95
Hollywood 144, 146, 148
home inspections (surveys) 44–5, 70
home inspectors 44, 45
  useful contacts 223
home security, useful contacts 223
horse riding 145
  hotspots 78–9
house inspectors, useful contacts 223
house prices 208
hurricanes 30
  Everglades 163
  Florida Keys 192
  Gulf Coast 109, 114
  and new builds 44–5
  South East Florida 146, 148

I

I-94W forms 53
immigration 56–60
Indian Creek 177
Indian River Lagoon Estuary 147
industry clusters 22
information technology 22
inheritance tax 49, 50, 65
insurance
  cars 67
  health 66
  title 48
  useful contacts 223
interest payments, taxation 63
interior design, useful contacts 224
Internal Revenue Service (IRS) 24, 39–40
international business 23
internet property search 25
Intracoastal Waterway 99, 112, 144, 148
investment 20, 26–7, 29, 58–9
taxation 63
IRS see Internal Revenue Service (IRS)
Islamadora 190, 192, 192
ITIN numbers 39–40

J

Jacksonville 30, 95, 96
Jacksonville Beach 96
John Pennekamp Coral Reef State Park 190, 192, 193

237

BUYER'S REFERENCE

K

Kennedy Space Centre 94
Key Biscayne 174, 175
Key Largo 190, 192, 193
Key Vaca 195
Key West 30, 190, 191, 192, 193
Kissimmee 126, 128, 129

L

Lake Kissimmee State Park 126
Lakeland 110
lakes 126, 129
language 24
law firms, useful contacts 224
lawyer-free purchases 36–7
Layton 192, 194
legal advisors 29, 34–5, 35–7, 39, 47
see also notaries
legal documentation 24, 46–7, 46–8
see also contracts; notaries
legal process 29, 34–5, 35–7, 39–48
legal restrictions 28–9
letting property see management companies; rental properties
lettings prices 26, 212–13
Liberty City 174
licences 48
driving 67
life sciences industries 22
Linderman Key 193
liquidated damages 36
Little Haiti 173, 174
Little Havana 173, 174
location 20
rental properties 26, 27, 28, 38–9, 55
Long Key State Park 194
long-term lets 26, 73
Looe Key Marine Sanctuary 192
Lower Keys 190
Lower Matecumbe Key 192
Loxahatchee Wildlife Refuge 146

M

management companies 26, 29, 40–1, 53, 55

Manatee 30
Manatee Village Historical Park 115
Marathon 190, 192, 195
marinas 73, 192
medical care see health care
medical centres see individual hotspots
Mexico Beach 84
Miami 171–87
getting there 172
hotspots 174–7
price guides 173, 178–87
profile 172–3
rental prospects 27
Miami Beach 172, 174
Miami-Dade 30
Miami Metro Zoo 174
Miccosukee Indian Village 162
Milton 84
mobile homes 161, 163
Monticello 84
mortgages 21, 25, 28, 42–4
credit rating 43–4, 52–3
points system 35, 44, 52
preapproval 34–5
sharing 29
sterling 25, 42
types available 41, 44
useful contacts 226
motor racing 94, 96, 99
motoring 30
driving licences 67
insurance 67
see also roads
Museum of Science and Industry 108
Myakka River State Park 110

N

Naples 108, 109, 110, 114
rental properties 27
National association of Realtors, Multiple Listing Service (MLS) 25
National Key Deer and Great White Heron Wildlife Refuge 190
National Wildlife Refuge 94
nature trails 126
Navarre Beach 84
Neptune Beach 96
new build vs resale 69–70
New Smyrna Beach 94, 96, 97
Niceville 83, 84
North East Florida 93–105

getting there 94
hotspots 96–9
price guides 95, 100–5
profile 94–5
North Miami Beach 172, 173, 174, 175
Norton Museum of Art 146
notaries 47, 52
useful contacts 226

O

Ocala 110
Ochopee 162
Okeechobee 146
Okeechobee (lake) 146, 160
one-stop shop companies 25
Orlando 26, 126, 127, 128, 128
rental properties 26, 27
rental prospects 27
Ormond 95
Ormond Beach 96, 99
outgoings and additional costs 21, 35, 38, 44, 73
rental properties 53, 55
see also taxation
overseas property exhibitions 53
Oviedo 128

P

Pahokee 146
Palm Beach 144, 145
Palm Beach County 144
Palm Beach Gardens 145
Palmdale 146
Panama City 30, 83
Panama City Beach 82, 83, 84, 86
Panhandle 81–91
getting there 82
hotspots 84–6
price guides 83, 87–91
profile 82–3
Pensacola 30, 82, 84, 85
pensions, taxation 63–4
Perry 84
pets 51
transportation 226
phone companies, useful contacts 228
Picayune Strand State Park 160
planning permission 69
Plantation Island 161, 162, 163

Point Washington 84
Polk City 110
Pompano Beach 146
Ponce de Leon Historical Park 115
Ponce Inlet 95
Ponte Vedra Beach 96, 99
population 15
Central Florida 125
Everglades 159
Florida Keys 189
Gulf Coast 107
Miami 171
North East Florida 93
Panhandle 81
South East Florida 143
Port Charlotte 110
Port Everglade 144
Port Orange 96
Port St Joe 84
Port St Lucie 145, 146, 147
ports 30
presence test 61–2
prices
Central Florida 127, 130–41
Everglades 161, 164–9
Florida Keys 191, 196–205
Gulf Coast 109, 117–22
how to use this guide 78–9
lettings 27, 212–13
matrixes 208–13
Miami 173, 178–87
North East Florida 95, 100–5
Panhandle 83, 87–91
regional comparisons 20
South East Florida 145, 150–6
properties
appraisal system 28, 44–5
finding a property 20–1, 25, 28, 38–9
historic 95
maintenance 53, 55
resales 28, 70
taxation 49–51
value appreciation 54, 74
see also buying a property; prices; rental properties
property fairs/exhibitions 53
property managers, useful contacts 228
property market 20–1, 26–7, 54, 73
Central Florida 127
Everglades 161
Florida Keys 191

238

BUYER'S REFERENCE

Gulf Coast 109
Miami 173
North East Florida 95
Panhandle 83
South East Florida 145
property search, useful contacts 228
Punta Gorda 110, 115

R

rabies, vaccinations 51
rail travel
 Central Florida 126
 Everglades 160
 Florida Keys 190
 Gulf Coast 108
 Miami 172
 North East Florida 94
 Panhandle 82
 South East Florida 144
 useful contacts 231
railways 30
realtors 25, 38, 52, 72, 75
 see also estate agents
regions 12–13, 23
 comparative property prices 20
religious retreats 86
relocation 50–1, 51
 useful contacts 228
removals 50–1
 useful contacts 228
renovation/restoration and conversion projects 69–70
 construction permits 43
 planning permission 69
rental properties
 buy-to-let 21, 26–7, 38–9, 54–5
 condominiums 38
 costs 53, 55
 income 55, 73
 legal requirements 48
 lettings prices 27, 212–13
 location and zoning 27, 28, 38–9, 55
 managing lets 26, 39, 40–1, 53, 55
 operating as a business 29
 registration 55
 taxation 48–50, 64
 see also individual hotspots; investment
resale homes 28, 70
residency 29, 56–60
 taxation 61–5
retirement 29

taxation of pensions 63–4
River of Grass 160
roads 30
 Central Florida 126
 Everglades 160
 Florida Keys 190
 Gulf Coast 108
 Miami 172
 North East Florida 94
 Panhandle 82
 South East Florida 144
 useful contacts 231
Rosemary Beach 83

S

St Augustine 94, 95, 96, 97
St Cloud 128
St Petersburg 30, 108, 109, 110, 111
sale of property 24–5, 74–5
 taxation 65
sales prices see prices
Sanford 128
Santa Rosa 84
Santa Rosa County 83
Sarasota 72–3, 108, 110, 111
 price increases 109
 rental prospects 27
Savannas preserve 147
schools see individual hotspots
sea travel 30
 useful contacts 231
Sea World 126, 128
Seacrest 83
Seaside 82, 83
Sebastian 145
Seminole Indian Reservation 144, 146
service-producing sectors 23
short–term lets 26, 55
Silver Springs 110
social groups
 Central Florida 127
 Everglades 161
 Florida Keys 191
 Gulf Coast 109
 Miami 173
 North East Florida 95
 Panhandle 83
 South East Florida 145
social security numbers 66
South Beach 172, 173, 174, 174
South East Florida 143–56
 getting there 144
 hotspots 146–8
 price guides 145, 150–6

profile 144–5
Space Coast 94, 95
space technologies 22
Steinhatchee 84
Sunny Isles 174
Sunnyside 84
surfing
 North East Florida 94, 97
 Sebastian 145
Surfside 174, 177
surveyors
 useful contacts 229
 see also home inspectors
surveys
 boundary 46
 home inspections 44–5, 70
 key checks 42
swimming pools 27, 54
 useful contacts 229

T

Tallahassee 82, 84
Tampa 30, 108, 109
Tarpon Springs 110
Tavernier 192, 194
tax advisors 34, 62, 64
tax services, useful contacts 230
taxation 33–4, 48, 48–50, 53, 55, 61–5
 capital gains 28, 49, 65
 income tax 27, 35, 40, 48–9, 62, 64
 inheritance tax 49, 50, 65
 property taxes 49–50
 stamp tax 44, 48
 US rates 61, 62
 wealth tax 50
 see also FIRPTA withholding tax
Ten Thousand Islands 160
termites 45
title insurance companies 24, 29, 33, 46, 48
 see also closing the sale
tourist attractions
 Central Florida 20, 26, 126
 Everglades 160
 Florida Keys 190
 Gulf Coast 72–3, 108
 Miami 172
 North East Florida 94
 Panhandle 82
 South East Florida 144–5
tourist offices 230
tourist taxes 64
trade 23

travel see air travel; buses; rail travel; roads; sea travel
Treasure Coast 144–5
tropical gardens 114, 174
trusts, taxation 64

U

Universal Studios 126, 127, 128
utility companies 231

V

Venice 110, 112
visas 29, 39, 53, 56–60
 useful contacts 231

W

W7 forms 24, 40
W8ECI forms 48
walking 82, 144, 160
walkthroughs 45–6, 53
Walt Disney World 26, 126, 127, 128
water sports
 canoeing 94, 126, 194
 Florida Keys 192, 194
 Gulf Coast 73, 108
 North East Florida 97
 Panhandle 85
 South East Florida 144
websites, finding homes 25
West Palm Beach 144, 146, 146
 rental prospects 27
Wet 'n Wild 126, 128
wildlife
 Everglades 160
 Florida Keys 190, 193, 194
 Gulf Coast 72
 North East Florida 94
 Panhandle 82
wills 50
Windermere 126
Winter Haven 126
Winter Park 128
work see employment
work permits 56–60

Y

Youngstown 84

Z

zoning 27, 28, 38–9

239

Contributors

Our panel of experts provide you with authoritative, practical information on all aspects of buying property – funding the purchase, tax implications and acquiring visas. All of our contributors are professionally qualified experts in their own field…

Kevin M. Burke
Kevin M. Burke, a partner with Bennetts Solicitors & Attorneys in Bristol, predominantly represents UK purchasers of Florida property. He has been a practising Florida attorney for 10 years and an English solicitor for five years. Kevin was admitted to Federal Practice in 1995 in Florida's Middle District Court.

Andrew Bartlett
A realtor with many years experience in understanding the Florida realty market, Andrew Bartlett has specialist knowledge of the quality of life and economic performance in this beautiful country. Andrew has written a number of articles on emigration, for relocation papers and journals and is a graduate of Surrey University.

Kevin Fleury
Kevin Fleury is Conti Financial Services' Regional Manager for the USA, Canada and the Caribbean. He has worked in the mortgage business for more than 10 years, in Canada, the Caribbean and now in the UK with CFS, for whom he travels extensively, negotiating with lenders on their behalf.

Garrett Kenny
Garrett Kenny entered the property business 13 years ago and has been involved in developing both domestic and commercial real estate. In 2002, he established the Coldwell Banker Team Realty franchise in Davenport, Central Florida. It has secured over $100 million in sales in its first 18 months of operation.

CONTRIBUTORS

Z. Joe Kulenovic
As the Senior Director for Strategic and Market Analysis, Z. Joe Kulenovic heads up Enterprise Florida's research team. Formerly an economist with the World Bank Group, Joe joined the organisation in 1999 and has since taken part in a wide variety of Florida's statewide economic and business development initiatives.

Nick Thake
Nick Thake is the UK sales director of Florida Choice Realty, one of Florida's largest and most successful rental and management companies. Since joining six years ago, Nick has dealt with well over 500 clients who have purchased buy-to-let properties in Florida. The company's UK office is based in Essex.

Janette Thorne
Janette Thorne set up Homes of America Ltd with her husband and daughter after spending years visiting and planning to buy a home in Florida. The company helps people to buy homes in the US and their sister management company looks after the properties when the owners are at home in the UK.

Lee Weaver
Lee Weaver was born and educated in the UK and, after serving four years with the British Army, came to the US to pursue a career in real estate and finance. As Director of Operations for the Mid-Atlantic Group in Orlando, Lee specialises in assisting UK residents acquire investment properties throughout Florida.

Liz Zitzow
An Enrolled Agent with 19 years of tax experience, Liz is the managing partner for British American Tax, a UK-based partnership founded in 2004. Liz is also a member of NAEA, NATP, and FSB. The firm specialises in US tax for individuals, corporations, partnerships, and trusts, conducting business on both sides of the ocean.

■ INDEX TO ADVERTISERS

Index to advertisers

Advertiser	Page
Abbey Global	170
AFM	188
American First Realty	149
Bella Homes	80
Bennetts Solicitors	219
British American Tax	219
British Homes Group	71
Calabay Homes	170
Classic Florida Realty	185
Coldwell Banker – Team Realty	155
Conti Financial Services	219
Destinations	32
Dolby Properties	106
Dream Homes Orlando	98
ERA America Realty	80
escapes2.com	92
Evans Florida Villa Sales & Rentals	92
Exclusively Florida	181
Florida Choice	6
Florida Connection	137
Florida Countryside	158
Florida Dream	137
Florida Mortgage Partners	227
Florida Properties	80
Florida Property Facts	157
Florida Villa Interiors	219
Florida Store	131
Freedom Homes USA	123
Gateway Overseas Homes	137
Global Property Group	179
HIFX	2
Homes of America	203
Homesearch Overseas	113
International Financing Consultants	106
Ideal Florida Homes	92
International Mortgages	227
IRM	197
JP Properties & Design	243
Just Florida	181
Katie Stack – RE/MAX Services	149
LynxBanc	157
MyUSALoan.com	227
NewSkys	17
Orlando Vacation Realty	215
Parson International	124
Select Destinations	149
SGM FX	113
Simply Florida	179
Sun Lakes Realty	98
Sunshine State Properties	98
Ultra Villas	142
Unique Internet Realty	181
World of Florida	183

To place advertisements in future versions of this guide or other **Red Guides**, please contact Barney Pearson, Assistant Ad Manager, Merricks Media, Cambridge House South, Bath BA1 1JT. Telephone 01225 786838; fax 01225 786801; e-mail barney.pearson@merricksmedia.co.uk